**This book should be cited as**

UNESCO, 2011, *Island as Crossroads: sustaining cultural diversity in Small Island Developing States.*
Edited by Tim Curtis, UNESCO: Paris, 224 pp.

**This UNESCO publication is a collaborative effort of**

The Division of Cultural Polices and Intercultural Dialogue, Culture Sector and
The Small Islands and Indigenous Knowledge Section, Natural Sciences Sector

**Editor**

Tim Curtis, Culture Unit, UNESCO Bangkok Office

**Project Support Team**

Khalissa Ikhlef, Stéphanie Ledauphin, Kremena Nikolova, Hans D. Thulstrup

**Copy-editing**

David McDonald

**Translation**

Colin Anderson, Lisa Maria B. Noudehou

**Design & Production**

Julia Cheftel

**Maps** reproduced courtesy of GEOATLAS® WORLD VECTOR – GRAPHI-OGRE® – France – 1997

**Cover image**

© Mark Edwards/Hard Rain Picture Library

Published in 2011 by the United Nations Educational, Scientific and Cultural Organization (UNESCO),
7 Place de Fontenoy, 75352 Paris 07 SP, France

ISBN: 978-92-3-104181-5

**For further information, please contact**

Katerina Stenou
Division of Cultural Polices and Intercultural Dialogue, UNESCO
1, rue Miollis, 75732 Paris Cedex 15 France

Douglas Nakashima
Small Islands and Indigenous Knowledge Section, UNESCO
1, rue Miollis, 75732 Paris Cedex 15 France
sids@unesco.org

# Islands as Crossroads

## Sustaining Cultural Diversity in Small Island Developing States

**Culture Sector**
**Natural Sciences Sector**

United Nations
Educational, Scientific and
Cultural Organization

# FOREWORD

by the President of the General Conference of UNESCO

Small island populations are among the most resourceful, innovative and adaptive in the world. These are the attributes that have allowed islanders to settle and thrive, often in geographically isolated and inhospitable locations.

To small islanders, however, islands are not insular in the sense of being isolated. For millennia, islands have been venues for encounters between different cultures. Rather than separating them, the ocean as the medium for voyaging has served to connect islands with each other as well as with the continents. From the earliest open ocean voyages to the slave trade, islands have been places of encounter and exchange, as well as conflict.

This continuum of interaction has defined small island cultures, resulting in the emergence of new traditions which are at once the products of synergies between cultures, yet at the same time intimately related to the island setting itself. Small islands are home to a wealth of linguistic and biological diversity, and have produced some of the world's most evocative cultural heritage, both tangible and intangible.

Nevertheless, small islands, their people and heritage are at risk. The last fifteen years have seen the continued expansion of global threats to which these islands are particularly vulnerable. These include climate change, inequalities in trade and finance, and the erosion of biological and cultural diversity.

To respond to these growing challenges, small island populations must rely on their cultures, at once unique and interconnected. In a time of growing vulnerability, the role of cultural heritage, local knowledge, societal structures and networks becomes ever more important. Culture is the foundation upon which small island societies must develop responses to address these unprecedented threats to their sustainability.

'Islands as Crossroads' explores the historical, cultural and economic dimension of small island responses to these global challenges. These responses, rooted in small island innovation and resourcefulness, provide lessons of urgent relevance to us all.

Davidson L. Hepburn

# FOREWORD

by the Director-General of UNESCO

IN January 2005, a high-level United Nations meeting was convened in Mauritius to review the implementation of and refine the 1994 Barbados Programme of Action for the Sustainable Development of Small Island Developing States. Prominent among the new emphases in the 2005 Mauritius Strategy is the role devolving upon culture, in particular cultural industries and related initiatives, in the development of small island developing states.

Ensuring the recognition of culture as an integral dimension of sustainable development is a challenge to which UNESCO is uniquely placed to respond. To take advantage of its multidisciplinary expertise in education, science, culture, communication and information, UNESCO proceeded in 2008 to establish an intersectoral platform on small island developing states to exploit the synergies generated by an interdisciplinary approach to development issues. Our Organization is engaged in this way in promoting, and demonstrating, new approaches to sustainable development that draw upon the rich cultural heritage of island societies.

'Islands as Crossroads' reflects the outcomes of a UNESCO symposium held in the Seychelles in 2007, which brought together small island specialists for discussions on the role of island cultures in sustainable development. The book highlights the diversity of these cultures while emphasizing their role as venues for the interaction of different societies. It draws attention in particular to the cultural bases of resourcefulness and inventiveness shared by all island nations.

Turning these attributes to account is crucial at the present time. More than ever, small islanders must rely on their resilience and determination to respond to a set of growing global challenges that include climate change, inequalities in trade and finance, and the erosion of the very cultural and biological diversity upon which their societies have been built. They may rely on UNESCO to support the whole spectrum of efforts upon which their sustainable development will necessarily depend.

Irina Bokova

# CONTENTS

# LIST OF CONTRIBUTORS

**C**laude Allibert is Professor of Indian Ocean Civilization at the Institut National des Langues et Civilisations Orientales, Paris. He was the Director of the Centre d'Etude et de Recherche sur l'océan Indien occidental (Paris) from 1996 to 2009 and Vice-President of INALCO from 2001 to 2005. He has directed several excavations in the Comoro Archipelago and edited *Etudes Océan Indien*. He is the author of some sixty articles and the books *Mayotte, plaque tournante et microcosme de l'océan Indien occidental* (1984), *Textes anciens sur l'océan Indien occidental* (1990) and *Histoire de la Grande Isle Madagascar de Flacourt* (1995, re-edition 2007). He is currently preparing a book about the Mirabilia in the Indian Ocean before AD 1000.

**A**boubakari Boina has held posts within the Ministry of Education of the Comoros, whilst consulting for the Planning Commission, UNDP, UNESCO, UNICEF, the European Union and the Indian Ocean Commission, parallel with his research in the fields of education, culture, governance and the environment. He was successively National Coordinator of the Cultural Programme CICIBA/European Union, a teacher and researcher and scientific coordinator of the National Centre for Documentation and Scientific Research (CNDRS) of the Comoros, before becoming Secretary General of the National Commission for UNESCO of the Comoros and a lecturer at the University of the Comoros. Aboubakari Boina is the author of numerous articles, papers, studies and reports.

**J**ocelyn Chan Low, historian and Associate Professor, is currently Head of Department of History and Political Science at the University of Mauritius. Former Director of the Mauritian Cultural Centre, he is a member of the International Scientific Committee of the Slave Route Project, UNESCO. He coordinated the inventory of memory sites of slavery in the Indian Ocean and has published several scholarly works on the political and social history of Mauritius.

**T**im Curtis is head of the Culture unit at the UNESCO Bangkok Office. He holds a PhD in Cultural Anthropology from the Australian National University, based on his work on the relationship between oral history and place amongst the Na'hai speakers in the island of Malakula, Vanuatu. Before taking up his duties in Bangkok, he served as programme specialist for Culture at the UNESCO Dar-es-Salaam Office, and served as a consultant to UNESCO's programmes in Intangible Cultural Heritage and Local and Indigenous Knowledge Systems.

**H**opeton S. Dunn is the Academic Director of the Caribbean Programme in Telecommunications Policy and Technology Management at the Mona School of Business, UWI Jamaica, where he holds an endowed Chair. He is Chairman of the Broadcasting Commission of Jamaica, Secretary General of the International Association for Media and Communication Research (IAMCR), and a Commissioner of the Jamaica National Commission for UNESCO. His five books and numerous academic papers cover the areas of new media and communications, ICT and cultural policies, theories of globalization, and the political economy of African and Caribbean media.

**T**homas Hylland Eriksen is Professor of Social Anthropology at the University of Oslo, and has carried out research in Mauritius and Trinidad. He has published extensively in many fields of anthropology, with a particular focus on globalization and the complexities of identity, nationalism and the politics of inclusion and exclusion. His textbooks *Small Places, Large Issues and Ethnicity* and *Nationalism* are widely used and translated. From 2004 to 2010, Eriksen directed the strategic research programme of the University of Oslo, entitled 'Cultural Complexity in the New Norway'.

**S**udel Fuma is the Professor of Contemporary History at the University of Reunion and Director of the UNESCO Chair in Reunion. He is the author of several works on the economic and social history of the islands and countries of the Indian Ocean, in particular, the question of slavery, which is his special field of study. He has founded a programme entitled 'Route de l'esclavage et de l'engagisme' on slavery and indentureship routes in the islands and countries of the Indian Ocean.

**M**ichael A. Mel is a performance artist, teacher and writer, and is currently Associate Professor in Indigenous Art and Education at the University

of Goroka, Papua New Guinea. Renowned for his expertise in the traditional arts and oral traditions of his people, he uses performance to explore issues of cultural identity and dispossession. For his contributions to the cultural development of Papua New Guinea, and for acting as a cultural bridge between PNG and the rest of the world, he received the Prince Claus Award in 2006.

**P**atricia Mohammed is Professor of Gender and Cultural Studies and Campus Coordinator at the School for Graduate Studies and Research, University of the West Indies, St. Augustine, Trinidad. Her most recent publication is *Imaging the Caribbean: Culture and Visual Translation* (2009). She has made ten films including the award winning short film *Coolie Pink and Green* (2009). She has worked and lived variously in England, The Netherlands, Jamaica, Namibia and the United States and currently lives in Trinidad.

**K**eith Nurse is Director of the Shridath Ramphal Centre for International Trade Law, Policy and Services, University of the West Indies, Cavehill Campus, Barbados. He has published numerous scholarly articles and papers on the political economy and trade policy dimensions of the clothing, banana, tourism, copyright and creative industries. He has also published on the development impact of migration and diaspora, HIV/AIDS and security, and development assistance and capacity development. Current research areas include the impact of climate change policies on the tourism sector in small island developing states and innovation and industrial policy in small states.

Ralph Regenvanu is the Member of Parliament for the constituency of Port Vila, the capital of the Republic of Vanuatu. He also holds the position of Director of the Vanuatu National Cultural Council. He was Director of the Vanuatu Cultural Centre (incorporating the National Museum of Vanuatu) from 1995 until 2006, and was also a founding Executive Board Member of both the Pacific Islands Museums Association (PIMA) and ICOMOS Pasifika. In recent years he has been a leading figure in the movement advocating for reform of national development policies, particularly in the areas of governance, land and economic empowerment. He was instrumental in the holding of the national 'Land Summit' in 2006 and the Government's declaration of 2007 and 2008 as 'Years of the Traditional Economy'.

Gordon Rohlehr is Emeritus Professor of Literature in the Department of Liberal Arts of the University of the West Indies, St. Augustine, Trinidad & Tobago, where he has taught for thirty-nine years (1968–2007). He has written more than 100 essays on West Indian literature, oral poetry, the calypso and popular culture in the Caribbean, and is the author of several publications, most recently *A Scuffling of Islands: Essays on Calypso (2004)*, *Transgression, Transition, Transformation: Essays in Caribbean Culture (2007)* and *Ancestories: Readings in Caribbean Culture (2010)*.

Matthew Spriggs is Professor of Archaeology in the School of Archaeology and Anthropology, College of Arts and Sciences at the Australian National University in Canberra. He is a Fellow of the Australian Academy of the Humanities and of the Society of Antiquaries of London. Professor Spriggs specializes in Island Southeast Asian and Pacific Island archaeology, and he has undertaken fieldwork in those regions for thirty-five years, most recently in East Timor and Vanuatu.

Katérina Stenou is the Director of the Division of Cultural Policies and Intercultural Dialogue, UNESCO in Paris. She holds a PhD in human and social sciences from the Sorbonne in Paris. She is a member of various research institutes such as observatories and centres devoted to cultural policies, intercultural communication and cultural diplomacy. Her publications, dedicated to issues concerning the formulation of policies to respond to the challenges of today's multicultural societies, include several articles and books.

Katerina Martina Teaiwa is Pacific Studies Convener in the College of Asia and the Pacific at the Australian National University. She also runs an outreach programme, Pasifika Australia, focusing on Pacific youth in the Australian diaspora. She has a PhD in Anthropology and was a founding member of the Oceania Dance Theatre at the University of the South Pacific. Her research focuses on phosphate mining on Banaba in Kiribati, the Banaban community of Rabi in Fiji, and contemporary Pacific popular culture. She has also undertaken cross-cultural training and debriefing with international aid and development volunteers, and worked on cultural mapping, planning and policy-making in Oceania with UNESCO and the Secretariat of the Pacific Community.

# INTRODUCTION

Tim Curtis, *UNESCO Bangkok Office, Thailand*

**IN** the early twentieth century, when the discipline of anthropology was emerging as the study of diverse human societies and cultures, Branislow Malinowski, often called the 'father' of contemporary ethnographic research, chose an archipelago of small islands off the eastern coast of Papua New Guinea to undertake his research, and pioneer the new methodology of 'participant observation'. The choice of small islands in relatively remote parts of the Pacific was not fortuitous, as it was assumed that such small islands, because of their relative isolation over time, would provide perfect 'laboratories' of 'untouched' or 'intact' cultures.

This came to be the dominant trend for the early investigators into 'human cultures', who were indeed rewarded for their ventures into the islands of the Pacific, where they found a remarkable diversity of languages and cultural practices. However, the assumption that somehow islands offered a 'natural' boundary for delineating supposed 'intact cultures' quickly began to fall apart. Instead, it became apparent that cultural and linguistic affinities exist that link small land masses spanning the thousands of miles of the turbulent Pacific Ocean, and that these affinities stretch far back in time. The islands of the Pacific Ocean, as it turned out, far from being 'natural incubators' of coherent cultural entities, were very much focal places, or crossroads, of manifold human interactions.

In the Caribbean as well as the Indian Ocean the historical context that led to the remarkable diversity of contemporary populations was marked primarily by the traumatic experiences of the slave trade and maritime warfare. The main exceptions to this are Madagascar and Comoro, where the cultural complexity in evidence today predates the era of European expansion. This is in marked contrast to the Caribbean, where the local indigenous population was virtually annihilated. In both of these regions the islands saw peoples from various parts of Africa, Asia and Europe cohabit in small terrestrial spaces through a complex network of social, political and economic interactions, thereby giving rise to new cultural forms. Here again, the islands were sites of intense social and cultural interaction exchanges, often both violent and oppressive.

Small islands have thus long been crossroads of human cultural interaction, rather than isolated or self-enclosed communities, as may be imagined by their 'insularity'. This notion of crossroads, therefore, draws on the historical situation of many Small Island Developing States, or SIDS, which for different reasons seemed to become 'encounter points' for different human populations and the cultures they embodied. These include issues related to geography (islands naturally served as crossroads during the times when most international travel was accomplished by sea), politics and economics (particularly colonialism and the slave trade), as well as the effects of different historical contexts, from pre-colonial through to colonial and post-colonial eras (many SIDS today find themselves in situations whereby a significant segment of their populations are living and working abroad, which continues to have important ramifications in terms of cultural diversity and dynamism).

The chapters presented here are the result of a conference held in Victoria, Seychelles, in April 2007. The conference brought together scholars from the three main island regions of the world, the Caribbean, the Indian Ocean and the Pacific Ocean, or Oceania. The aim was to develop greater reflection on the issues of cultural diversity in Small Island Developing States (SIDS), from an inter-regional and pluri-disciplinary viewpoint. UNESCO organized the conference as a follow up to the United Nations 2005 Mauritius International Meeting to Review Implementation of the Programme of Action for the Sustainable Development of Small Island Developing States. In that meeting the 54 Small Island Developing States, or SIDS, had identified culture as a priority for their sustainable development. They stressed 'the importance of protecting cultural diversity and promoting cultural industries as a vital component of sustainable development in SIDS'.[1]

By bringing together multi-disciplinary expertise from the three main SIDS regions, the conference sought to explore whether there were underlying commonalities across SIDS and these regions in relation to their experiences of cultural diversity, and how this might relate to their sustainable development. Moreover, did their 'islandness' specifically set them apart from larger, continental countries? Ultimately, as could be expected, no neat all-encapsulating formulation could capture the complexity and diversity of situations facing SIDS. Nor did the issues explored necessarily neatly fit into discrete 'regional' schemes. Nevertheless, some broad patterns across the regions did emerge. For example, during initial discussions at the Mauritius international meeting in 2005, one could sense that, issues of indigeneity and traditional knowledge or intangible heritage lay at the forefront of people's concerns in the Pacific. For the Caribbean, the issues concerning cultural industries and the role of Diasporas were touched upon. In the Indian Ocean SIDS, cultural pluralism and intercultural dialogue appeared high on the agenda. However, as these issues were unpacked more rigorously during the Seychelles meeting it became apparent that there were differences within regions as well as linkages between specific island states across regions. Mauritius' experience of *Creolité* seemed to echo more strongly with the experiences of Trinidad and Tobago in the Caribbean, than with its Indian Ocean neighbours of Seychelles and Reunion. Traditional knowledge and values, high on the Pacific islands agenda, were also at the core of issues discussed for the Comoros, and indeed in Madagascar. The influence and effects of the various island diasporas, identified as a key issue for Caribbean islands, were also crucial to understanding the situation of the Comoros, as well as the Polynesian islands of the Pacific.

This book is therefore the product of an inter-island, inter-regional and inter-disciplinary exchange, which provided an opportunity to dig deeper into the ways in which the people of small islands have constructed and live in their diverse societies and cultures. The book is divided into three parts: the first looks at the historical and social dimensions of cultural diversity in Small Island States, the second at how different island communities have developed strategies for retaining their cultural uniqueness in the face of cultural globalization, and the third at the relationship between the cultures of Small Island Developing States and their economies.

**Part 1** of the book brings together archaeological and historical perspectives on the ways in which islands have served as points of human intercultural exchange in different contexts. Matthew Spriggs and Claude Allibert explore how inter-island travel can be found in the archaeological records far predating written history. On the trail of Lapita pottery, Spriggs shows how people criss-crossed the Pacific islands as early as 3,000 years ago, establishing trade networks across vast areas of ocean. Allibert introduces genetic and archaeological evidence to demonstrate how the island of Madagascar was populated by a complex interplay of cross-cultural encounters including Austronesian, Bantu, Arab and possibly Indian populations, centuries before the vassals of colonial empires displaced and intermingled people around the globe.

Sudel Fuma, looking at the Indian Ocean, argues that the process of what he calls *Créolisation* in Reunion and the Seychelles, spread beyond its original identification with the descendents of slaves to include the broader society, incorporating the former slave owners themselves. He refers to the fact that the Creole language – originally the cultural 'marker' of the enslaved and oppressed section of society – eventually came to serve as the identifier of the whole society as the 'Creole Miracle'. In the following chapter, Jocelyn Chan Low, focuses on a very different scenario in another Indian Ocean Island, Mauritius, where heritage is a means of demarcation between different ethnic groups, and the notion of *Creolité* continues to be specific to the descendants of slaves. Finally, Thomas Eriksen draws on his work both in Trinidad and Mauritius to explore the relation between cultural complexity and social cohesion in small islands, where, he argues, 'social epidemics' are more likely to occur due to social proximity and cultural complexities linked both internally and externally to places of origin.

**Part 2** of the book moves on to explore different mechanisms by which people in Small Island Developing States are attempting to secure a sense of cultural identity and specificity in the context of cultural globalization. Indeed, one might think that by their very 'smallness' islands are perhaps more vulnerable to rapid socio-cultural submersion of ever-expanding cultural forms and expressions emanating from the centres of political and economic power. Yet, the chapters in this book testify to ingenious strategies, some 'conscious', others less so, which islanders are using to retain, reclaim and reinvigorate their cultural uniqueness in moving into the twenty-first century.

Gordon Rohlehr explores the meta-events of UNESCO global conferences on cultural policies to see how they interplay with the actual occurrences, or not, of Caribbean cultural governance, in particular, in Trinidad and Tobago. In doing so, he reflects on general trends facing the people of the Caribbean in relation to their cultural identities. Michael Mel then takes us to the highlands of Papua New Guinea to expose the tensions that emanate from an education system which can alienate people from their own cultural roots. There, he examines a project that uses chanted tales as a potential way of broadening the educational framework, enabling people to both feel comfortable with their own communities and engage in the complexities of the modern world. Patricia Mohammed undertakes a 'history of aesthetics' of Haitian art and religion, to accommodate a new reading of Caribbean cultural history and thus create an aesthetic that shifts from Western tastes and notions of what is beautiful, towards a local reading of the aesthetic. Katerina Martina Teaiwa closes the section by arguing for the use of dance as a space for theorizing and understanding the relationship between a people's culture and the land, thus exploring issues of displacement, migration and contemporary identity in the Pacific and beyond.

**Part 3** looks at the different ways in which SIDS communities are deploying cultural strategies to engage with the demands and pressures of modern economic development. In Vanuatu, Ralph Regenvanu, explains local attempts to reposition the economy as integral to culture, rather than using culture as an economic 'good'. In this sense, through the declaration of the year of the 'traditional economy', the people of Vanuatu have deployed a strategy to counter classic economic development approaches, building on the traditional economic system that has served for centuries, and which provides food security and protection against extreme poverty. In the Comoros, Aboubakari Boina shows how a traditional cultural practice, the *grand marriage*, also serves as a key mechanism for ensuring ongoing social and economic linkages between the inhabitants of the Grand Comoros Island and the vast Comorian Diaspora, residing largely in France. The two Caribbean contributions, by Hopeton Dunn and Keith Nurse, focus on the potentialities of the cultural industries for economic development in SIDS, and in the Caribbean in particular. Dunn demonstrates how Jamaicans have drawn upon Maroon and Rastafarian culture to make significant inroads into the global cultural industries market, specifically music. He demonstrates the comparative advantage available to a small island in a particular creative sphere, as a result of its own local cultural expressions. Finally, Keith Nurse takes a broader view, arguing that SIDS have the potential to exploit the cultural industries as a viable mechanism for sustainable development, and in many cases with a potential for comparative advantage by drawing on the diversity of island cultures, thus giving local value added in the context of international markets.

As we will see throughout this book, Small Island Developing States seem by and large to be places where cultural diversity has, and continues to be, a highly significant element of the local social, political and economic life of people. Is this specific to small islands? Surely not, as there are many other land-bound areas where cultural diversity is paramount in people's daily lives. Yet, the chapters collectively suggest that all the islands from all the regions represented in the meeting had important stories to tell of the central role of diverse cultural interactions, both past and present, in the very fabric of their societies.

# Endnote

1   The report of the Secretary-General on the Strategy for the Implementation of the Programme of Action for the Sustainable Development of Small Island Developing States (Introduction, para. 5).

# Acknowledgements

The papers published in this book were first presented at an Inter-regional Expert Meeting on Cultural Diversity in SIDS, held in the Seychelles from 11 to 13 April 2007. The meeting was a direct follow up to the plenary panel on culture that UNESCO organized at the Mauritius International Meeting to Review Implementation of the Programme of Action for the Sustainable Development of Small Island Developing States, which took place in 2005. Speakers came from the three main SIDS regions: the Pacific, the Caribbean and the Indian Ocean as well as the AIMS Region.

We would like to take this opportunity to thank all those who contributed to the success of the event and chaired the individual sessions. Special mention should be made of Bernard Shamlaye, former Secretary-General of the Seychelles National Commission for UNESCO (now Minister of Education), Cheikh Tidiane Sy, former Director of the UNESCO Dar-es-Salam Office, Katerina Stenou, Director of the Division of Cultural Policies, Dirk Troost, former Chief of the Coastal Regions and Small Islands Platform, Mali Voi, former programme specialist for Culture Officer at the UNESCO Apia Office, and Tim Curtis, former Programme Specialist for Culture at the UNESCO Dar es Salaam (now at the UNESCO Bangkok Office). For their efforts in organizing the conference and follow up we would also like to thank Gabriel Essack, Lydia Charlie and Vicky Michelle from the Seychelles as well as Marie Aude Fouéré and Stella Rwechungura from the UNESCO Office in Dar es Salaam.

# MAPS Caribbean

ATLANTIC

OCEAN

Turks and
Caicos Islands

Haiti        Dominican
             Republic

British Virgin
Islands

Anguilla

Puerto Rico              St Martin   St Barth.

US Virgin                            Antigua and Barbuda
Islands          St Kitts
                 and Nevis
                 Montserrat

                                     Guadeloupe

                              Dominica

A  N      S  E  A            Martinique

                                     St Lucia
                                             Barbados
                           St Vincent and
                           the Grenadines

Aruba                                  Grenada
      Curaçao   Bonaire

              Margarita            Trinidad
                                   and
                                   Tobago

bia        V  e  n  e  z  u  e  l  a

# Indian Ocean

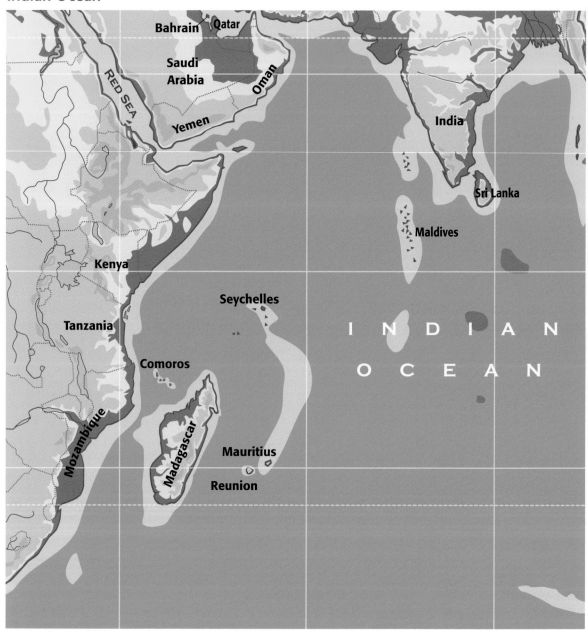

Bahrain · Qatar

Saudi Arabia

Oman

RED SEA

Yemen

India

Sri Lanka

Maldives

Kenya

Seychelles

Tanzania

INDIAN

OCEAN

Comoros

Mozambique

Madagascar

Mauritius

Reunion

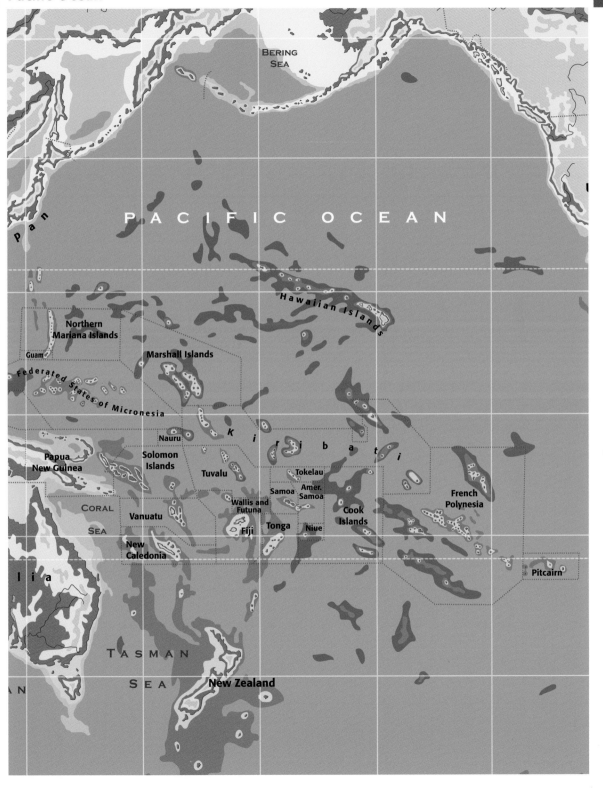

BERING
SEA

p a n

PACIFIC OCEAN

Hawaiian Islands

Northern
Mariana Islands

Guam

Marshall Islands

Federated States of Micronesia

Nauru

Papua
New Guinea

Solomon
Islands

Tuvalu

K      i      r      i      b      a      t      i

Tokelau

Samoa

Amer.
Samoa

Wallis and
Futuna

CORAL

Vanuatu

SEA

Fiji

Tonga

Niue

Cook
Islands

French
Polynesia

New
Caledonia

l i a

Pitcairn

TASMAN

SEA

New Zealand

AN

# PART 1

## ISLAND CULTURES THROUGH TIME

*So much as you can see in the heavens ... so much as the earth reveals to you ... is not to be compared with what is concealed in the earth* – Rabelais

UNESCO/Anthony Na'alehu

UNESCO/Peter Coles

UNESCO/Rocky Roe

UNESCO/Peter Coles

UNESCO/Hans Thulstrup

UNESCO/Eric Hanauer

# PACIFIC ISLANDS AS CROSSROADS
## Ancient connectivities in an island world

Matthew Spriggs, *The Australian National University, Canberra, Australia*

The settlement of the islands of the vast Pacific Ocean, stretching some 10,000 km from east to west, was the greatest sea migration ever undertaken. The Pacific was the first of the world's great oceans to be explored. The story of this migration has the potential to provide a powerful 'origin myth', with the capacity to unite the peoples of the many Small Island Developing States (SIDS) situated there; but as yet, it is a story better known outside the region than within.

Oral traditions attest to widespread interaction up to European contact across much of the Pacific, even if only on an occasional basis. Archaeological research taken, in particular, from the movement of stone artefacts and pottery, as well as isotopes in the teeth of skeletons of the earliest generations of inhabitants on particular Pacific islands, extend our knowledge of such long-distance interaction back into the remote past of the earliest Pacific voyagers and settlers: more than 40,000 years for the islands closest to New Guinea, and at least 3,000 years for the region between the Southeast Solomons and Tonga and Samoa. Recent studies reveal an ancient shared history. The new knowledge gained from such studies shows that the conventional colonial European division of the Pacific into Melanesia, Micronesia and Polynesia

has no basis in biological or cultural reality, with the partial exception of Polynesia. This chapter argues that greater knowledge within the region of an ancient shared history helps to break down old racial stereotypes that have not only been imposed by outsiders, but also seemingly internalized by some Pacific Islanders. Such knowledge also helps to shift the focus away from isolation and smallness – a focus found in much of the historical and development literature on the Pacific – towards wider visions of potential cooperation and interaction.

## Traditional geographic knowledge in the Pacific

During a sojourn on Tahiti in 1769, the English explorer Lieutenant James Cook and other members of his crew were impressed by the wide knowledge held by the priest-navigator Tupaia of other islands and island groups of the eastern part of the Pacific Ocean (Cook [Beaglehole], 1957: 117). His knowledge was distilled (and inevitably filtered) into a notional chart of the Pacific with the islands marked on it (Lewthwaite, 1970). Tupaia could list the names of 130 islands and 74 of these were presented on the chart, which gave their direction and notional distance (in terms of days' sailing) from Raiatea in the Society Islands.

Many of the islands can be identified, but the pronunciation of the names of some – and thus the spellings that have come down to us – were garbled by European recorders. The names of certain islands were archaic, suggesting that these were preserved for many generations through oral tradition rather than actual contact. The names of others remain obscure, and have led to controversial or contested interpretations – among them the idea that one such name refers to New Zealand, designated 500 or so years earlier by settlers from the Tahitian region (see discussion in Dening, 1962; Lewthwaite, 1970; and references therein).

Tupaia had himself visited some twelve of the islands, eight in the Society Group, two in the Austral Islands to the south, and two whose identification is uncertain. Various authors have suggested that he travelled to places in Samoa or Tonga, or less likely, in the Cook Islands. As the geographer Oskar Spate (1988: 26) noted, Tupaia's chart covered about 4,700 km, some 43 degrees of longitude between the Marquesas and Rotuma, to the north-west of Fiji. Given the weather systems of this part of the Pacific, the latitudinal range was nowhere near as great – some 15 degrees or 1,650 km. It extended south, possibly as far as Mangareva and Pitcairn, but more likely only as far as the Austral Islands, and to the north to the Marquesas.

David Lewis (1978: 68) wrote that 'every major island group in Eastern and Western Polynesia and Fiji, except Hawaii, New Zealand and Easter Island is indicated. The Tahitians' geographical sphere, which spanned 2,600 miles, the width of the Atlantic or more than the width of the United States, far exceeded their then voyaging range'.

Some centuries before, Hawaiian oral traditions record culture-changing visits by chiefs from Tahiti, perhaps in the thirteenth century. These visits had long ceased by the eighteenth century and appear to have been forgotten in Tahiti (Cachola-Abad, 1993). It seems that a period of inter-island voyaging followed initial colonization of the region, but regular voyaging between distant archipelagos largely ceased by the time of European contact in eastern Polynesia. It did continue, however, in western Polynesia and other parts of the Western Pacific.

Polynesians of course soon took to voyaging to distant lands again. Tupaia went with Cook to New Zealand, and was able to immediately understand Maori and provide translations into English. He then travelled on to Australia, before sadly dying in Batavia (present-day Jakarta), while on route to England. Before dying, his unerring accuracy was underlined once more by his ability to point back in the direction where Raiatea lay. Other Polynesians soon voyaged further. As well as the celebrated Omai, a Tahitian who cut a fine figure in London in 1774–77, two Tahitian adventurers took part in local European disputes and were recorded as fighting as British soldiers at the Battle of Waterloo in 1815 (Tagart, 1832: 284–92, cited in Lewis, 1972: 298).

Cook also visited Tonga and there recorded the names of 153 islands, including all the islands in the Tongan chain, the Samoan and Fijian archipelagos, (East) Futuna, Rotuma and Vaitupu in Tuvalu – the latter some 1,000 miles to the North-north-west (as quoted by Dening 1962: 110). The people who provided the names apparently did not know of Tahiti, although the Tahitians were certainly aware of the Tongans, there being some considerable overlap in geographical knowledge between the traditions of east and west Polynesia.

Our knowledge of interactions between the islands of the Pacific now extends back considerably further than the memory of oral traditions recorded in the early years of European contact. The evidence is predominantly archaeological, backed up by linguistic and genetic data (see Kirch, 2000 for a general overview of Pacific archaeology).

# Melanesia, Polynesia and Micronesia: a colonial typology

Before we examine the archaeological evidence for past interactions between different Pacific Island groups, we need to address the utility of the European categorization of Pacific peoples into Melanesians, Polynesians and Micronesians. This is an early nineteenth-century division based on a combination of geography and racial typology, derived linguistically from Classical Greek: Melanesia means 'black islands', Polynesia means 'many islands' and Micronesia means 'small islands'. Although he did not invent the individual terms used, Dumont D'Urville is credited with the definitive setting forth of this threefold division in an 1831 lecture, published in French the following year (Tcherkezoff, 2003). (Despite the enduring influence of Dumont D'Urville's essay it was published in English only in 2003).

D'Urville took his cue from earlier attempts to categorize the people of the Pacific into two races: 'copper-skinned' and 'black'. The primary division lay between the lands of the former, Polynesia and Micronesia, and the Melanesian lands of the latter, which in his conception included Australia. The Polynesians were those 'peoples who observe the *tapu*, speak the same language, and belong to the first division of the copper-skinned or swarthy race' (Dumont D'Urville, 2003: 165). Micronesians differed from them, having

> a slightly swarthier skin colour, finer facial features, more wide-open eyes, and a slimmer build. They seemed ignorant of the custom of tapu. Their language varies from one archipelago to another, and is totally unrelated to the language common to the eastern nations. The only similarities between the two divisions are the caste system, the absence of bows and arrows as offensive weapons, and the use of kava on some islands (2003: 165).

After a series of very unflattering observations about the inhabitants of Melanesia, Dumont

D'Urville notes that

> *There are countless variations in their very limited*
> *languages, even sometimes within the same island.*
> *These black people almost always live in very small*
> *tribes whose chiefs wield an arbitrary authority*
> *that they exercise just as tyrannically as any small*
> *African despot. Much closer to the barbaric state*
> *than the Polynesians and the Micronesians, they*
> *have no governing bodies, no laws, and no formal*
> *religious practices. All their institutions seem to be in*
> *their infancy (2003: 169).*

Of the 'Melanesians', the Australian Aboriginals and Tasmanians ranked lowest, and the Fijians ranked highest. Contact with neighbouring Polynesians was the explanation for the elevated rank of the Fijians, who 'obviously owe these qualities to the proximity of the Tongan people and to their frequent contacts with the Polynesian race' (2003: 170).

Although sometimes today excused as merely geographic terminology, the tripartite division of the Pacific Islands was based from its inception on perceived cultural differences, a putative culture history whereby Melanesians were progressively replaced throughout the Pacific by Polynesians, and a racial hierarchy with the Polynesians at the top. The Micronesians were second, mainly because only in Polynesia were 'well-ordered monarchies' (2003: 166) found. Then, after the Fijians came the rest of the Melanesians, and finally the Australians and Tasmanians who were condemned by their technological simplicity, their environment and

hunter-gatherer lifestyle to be placed on the lowest rung of so-called civilization.

As noted by Clark (2003a: 161), the tripartite division of Dumont D'Urville contains 'racist, essentialist and socio-evolutionary elements which are now submerged and seldom obvious due to the entrenchment of the terms resulting from their frequent use over 170 years'. Submerged perhaps, but still influential on the political alliances and divisions both between and even within Pacific Island nations; and still very much informing the academic understanding of the region's history, despite recent attempts at critique (see Clark, 2003b; D'Arcy, 2003, and references therein). We can use these divisions today as geographical shorthand, but as noted above (with the partial exception of Polynesia) they have no biological or cultural basis in reality.

## An ancient history

The first true Pacific Islands to be reached by human beings were probably New Britain and New Ireland, just to the east of New Guinea (Spriggs, 1997: Ch. 2). This was because 40,000–50,000 years ago New Guinea was part of the continent of Sahul and not an island at all. It was joined to Australia, the Aru Islands in Eastern Indonesia and Tasmania. The Torres Strait between Australia and New Guinea did not exist at this point in time; in fact, the ancient land connection between New Guinea and Australia was only severed about 8,000 years ago. While today the indigenous people of

New Guinea (in the Indonesian province of Papua and the independent nation of Papua New Guinea) and the Australian Aboriginals have little obvious cultural connection, they were once a single people (White and O'Connell, 1982).

The colonizing movements of early modern humans, originally from Africa through South and Southeast Asia and onto the continent of Sahul and beyond to the Pacific Islands of the time, soon reached as far as the end of the main Solomon Islands chain. Although our earliest dates for the Solomons, at present, only go back about 29,000 years, this probably occurred a little under 40,000 years ago (Wickler and Spriggs, 1988). Island-hopping along the entire route between intervisible islands was possible at the time, with many of the Solomon Islands forming part of a longer island, which specialists in this period have termed 'Greater Bougainville' after the largest remnant of this island mass (Spriggs 1997: 25). Not all islands of the Solomons chain were joined to this landmass, but all the main islands would have been intervisible.

During 'Ice Age' or Pleistocene times, people continued to travel between these islands. Obsidian, a black glass-like stone used for knives, travelled from New Britain to New Ireland 20,000 years ago, and by at least 6,000 years ago had reached as far south as Nissan, a raised atoll in sight of the main Solomons chain (Spriggs, 1997: Ch. 3).

As noted previously, all of these islands were potentially visible from others along the route out from Southeast Asia. But there was one exception: the crossing to Manus or the Admiralty group – either from New Ireland, New Britain or what was then the northern coast of Sahul (present-day New Guinea). Manus was reached over 26,000 years ago; however, this was not a one-off event as evidence exists of the introduction of animals – bandicoots and possums – from Sahul many thousands of years later. The significance of this event rests on the fact that Manus has never been visible from any other location: it is our first evidence of a 'blind crossing'. The people who set off on that 200–230 km journey had no idea of where they were heading. Moreover, for 60–90 km in the middle of the journey, they also lost sight of the lands they had left behind, with still no sight of a destination (Spriggs 1997: 29). To my mind, this Ice Age episode of human voyaging is of greater significance than the first Moon landing; while the Moon has been a constant, visible presence in our lives, for 60–90 km those early voyagers truly ventured into the unknown.

Such ancient chains of interconnections are traced by archaeologists using artefacts, animal bones and other evidence of the past. Traces of more recent interconnections can be found in oral traditions.

Although the Manus group was found more than 26,000 years ago, the next blind crossings in the Pacific took place just over 3,000 years ago. The bearers of the Lapita culture, named after an archaeological site in New Caledonia, colonized approximately 4,500 kilometres of the Pacific Ocean within only eight to ten generations (Kirch, 1997).

# The Lapita culture

The people of the Lapita culture were the first to venture beyond the end of the main Solomons chain, their advantage being an agricultural lifestyle and more advanced boat technology than had hitherto existed. They discovered the southeast Solomons, Vanuatu, New Caledonia, Fiji, Tonga and Samoa. The Lapita colonizers were the first to break out of what specialists term 'Near Oceania' (the present-day island of New Guinea, the Bismarck Archipelago and the main Solomons), which was settled tens of thousands of years ago by the first Pacific islanders. The rest of the Pacific, very largely pioneered for settlement by the Lapita people and their descendants, is often called 'Remote Oceania' (Green, 1991) to mark the area as one only reached by humans during the last 3,000 years.

The Lapita 'homeland' is often described as being located in the Bismarck Archipelago, centred on New Britain, New Ireland and Manus, as this is where all of its cultural elements came together and where the earliest sites are found. But its roots are a mixture of Near Oceanic cultural patterns and elements that arrived with Neolithic voyagers from Island Southeast Asia, speaking Austronesian languages derived from Taiwan, and presumably originally from what is now southern China (Green, 2000).

All indigenous groups in Remote Oceania speak Austronesian languages, as do many communities along the route from Taiwan (Pawley, 2004). The other major language groups consist of Non-Austronesian or Papuan languages, descended no doubt in a direct line from the languages of those first human settlers of New Guinea, the Bismarcks and Solomons. As direct descendants of a very ancient migration or set of migrations these languages have diverged so that links between many of them can no longer be traced by linguistic studies. It is these two processes, embedded long-lived cultural traditions combined with more recent movements of people spreading out across the vast Pacific Ocean, that make this region the most linguistically diverse in the world, with about a quarter of the world's individual languages spoken there.

All Polynesians, many Micronesians, the inhabitants of Fiji, Vanuatu and New Caledonia, and many of the coastal peoples of Near Oceania all descend linguistically and (to varying extents) culturally from the Lapita people of 3,000 years ago. I say 'many' Micronesians, because the indigenous inhabitants of Palau and the Mariana Islands in western Micronesia, although also speaking Austronesian languages, derive *directly* from Island Southeast Asia, at about the same time period as other Neolithic Southeast Asians were venturing along the north coast of New Guinea to form part of the foundational Lapita culture in the Bismarck Archipelago (Craib, 1999; Rainbird, 2004). This was followed by a further 3,000 years of mixing of Austronesian and Papuan cultures in New Guinea, the Bismarcks and the Solomons – mainly in coastal areas, but also extending up major river systems, such as the Markham Valley in New Guinea, and into the fringes of the Eastern Highlands.

To reiterate, all Pacific Island cultures derive from two great movements: that of Papuan speakers some 40,000 to 50,000 years ago, and the movement into the area of Austronesian speakers from Southeast Asia some 3,300 to 3,500 years ago. A further 3,000 years of cultural interaction between these two groups produced the cultural diversity seen today in areas of Near Oceania, where speakers of both languages are found. In the rest of the Pacific – Remote Oceania – all indigenous populations derive from the initial mixing of Papuan and Austronesian cultures, which occurred around 3,000 years ago in the Lapita 'homeland' and areas further west along the north coast of New Guinea. There is thus a shared history of *all* Pacific Islanders, a point that is not always appreciated.

One example of this is the painted rock art of the New Guinea Highlands, much of which derives from Austronesian art styles that entered the region over the last 3,000 years. Another example is the wide variety of crops enjoyed today by people all over the Pacific Islands and exported worldwide, such as taros, yams and sugarcane, all of which are thought to have been first cultivated by the Papuan speakers of the New Guinea area (Lebot, 1999). Indeed, some of the earliest physical evidence for agriculture anywhere in the world comes from the site of Kuk in the New Guinea Highlands (Denham et al, 2003).

As mentioned earlier, the existence of obsidian provided evidence that people in New Britain were in contact with people hundreds of kilometres away in New Ireland approximately 20,000 years ago. Obsidian was equally valued by the Lapita people who extended the distribution of New Britain and Manus obsidian as far south and east as Vanuatu, New Caledonia and Fiji, and as far back west into Island Southeast Asia as modern-day Sabah in Malaysian Borneo. This is among the longest distance exchange of a commodity in Neolithic societies anywhere in the world (Bellwood and Koon, 1989). Moreover, regarding Central Vanuatu at least, this was not a case of early settlers carrying a valued stone with them on initial voyages of discovery, but of a continuing exchange network bringing obsidian from the Bismarcks over a period of more than 100 years (Bedford et al, 2006).

The Lapita people were the Pacific's first pottery makers and their distinctively decorated pot designs spread from New Guinea out as far as Tonga and Samoa. Along with designs on more perishable media such as tattooed skin, barkcloth, and so on, these pots form the basis of many of the traditional art styles found in the Pacific today. One of the most remarkable aspects of Lapita culture was that the vast majority of pottery found was *not* moved from island to island, but was made on the island where it was discovered (Dickinson, 2006). The designs themselves and their meanings were carried from island to island, but in the majority of cases the pots were not.

There are exceptions, which provide us with further clues to the long voyages of the Lapita people: some pottery in Tonga is made from clay from the same source as pottery in the Reefs-Santa Cruz Islands of the southeast Solomons. The source has not yet been identified, but it may well be somewhere in northern Vanuatu. Some pottery from Central Vanuatu comes from the same source as pottery from the Reef Islands in the southeast Solomons, but this source is thought to be either the main Solomon Islands or the Bismarck Archipelago. Some Lapita pots manufactured in New Caledonia have been found in south, central and northern Vanuatu. The existence of individual Lapita pots exchanged between Fiji and Tonga also demonstrates the connections between these island groups (Dickinson, 2006 and *pers. comm.*).

We also have the evidence of the people themselves. In 2004, staff of the Vanuatu National Museum located what is to date the earliest cemetery site in the Pacific, dating from approximately 3,100 to 3,000 years ago, and belonging to the first generations of Lapita settlers on Vanuatu. This is the site of Teouma, just outside Port Vila, the capital of Vanuatu (Bedford et al, 2006). Analysis of Strontium isotopes and trace elements in the bones of this population have shown that at least four of the eighteen skeletons tested so far spent their childhoods elsewhere, and were first-generation migrants to Vanuatu (Bentley et al, 2007).

It would seem to be the case that about 3,000 years ago, people from New Guinea out as far as Tonga and Samoa were more closely interconnected than at any time until the beginning of the age of mass transportation, some two centuries ago. People travelled between islands, on occasion pots moved from one island to another, obsidian was exchanged, and art styles developed in one area and spread across many thousands of kilometres. The Lapita culture is the fundamental cultural heritage of almost all Pacific Islanders today, and provides a powerful message of shared values and connections.

As mentioned earlier, Palau and the Marianas Islands were settled from Island Southeast Asia by Neolithic cultures broadly similar to the Lapita culture and at about the same time, or slightly earlier, than the Lapita expansion. Yap would appear to have been settled as part of the Lapita phenomenon, and from the Bismarck Archipelago – a theory advanced on linguistic grounds and based upon evidence of human environmental impacts about 3,000 years ago. At this point, no sites this early have been found, but I suggest that their discovery is likely. Most of the rest of Micronesia, where 'Nuclear Micronesian' languages are spoken today, appears to have been settled in the immediate post-Lapita period. Lapita descendants from somewhere in the region between Manus and central Vanuatu arrived approximately 2,300 to 2,800 years ago (Rainbird, 2004).

# The final chapter: settlement of Eastern Polynesia

Western Polynesia was settled by the Lapita people, but there was then a pause of over 1,000 years before people moved further out beyond Tonga, Samoa and Wallis and Futuna to settle Eastern

Polynesia. During that pause the distinctive features of the Polynesian language sub-group developed (Pawley, 1996). Then, starting perhaps 1,500 years ago, there was another explosive movement of people who settled all of Eastern Polynesia, except New Zealand, within about 500 years. This amazing feat of trans-oceanic settlement reached as far as Hawaii to the north-east and Easter Island to the south-east. The settlers must also have reached South America as they brought back with them the sweet potato, found as 1,000-year-old charred remains at a site in the Cook Islands, and widespread in Eastern Polynesia by the time of European contact (Kirch, 2000).

Some 700 to 800 years ago, the final chapter in Pacific settlement was written when Eastern Polynesians headed south-west from the region of the Cook Islands towards the third apex of the 'Polynesian triangle'. They arrived at New Zealand (Hogg et al, 2003) and its neighbouring islands, which included the Chatham Islands and the Sub-Antarctic islands way to the south at 50 degrees latitude (for evidence of Polynesian visitors to these latter islands see Anderson and O'Regan, 2000).

These descendants of the Lapita voyagers visited almost every island in the Pacific Ocean, and on most of them stayed as permanent settlers. The settlement of Eastern Polynesia occurred relatively recently – within the last 700 to 1,500 years. As such, oral traditions relating to the initial settlement of many island groups, including Hawaii, Easter Island and New Zealand, are still recounted and name some of the heroic navigators involved.

However, some of those stories must also relate to subsequent long-distance interactions between island groups in the Polynesian region and beyond. Tupaia's map shows us that voyaging continued between islands, sometimes long after they were first settled.

Low-grade obsidian does occur naturally in Polynesia, but was not exchanged as widely as that from the Bismarck Archipelago. It was usually only moved – if at all – between islands of the same archipelago, as in Hawaii. By the time Eastern Polynesia was settled, pottery-making had either died out or was in decline in Western Polynesia. Apart from a few pieces from the Cook Islands and (more surprisingly) the Marquesas, pottery did not find its way out to these more scattered and remote archipelagos (Dickinson, 2006).

So our two main markers of ancient interaction, pottery and obsidian, are either not present or not informative for central and eastern Polynesia. But we do have some 'hard evidence' in the form of basaltic stone adzes that *were* exchanged between archipelagos quite extensively. This included transport of adzes from Tutuila in the Samoan Islands of Western Polynesia to Mangaia in the Cook Islands in Eastern Polynesia, some 1600 km away (Weisler and Kirch, 1996). Cultural differences between West and East Polynesia are often explained as being caused by isolation after initial settlement of the East, but the adze evidence shows that interaction probably continued throughout the pre-contact period. Society Islands adzes have also been found on Cook Islands sites, further demonstrating the existence of continuing links to the east (Allen and Johnson, 1997).

# Polynesia, Micronesia and Melanesia revisited

It is often thought that Polynesia, Micronesia and Melanesia form distinct cultural regions with perhaps distinct histories. Moreover, it is claimed that these terms demarcate separate 'races'. Indeed such views have become internalized to various degrees among Pacific Islanders. However, the early history of the Pacific, which is being revealed by archaeologists, shows that these divisions are colonial creations and have no clear basis in ancient history.

It is true that there is a well-marked subgroup of Austronesian languages labelled 'Polynesian' (Pawley, 1996). All indigenous people in geographical Polynesia speak or spoke a Polynesian language. As a cultural term it means more than Micronesian or Melanesian. But this language subgroup has arisen within Polynesia *since* the Lapita period. Around 3,000 years ago, people in Tonga and Samoa would have understood the speech of Lapita-associated groups as far away as New Britain and New Ireland just to the east of New Guinea: they were all speakers of dialects of Proto-Oceanic. Polynesian languages derive from this through a language stage shared with the indigenous people of Fiji – who are usually identified as 'Melanesian' in culture. Fijians and

Polynesians share a similar cultural origin in the Lapita culture, as do many other 'Melanesians'. The Melanesia-Polynesia division did not exist 3,000 years ago.

While linguistically Fiji and Polynesia did diverge over the succeeding centuries, this was not a result of absolute isolation between these areas. Fiji had a much closer relationship throughout its history with Western Polynesia than with the rest of what we call Melanesia. On current archaeological evidence, the 800 km or so gap between Vanuatu and Fiji was very rarely crossed from Lapita times up until European contact, but a complex exchange network did link Tonga, Samoa and Fiji during much of this period (Weisler, 1997).

Geographical Melanesia is extremely diverse linguistically and culturally. It is hard to think of anything that unites it as a cultural region. In the Remote Oceanic parts – the south-east Solomons, Vanuatu, New Caledonia and Fiji – the foundation culture is Lapita, and languages again derive from Proto-Oceanic Austronesian. But in Near Oceania, settled many tens of thousands of years prior to the Lapita culture, we find both Austronesian and Papuan languages, the greatest genetic diversity among humans outside of Africa, and a bewildering variety of distinct cultures and cultural expressions.

Something of a new Melanesian identity has been created during and after the period of colonial domination of the nineteenth and twentieth centuries. There are elements of shared colonial histories and shared histories of sometimes-forced indentured labour on plantations on various Pacific islands and in Queensland, Australia. People in Melanesia often identify each other with the term 'wantok', literally 'people of one language'. New Guinea *Tok Pisin*, Solomon Islands *Pidgin* and Vanuatu *Bislama* are indeed all closely-related forms of plantation-era Pidgin English and form a *lingua franca* across much of the region – but by no means all. In New Caledonia the common language is French, in (West) Papua it is in large part Indonesian, and in Fiji the languages of intercultural communication are Standard Fijian and English. Many people in the region of Papua New Guinea around the capital Port Moresby use another pidginized language, *Motu* (sometimes called *Police Motu*), derived from a local Austronesian language rather than English vocabulary.

Based on an anthropological stereotype in part going back to D'Urville and earlier, it is sometimes said that traditional Melanesian leadership was based on the acquired skills of a 'Big Man' as opposed to the hereditary chiefship seen as typical of Polynesia (Sahlins, 1963). It is true – as noted by D'Urville in the 1830s (2003: 166) – that the Pacific's most powerful chiefs at the time of European contact were found in Polynesia, in places such as Tonga, Tahiti and Hawaii. But there were also certainly chiefs in parts of Island Melanesia, such as Fiji, New Caledonia and Vanuatu. At least some of the 'Big Man' societies described by white anthropologists and missionaries in parts of Melanesia, appear to have resulted from the breakdown of more hierarchical societies as a result of European contact, depopulation and colonial pacification (Spriggs, 2008 and refs therein). As has been realized more recently, the term 'Big Man' does not do justice to and does not adequately capture the many forms of non-chiefly leadership found in Melanesia. Diversity and innovation are again features that we find there (Godelier and Strathern, 1991).

Of the three named divisions in the Pacific, Micronesia or 'small islands' is the least commented upon. The area is not as culturally diverse as Melanesia and not as seemingly homogeneous as Polynesia (see Rainbird, 2004). It was settled between 2,000 and 3,500 years ago, but not from one single location. At approximately the same time as the Lapita expansion into the Remote Oceanic parts of Melanesia and on into Western Polynesia, separate migrations took place from Island Southeast Asia to the Mariana Islands and Palau. It is almost certain that the islands of Yap were reached during the Lapita expansion, although we have yet to find any sites that early there.

As previously noted, the rest of Micronesia was seemingly settled between about 2,300 and 2,800 years ago by Lapita descendants from somewhere in the area between Manus and central Vanuatu. Sometime within the last 2,000 years there was contact between the Polynesians of Tuvalu and the Micronesians of Kiribati, and new sailing technologies and fishhook types were introduced into Polynesia. Contact was not just one-way: the narcotic drug kava was introduced to Kosrae and Pohnpei from a Polynesian source, and two

Polynesian-speaking islands, Kapingamarangi and Nukuoro, exist in the southern fringes of Micronesia (Crowley, 1994).

The origins of the people of the Micronesian region can therefore be traced to at least five separate migrations, over a period of about 500 to 3,500 years ago, from five distinct areas of Island Southeast Asia, Melanesia and Polynesia. Culturally, Micronesia does not exist, although most (but not all) of it shares a recent history of Japanese and American colonial administration, which has tended to impose a superficial degree of unity.

That said, archaeological evidence and oral tradition demonstrate widespread interaction between island groups across the region (Lewis, 1972: 33). Over the last 2,000 or so years, Micronesia has also formed an entry point into the Pacific from Southeast Asia, with cultural items such as the backstrap weaving loom and kite fishing spreading into Micronesia and then further out into the Pacific (Intoh, 1999).

Certain traditional island interactions within Polynesia have been recently revived by the building (usually using modern materials) and sailing of large voyaging canoes such as the *Hokule'a*. These craft approximate traditional canoes in appearance to various degrees but their value is *not* as true representatives of ancient canoes; it lies instead in the cultural re-uniting of long-separated parts of Polynesia, such as Easter Island and Tahiti and other central-eastern Polynesian islands, Hawaii and Tahiti, and the Cook Islands and New Zealand (Finney, 1994; 1997). However, this cultural revival has not led to a renewal of earlier Lapita culture interactions which united Island Melanesia and Western Polynesia.

To my mind this is a lost opportunity, the absence of any appreciation of the Lapita culture merely reinforcing old nineteenth-century prejudices. Lapita constitutes the founding culture for much of the Pacific. The languages, arts and many aspects of traditional culture and social organization in the Pacific Islands derive directly from Lapita, with its proximate 'homeland' in the Bismarck Archipelago off the eastern end of New Guinea. As we have seen, all Polynesians and Island Melanesian cultures in Remote Oceania derive directly from Lapita; this is also the case for many of the Near Oceanic parts of Island Melanesia and most peoples and cultures in Micronesia – with the exception of Palau and the Marianas. These latter countries trace their cultural ancestry back to Island Southeast Asian Neolithic cultures not much different than Lapita, and represent the eastwards expansion of these cultures out into the Pacific.

This viewpoint might be seen to exclude New Guinea and the original inhabitants of the Bismarck Archipelago and the Solomons, however, this is not really the case. Lapita itself was to some extent a hybrid of Island Southeast Asian and the earlier cultures of Continental and Island Melanesia. Many coastal populations of New Guinea which today speak Austronesian languages can trace direct cultural roots to Lapita – in particular, populations along both the northern and southern coasts of what is today Papua New Guinea. Lapita technologies such as pottery-making spread beyond Austronesian-speaking groups into areas such as the Sepik River, while Lapita or Island Southeast Asian Neolithic art styles spread up into the interior of New Guinea into the New Guinea Highlands.

As noted earlier, many of the crops and some cultural practices seen in Lapita, such as the use of the ground or earth ovens for cooking and obsidian exploitation and exchange, pre-date Lapita in the New Guinea region (Spriggs, 1996). Lapita is thus not exclusively Southeast Asian in origin.

Some progress has been made in re-uniting the peoples of the ancient Lapita realm, stretching from New Guinea to Tonga, Samoa, Uvea and Futuna, and this is encouraging. Lapita culture draws its name from the site of Lapita in New Caledonia, and in 2002 a moving ceremony was held there to comemorate the fiftieth anniversary of the site's excavation by Gifford and Shutler (Sand, 2003). The traditional Kanak tribal owners of the Lapita site area welcomed onto their land representatives from all areas where examples of Lapita culture have been found. Gifts were exchanged and hopefully some of that ancient unity was re-established. A new Pacific group – the archaeologists – was represented at the ceremony by Kanak archaeologist Jacques Bole. Hopefully, this group will spearhead many further episodes of rediscovery and reconnection.

The participation at the ceremony of Western Polynesian representatives was a very good sign, given the colonial history of antagonism by Polynesians to the idea of any shared ancestry with the peoples of the Melanesian region. The 1930s map of supposed Polynesian migrations by the New Zealand Maori scholar Peter Buck or Te Rangi Hiroa illustrated this antagonism (Buck, 1938). It studiously avoided marking a route out of Asia for the Polynesians that included any Melanesian islands, with the exception of Fiji. Buck, like many Polynesians of his generation, had clearly internalized D'Urville's ideas of racial hierarchy. Thus, it was particularly heartening that the Western Polynesians in attendance at the Lapita site were joined by an eastern Polynesian representative in the person of a Maori woman potter from New Zealand, Colleen Waata Urlich.

Colleen has been inspired by Lapita pottery designs and forms to create beautiful modern pots whose production is rooted in a Maori cosmogony that recognizes and is legitimized by ancient uses of clay in New Zealand (Urlich, 2003). She notes that knowledge of the ancient links between contemporary Maori workers in clay and Lapita ceramicists provides 'a sense of history, of continuity and an ancient *whakapapa* or genealogy, for the contemporary Maori clay movement' (2003: 391).

## Conclusion

This chapter has sought to bring to the fore the deep history of connections between populations across the Pacific Islands. First noticed by the earliest European explorers who recorded oral histories of such long-distance interactions, modern archaeology has shown that such connections date back to the earliest human settlement of islands in this region. In so doing, it has also demonstrated that European colonial divisions, in particular for Melanesia and Micronesia, have little salience as one goes back in time, and represent a history tainted by racist thought that we should be aware of when using these strictly geographical terms.

Wider knowledge of the ancient shared history of the peoples of the Small Island Developing States (SIDS) of the Pacific Islands and their relatives in larger countries and territories in the region, such as New Zealand, French Polynesia and Hawaii, can only be to the good. Such knowledge helps to reframe our experience of the region away from seeing 'small islands in a big sea' and towards a view of the Pacific Ocean as a 'sea of islands' – a perspective reiterated by Tongan scholar Epeli Hau'ofa in his writings (see, for example, Hau'ofa, 1993). This shifts the cultural focus away from smallness and isolation towards wider visions of cooperation and interaction. It also helps break down the lingering insidiousness of views of racial hierarchy within the Pacific, still held by outsiders and internalized by some Pacific Islanders themselves to the detriment of all.

## References

Allen, M.S. and Johnson, K.T.M. 1997. Tracking ancient patterns of interaction: recent geochemical studies in the southern Cook Islands. M.I. Weisler (ed.) *Prehistoric Long-distance Interaction in Oceania: an interdisciplinary approach. New Zealand Archaeological Association Monograph* 21, pp. 111–33.

Anderson, A. and O'Regan, G. 2000. To the final shore: prehistoric colonisation of the Subantarctic Islands in South Polynesia. A. Anderson and T. Murray (eds) *Australian Archaeologist: collected papers in honour of Jim Allen.* Canberra: Coombs Academic Publishing, ANU, pp. 440–54.

Bedford, S., Spriggs, M. and Regenvanu, R. 2006. The Teouma Lapita site and the early human settlement of the Pacific Islands. *Antiquity* 80: 812–28.

Bellwood, P. and Koon, P. 1989. 'Lapita colonists leave boats unburned!' The question of Lapita links with Island Southeast Asia. *Antiquity* 63: 613–22.

Bentley, R.A., Buckley, H., Spriggs, M., Bedford, S., Ottley, C.J., Nowell, G.M., Macpherson, C.G. and Pearson, D.G. 2007. Lapita migrants in the Pacific's oldest cemetery: isotope analysis at Teouma. *American Antiquity* 72(4): 645–656.

Buck, P. 1938. *Vikings of the Sunrise.* New York: Frederick Stokes.

Cachola-Abad. C.K. 1993. Evaluating the orthodox dual settlement model for the Hawaiian Islands: an analysis of artefact distribution and Hawaiian oral tradition. M.W. Graves and R.C. Green (eds) *The Evolution and Organisation of Prehistoric Society in Polynesia. New Zealand Archaeological Association Monograph* 19, pp. 13–32.

Clark, G. 2003a. Dumont D'Urville's Oceania. *Journal of Pacific History* 38(2): 155–61.

Clark, G. 2003b. Shards of meaning: archaeology and the Melanesia-Polynesia divide. *Journal of Pacific History* 38(2): 197–215.

Cook J. [J.C. Beaglehole ed.] 1957. *The Journals of Captain James Cook on his Voyages of Discovery*, Vol. I. Cambridge: The Hakluyt Society.

Craib, J. 1999. Colonisation of the Mariana Islands: new evidence and implications for human movement in the Western Pacific. J-C. Galipaud and I. Lilley (eds) *The Pacific from 5000 to 2000 BP: Colonisation and transformations. (Le Pacifique de 5000 à 2000 avant le présent: Suppléments à l'histoire d'une colonisation.)* Paris: IRD, pp. 477–85.

Crowley, T. 1994. Proto who drank kava. A. Pawley and M. Ross (eds) *Austronesian Terminologies: continuity and change.* Canberra: Department of Linguistics, RSPAS, Australian National University. Pacific Linguistics C-127, pp. 87–100.

D'Arcy, P. 2003. Cultural divisions and Island environments since the time of Dumont D'Urville. *Journal of Pacific History* 38(2): 217–35.

Denham, T.P. Haberle, S.G., Lentfer, C., Fullagar, R., Field, J., Therin, M., Porch, N. and Winsborough, B. 2003. Origins of agriculture at Kuk Swamp in the Highlands of New Guinea. *Science* 301: 189–93.

Dening, G. 1962. The geographical knowledge of the Polynesians. J. Golson (ed.) *Polynesian Navigation: a symposium on Andrew Sharp's theory of accidental voyages. Polynesian Society Memoir* 34, pp. 102–36.

Dickinson, W.R. 2006. Temper sands in Prehistoric Oceanian pottery: geotectonics, sedimentology, petrography, provenance. *Geological Society of America Special Paper* 406.

Dumont D'Urville, J-S-C. 2003. On the islands of the Great Ocean. *Journal of Pacific History* 38(2): 163–74.

Finney, B. 1994. *Voyage of Rediscovery.* Berkeley: University of California Press.

Finney, B. 1997. Experimental voyaging, oral traditions and long-distance interaction in Polynesia. M.I. Weisler (ed.) *Prehistoric Long-distance Interaction in Oceania: an interdisciplinary approach. New Zealand Archaeological Association Monograph* 21, pp. 38–52.

Godelier, M. and Strathern, M. (eds). 1991. *Big Men and Great Men: personifications of power in Melanesia.* Cambridge and Paris: Cambridge University Press and Editions de la Maison des Sciences de l'Homme.

Green, R.C. 1991. Near and Remote Oceania: disestablishing 'Melanesia' in culture history. A. Pawley (ed.) *Man and a Half: essays in Pacific anthropology and ethnobiology in honour of Ralph Bulmer. Polynesian Society Memoir.* Auckland: The Polynesian Society, pp. 491–502.

Green, R.C. 2000. Lapita and the cultural model for intrusion, integration and innovation. A. Anderson and T. Murray (eds) *Australian Archaeologist: collected papers in honour of Jim Allen.* Canberra: Coombs Academic Publishing, ANU, pp. 372–92.

Hau'ofa, E. 1993. Our sea of islands. *A New Oceania: rediscovering our sea of islands.* Suva: School of Social and Economic Development, The University of the South Pacific, pp. 2–16.

Hogg, A.H., Higham, T.F.G., Lowe, D.J., Palmer, J.G., Reimer, P.J. and Newnham, R.M. 2003. A wiggle-match date for Polynesian settlement of New Zealand. *Antiquity* 77: 116–25.

Intoh, M. 1999. Cultural contacts between Micronesia and Melanesia. J-C. Galipaud and

I. Lilley (eds) *The Pacific from 5000 to 2000 BP: colonisation and transformations.* (*Le Pacifique de 5000 à 2000 avant le présent: suppléments à l'histoire d'une colonisation.*) Paris: IRD, pp. 407–22.

Kirch, P.V. 1997. *The Lapita Peoples: ancestors of the Oceanic world.* Oxford: Blackwell.

Kirch, P.V. 2000. *On the Road of the Winds: an archaeological history of the Pacific Islands before European contact.* Berkeley and Los Angeles: University of California Press.

Lebot, V. 1999. Biomolecular evidence for plant domestication in Sahul. *Genetic Resources and Crop Evolution* 46: 619–28.

Lewis, D. 1972. *We, the Navigators: the ancient art of landfinding in the Pacific.* Canberra: ANU Press.

Lewis, D. 1978. *The Voyaging Stars: secrets of the Pacific Island navigators.* Sydney: William Collins.

Lewthwaite, G.R. 1970. The puzzle of Tupaia's map. *New Zealand Geographer* 26(1): 1–19.

Pawley, A. 1996. The Polynesian subgroup as a problem for Irwin's continuous settlement hypothesis. J. Davidson, G. Irwin, F. Leach, A. Pawley and D. Brown (eds) *Oceanic Culture History: essays in honour of Roger Green.* Dunedin: New Zealand Journal of Archaeology, pp. 387–410.

Pawley, A. 2004. The Austronesian dispersal: languages, technologies and people. P. Bellwood and C. Renfrew (eds) *Examining the Farming/Language Dispersal Hypothesis.* McDonald Institute Monographs. Cambridge: McDonald Institute, pp. 251–73.

Rainbird, P. 2004. *The Archaeology of Micronesia.* Cambridge: Cambridge University Press.

Sahlins, M. 1963. Poor man, rich man, big-man, chief: political types in Melanesia and Polynesia. *Comparative Studies in Society and History* 5: 285–303.

Sand, C. 2003. Introduction to the conference: commemorating the first excavation at Lapita. C. Sand (ed.) *Pacific Archaeology: assessments and prospects.* Proceedings of the International Conference for the 50th Anniversary of the first Lapita Excavation, Koné-Nouméa 2002. Le Cahiers de L'Archéologie en Nouvelle-Calédonie 15, pp. 1–10.

Spate, O. 1988. *Paradise Found and Lost: the Pacific since Magellan*, Vol. III. Minneapolis: University of Minnesota Press.

Spriggs, M. 1996. What is Southeast Asian about Lapita? T. Akazawa and E. Szathmary (eds) *Prehistoric Mongoloid Dispersals.* Oxford: Oxford University Press, pp. 324–48.

Spriggs, M. 1997. *The Island Melanesians.* Oxford: Blackwell.

Spriggs, M. 2008. Ethnographic parallels and the denial of history. *World Archaeology* 40(4): 538–52.

Tagart, E. 1832. *A Memoir of the late Captain Peter Heywood*, R.N. London: Effingham Wilson.

Tcherkezoff, S. 2003. A long and unfortunate voyage towards the 'invention' of the Melanesia/Polynesia distinction 1595–1832. *Journal of Pacific History* 38(2): 175–96.

Urlich, C.E. Waata. 2003. A new perspective: new blooms from ancient seeds. C. Sand (ed.) *Pacific Archaeology: assessments and prospects.* Proceedings of the International Conference for the 50th Anniversary of the first Lapita Excavation, Koné-Nouméa 2002. Le Cahiers de L'Archéologie en Nouvelle-Calédonie 15, pp. 387–92.

Weisler, M.I. 1997 Introduction. M.I. Weisler (ed.) *Prehistoric Long-distance Interaction in Oceania: an interdisciplinary approach.*

New Zealand Archaeological Association Monograph 21, pp. 7–18.

Weisler, M.I and Kirch, P.V. 1996. Inter island and interarchipelago transfer of stone tools in prehistoric Polynesia. *Proceedings of the National Academy of Sciences* 93: 1381–85.

White, J.P. and O'Connell, J.F. 1982. *A Prehistory of Australia, New Guinea and Sahul*. Sydney: Academic Press.

Wickler, S. and Spriggs, M. 1988. Pleistocene human occupation of the Solomon Islands, Melanesia. *Antiquity* 62: 703–06.

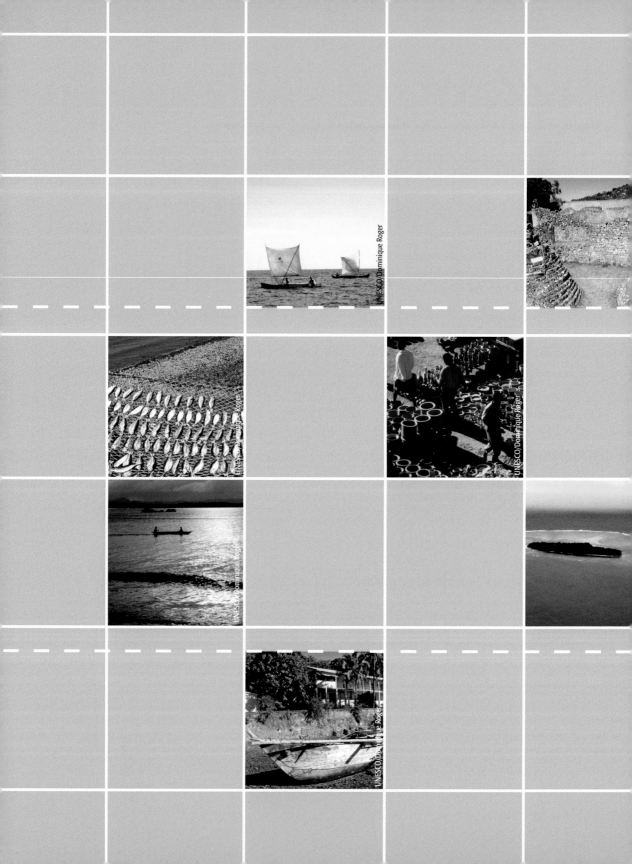

# Austronesian migration and the establishment of the Malagasy civilization

## Contrasted readings in linguistics, archaeology, genetics and cultural anthropology[1]

Claude Allibert, *Institut National des Langues et Civilisations Orientales, Paris, France*

Malagasy studies have been dominated, rightly or wrongly, by the work of two great pioneers, Grandidier and Ferrand, who adopted opposing stances on the question of the peopling of Madagascar.

Grandidier (1908) represents a viewpoint privileging Hindo-Austronesian and even Melanesian origins. Ferrand (1908), over and beyond an initial undetermined settlement from Africa which he nevertheless supports, perceives there to have been a second wave of settlement from Africa followed by migrations of Austronesians with some Persian/Arab admixtures.

The major difference between these two viewpoints is that, for Grandidier, Africa played only a minor role late in the process, which he is inclined to relegate to recent slaving episodes, whereas the black element in the population he attributes to a Melanesian component. We show here that this reading is faulty. This position may perhaps be put down to the fact that Grandidier himself arrived in Madagascar from the east: health reasons caused him to leave India to recuperate in the Mascarene Islands (Mauritius and Reunion), from where he travelled to Madagascar.

Ferrand, on the other hand, from the very beginning asserted the involvement of a Bantu element in the earliest periods of settlement. The Persian/Arab adjuncts are represented as occurring over a period of centuries, from around the tenth to the sixteenth. The Austronesian component, which he traces to the Indonesian archipelago, has long been established, but he asserts that this was preceded by the Bantu element. Although his views evolved somewhat between the end of the nineteenth century and his death in 1935, they continued to conform to this general schema.

These two authors, who both enjoyed great scientific reputations, were followed to a greater or lesser extent by other researchers throughout the twentieth century, who tended to line up behind one or the other. In the second half of the century, however, a greater number of them sub-scribed to Ferrand's positions. First Deschamps (1960), then Kent (1970) and Verin (1980), demonstrated the antiquity of the Bantu ele-ment, and further, that certain populations of the Madagascan west coast consisted entirely of this element – an observation noted and confirmed by the reports of sixteenth and seventeenth-century Portuguese navigators.

Fewer followed Grandidier, no doubt because the Hindo-Melanesian theory failed in general terms to catch on. It was undermined, among other reasons, by the linguistic evidence estab-lished by Dahl (1951), but also because the study of Arab writings undertaken by Ferrand (1913–14) revealed the part played by Arabs in popula-tion movements of the Mozambique Channel as far as Madagascar, long before the existence of the European-operated slave-trade. However, it should also be remembered that Grandidier (1836–1921) was older than Ferrand and put forward his theories and hypotheses earlier. The latter then used these as a point of contrast for his ideas, in part incorrectly, for example, when he took issue with Grandidier over the occurrence of Arab occupation in the Comoro islands in the tenth century, an event which was later confirmed by archaeologists.

But in the end, the only problem which remained, and which perhaps remains still, is that of estab-lishing which of the two main groups, one of African origin, the other Austronesian, settled in Madagascar first.

The aim of this chapter is to try to make some progress in understanding the settlement patterns of populations which contributed to the forma-tion of Malagasy culture, but equally to that of the island regions of the western Indian Ocean. To accomplish this, this chapter re-evaluates the migrations that were effective in establishing the patterns of human settlement in the area by bringing forward evidence derived from certain cultural and physical anthropology studies. This also provides an opportunity to reflect on the concept of migration and on the link between this concept and the vectors that underlie it, which are often cited in order to equate the ethnic origin of migrant peoples with the artefacts, technologies, religious practices and even language(s) that they bring with them.

The first task is to review the knowledge which has become available to us in the fields of linguis-tics, archaeology and, recently, genetics over the half-century that has elapsed since the deaths of these two famous researchers. Where appropri-ate, theories of technological diffusion and cul-tural anthropology are also taken into account. The overall study attempts to find responses to the questions: who, when and why?

## Linguistics: the major literature

It is generally recognized that Otto Dahl's 1951 publication, *Malgache et Maanjan* (Malagasy and Maanjan) demonstrated the links between the former and the latter – the latter belonging with the

Barito group of languages of South-East Kaliman-tan (Borneo) – and formed a key turning-point in the development of Malagasy and Austronesian linguistic studies. Admittedly, the connection be-tween Malagasy and Malay had been recognized by the Portuguese since the early decades of the sixteenth century (well before van Houtman in 1595 and Luis Mariano in 1614). Adelaar (1995) drew attention to the close proximity between Malagasy and Samihim (also belonging to the Barito group), but signalled likewise the presence of borrowings from Javanese and Malay. He also pointed to links with the Toradja and Buginese languages of Sulawesi.

However, Dahl was also the author of two other significant contributions to this field: the first (1988) considered the idea of a Bantu substra-tum to Malagasy,[2] while the second, which ap-peared in 1991 shortly before his death, revisited the hypotheses formulated at the conclusion of his very first book. In this early work he attrib-uted the proto-Malagasy migration to an Austro-nesian population, placing its beginning around the fifth century. In his latter work, he brought forward the date of this migration to the seventh century, associating it with the beginnings of the Srivijaya thalassocracy. Adelaar in turn also adheres to this date, but construes a sea-going Malay culture exercising an attraction for the neighbouring Austronesian populations (which would explain the diversity of borrowings).

Dahl's third stand is the assertion of an initial Bantu presence in Madagascar, by which the Austronesian language of the Malagasy became modified though linguistic interference. But this viewpoint has not met with universal acceptance. Other linguists willingly admit Bantu borrow-ings into Malagasy at a more or less early period, whether pre-Swahili or under Swahili influence, but refuse to recognize a structural incidence on the language.

Beaujard (2003) re-evaluated the Sanskrit element, limited to seventy-five words in Malagasy. Solange Bernard-Thierry (1959) had already demonstrated that thirty-four words of Sanskrit origin, which did not constitute a vocabulary, had transited via Southeast Asia before passing from the Indian sub-continent to Madagascar by the direct route. An-other recent contribution to this debate is that of Beaujard (unpublished) relating to plants and their associated terminology (see also Allibert, 1991 and 1992, on the early introduction of bamboo and the coconut). Their Austronesian origins extend over a vast oceanic territory, as shown by Waruni Mahdi, who examined the spread of the outrigger canoe over a large part of the Indian Ocean (this point is discussed later in the chapter).

Just as interesting (but open to debate) is the thesis of Pierre Simon (2006), who sees in Mala-gasy an initially Austronesian language which underwent phases of creolization and relexicali-zation. Simon characterizes the proto-Malagasy population as a people of Austronesian language coming into contact with proto-Bantu peoples (speakers of Sabaki) from around the first centu-ries of the Common Era.

Finally, it is important to note the interesting discovery made by Ferrand (1932) (reprised by Hébert [forthcoming]) and the inscription on the Bangka stele (686 CE), which he has dubbed the Indonesian Rosetta Stone. There are inscriptions in Sanskrit and proto-Austronesian (might one even say proto-Malagasy?) concerning the curse directed at those who refused to yield to the new masters conquering the land. The interpretation of this text attracted close attention from the leading linguists (Ferrand, 1932; but also Coedès 1931) and epigraphists in the field. Ferrand claimed to have detected a Malagasy proto-language in which figured the word *tafika* (army), which to this day has not been found in any Austronesian language other than Malagasy. But this proposition has not met with universal adherence despite the interest raised by the occurrence of the term.[3]

# Archaeology:
# Austronesian or African tracks?

Given the evidence of the Malagasy language's Austronesian origins, archaeologists have been led to search for forms of pottery presenting typological linkages with those of the Austronesian world. Unfortunately, up to the present day no typological relationship in any formal sense has been shown, in the way that has been achieved for pottery of the *lapita* type in Oceania, even if *lapita* pottery does present variants in which researchers have noted a 'dynamic conservatism' (Gosden, 1992).

Austronesian pottery of the first millennium CE is not well known as far as the western sector of its diffusion zone is concerned. One single decorative type, found in the south of Sulawesi (Allibert, 2002: 23, n. 34) has suggested a possible correspondence associated with ornamental interlacing figures on the neck of the pots, but the degree of relevance of this decoration is uncertain. Moreover, the dating of this particular pottery is very imprecise (first millennium CE).

Furthermore, in ninth and tenth-century sites in Sumatra, for example, local pottery examples are quite low in number, and those that exist do not correspond to Malagasy pottery. In contrast, there is frequent and widespread evidence of imported ceramics (Chinese, Arab and even Indian). These are found throughout the Indian Ocean and could well indicate their general usage. Finally, the Austronesian culture relied predominantly on plant materials (bamboo and leaves as receptacles) and such usage would not have left many traces.

It might well be more profitable to approach the problem of detecting pottery of Austronesian origin by looking along the western shores of the Indian Ocean, rather than trying to rediscover pottery from Southeast Asia by searching for its diffusion in Madagascar and the Comoro Islands. One might ask whether examples of pottery can be found in Madagascar which bear no relationship to those of Africa, and whose origin must therefore be sought with those of Austronesia. This would presuppose that its typology has not been totally lost and that such Malagasy pottery of non-African appearance is not of specifically indigenous creation.

The discovery in the Comoros (in Mayotte in particular, at Koungou and Majikavu) of two different types of pottery is noteworthy. One is the so-called 'triangular incised ware' (TIW), dated from the sixth to the eighth centuries, and indisputably of African origin (Chami and Msemwa, 1997). The other has a decorative pattern of large shell impressions and is from the same period (though not precisely dated); its percentage occurrence rate steadily increases from the coast of Africa to Madagascar, or steadily decreases if read in the opposite direction, and could well be the proto-Malagasy pottery, if not the proto-Austronesian pottery, of the western Indian Ocean.

Finally, there exists another pottery of exceptional quality (cups with alternating graphite and/or red ochre coats) dated to the ninth and tenth centuries, whose origin is unknown, but which English-speaking archaeologists attribute to the 'Swahili corridor'.[4]

# Cultural markers

Although it is always a little delicate to speak of cultural diffusionism, there are cases where connections show that this idea has indisputable relevance. Four examples, covered here, closely associate Madagascar with the Austronesian world:

1.  The role of the maternal uncle (*zama* in Mayotte and in the north of Madagascar), has a central function in the rites of a nephew's circumcision (see Flacourt, 1995). The Austronesian root (*iama*) of this term has been confirmed by Waruno Mahdi (pers. comm.).

2.  The rite of second burial (*famadihana* in Madagascar, both among the Merina and Sakalava peoples) (Aujas, 1927) is also found in the Philippines (the Mangyan Patag people), in Borneo (among the Dayaks) and as far away as Samoa. In this regard, a recent thesis defended by Luquin (2004) on the Mangyan Patag has brought to light the fundamental significance of the number eight among the Autronesians. One must correlate the practice of the *taolambalo* – the eight key bones which must be brought back to the tomb according to the Malagasy (Allibert, forthcoming) – with the eight generations of dead ancestors needed to personally attain the status of ancestor among the Philippine ethnic group.

3.  Also relevant is the Austronesian terminology used to designate the single or double-outrigger canoe – *gala-gala* (Oceania) / *kolavə* (Sri Lanka) / *galawat* (Gujerat) / *ngalawa* (Swahili zone and Comoros) and *lankang* (Indonesia) / *laka* (Madagascar) (Allibert, 1996). These examples imply a double diffusion pathway: one directly to Madagascar, the other by shorter sea-borne stages. We might also note the use made of

the canoe as a coffin in the Austronesian dispersal zone.

4. The final example constitutes the ritual pairing that associates a child with a reptile (monitor lizards, crocodiles and Komodo dragons), as practised among the Buginese (Hamonic, 1987: 9). Flacourt, in the celebrated Chapter XVI of his first book, tells the tale of the Malagasy princess Zafiramini who learned she had given birth to a crocodile. Here, one sees the belief that the spirits of the ancestors reside in these animals. Any such animal that is presented as the child's twin is brought up alongside it. This interpretation better elucidates the relationship of the Malagasy with crocodiles, especially among the Sakalava, and derives from a practice that is in no way African but Austronesian.

## Genetics: a fundamental tool to be handled with care

Genetic analysis is a technique whose use can be dangerously misleading, but which is also genuinely promising, on condition that it is applied only after an indispensable prior analysis relating to genealogies has taken place. The main danger relates to confusion of concepts of ethnicity with designated social groupings. In this respect, the persistence of the idea of distinct ethnic groups in Madagascar is problematic (these distinctions are more than 100 years old, but already in the time of

Gallieni's governorship were not universally accepted because of the extent of the migration of human populations towards the interior of the island).

The best example of such debatable research is a recent study (Hurles et al, 2005) on 'Merina ethnicity'. This was undertaken by an Anglo-Saxon team, which took as its research base a group of 362 men from four Malagasy 'ethnic groups', and ten populations potentially associated with Madagascar, located in the islands of Southeast Asia and the Pacific.

The main points derived from the study are raised briefly here in advance of a more detailed discussion.

- Genetic heritage from maternal and paternal lines was attributed to an initial geographic zone, specifically the area of South-Eastern Borneo.

- The contribution was more or less evenly divided between Asian and African heritage, as much from paternal as from maternal branches.

- The Southeast Asian admixture most probably occurred in a single migration episode (historians and cultural anthropologists do not agree with this view).

These results present little new information, since there is general agreement on the ethnic links of the Malagasy with Austronesian and African groups.

Questions remain as to what meaning can be attributed to the term 'ethnic groups'[5] at a time when, for example, all inhabitants of the Imerina region are called Merina – that is to say, in circumstances where the concept of genetic group markers is no longer observable under a designation which is essentially geographic and no longer genetic.

What conclusions can be drawn from this? Supposing that it is still possible to establish a point of departure within a population that is genetically more Austronesian than African (or vice versa), the appropriate approach would not be to begin from randomly chosen study subjects, but to work from the studies of genealogical anthropologists, historians, geographers and sociologists. In this way one would secure the possibility of taking blood samples from groups with a higher chance of obtaining authentically significant results from a historic perspective. However, this approach was not the one taken, or if it was taken, it has not been explicitly so stated by this team of geneticists. Will the 50:50 result obtained be robust enough for the purpose of defining the genetic characteristics of all Merina groups (considering the different origins of the Andevo, etc.)? It would have been preferable had preliminary anthropological research into the lines of descent been carried out in well-defined groups.

The other two results to claim attention are of some interest (if the limited relevance that we have been led to accord to the preceding observations can be relied upon). The first, almost too precise to be true, confirms the south-eastern Barito (Borneo) origin of the population studied, defined half a century ago by Dahl on the linguistic level. The second postulates a single migration arrival.

A second study (Soodyall et al, 1996) encompassing further research into the postulated ethnic groups (p. 18), has brought out the fact that the Sakalava group is largely Bantu, but deriving from Mozambique rather than from the Kenyan coast. The Merinas are shown as being more Austronesian.

This particular study, even if it once again presents the disadvantage of relying on a concept of ethnic groups without attesting a prior methodology based on cultural and genealogical anthropology (the designation of Sakalava is given to those living in the Sakalava region), at least makes the case for this erroneous principle.

Nevertheless, one important piece of information should be retained from this study: the authors affirm that no Indian genetic marker was found. The conclusion to be drawn is that the migratory passage to Madagascar was not accomplished in short coast-bound or island-hopping stages, but by a direct route – a finding which confounds the hypotheses of Deschamps (1960). But which were the population groups studied? Among those included, were there any of the populations from the south-east coast, described by Flacourt (1995), which in the seventeenth century may have presented certain Indian or Persian traits? The third study (Ducourneau et al, forthcoming), addresses the island of Grand Comoro. It is general knowledge that the Comoro archipelago is considered a conservatory of the cultures of the Indian Ocean. The research for this study was based on ninety-three Grand-Comoran men living in Marseille, whose genealogical history had been established. Several genetic markers were observed:

- a very dominant Bantu marker, against an African background

- a marker from the area of the Persian Gulf, Arab or Persian (probably Shirazian) at 5–6 per cent

- an Austronesian marker (about 5 per cent) unexpected in Grand Comoro, perhaps a little over-dimensioned because of the notion of drift due to insularity, but definitively present, and

- a noted total absence of markers from South India.

# Conclusion: comparing and contrasting data

If a corroborative contrasting of the data obtained from archaeological and linguistic studies has proved difficult to substantiate, one which sets the results obtained from genetics against the linguistic evidence is indeed possible. Thus, as we have seen, the linguistic connection of Malagasy to the Barito language of Kalimantan has been confirmed by genetic studies. Similar genetic analysis applied to plants, set against the terminologies used to name them,[6] can explain their spread. Genetics and archaeo-technology can be equally complementary. The comparison of technological typologies with genetic markers can prove eloquent, even if a human group is not necessarily the manufacturer of the technology that it carries: it was not the Chinese who brought the Chinese pottery (tang and song) into the region. This is why one cannot assert with total conviction the existence of an ethnic migration under the blanket of a diffusion of technologies. But it cannot be completely ruled out either. Attempts to contrast the percentage of potsherds with the shell-impression pattern (fairly rare on the African coast and gradually increasing in number the more one approaches Madagascar) with the Austronesian genetic marker (haploid group O), which similarly increases in percentage terms from the Comoros to Madagascar, need to be taken into account in any future plan of study.

In conclusion, it seems that:

- Austronesians never reached Africa (or at least not as far as Mozambique), and hence the Austronesian technologies found in Africa are a result of simple diffusion. No linguistic or genetic trace has been detected there,[7] nor have any archaeological typologies. However, it will be important to see whether the same conclusion applies to the north-eastern region of Africa, from Somalia to Tanzania, and around the coasts of South Africa, or even further a field in west Africa.

● The genetic data from the Comoros confirms an early Austronesian presence there, which conceivably became more marked in moving from west to east. This would not be surprising, but leaves open the problem of the direction of migratory movements preceding sedentarization (east–west or west–east?). If the shell-impression typology is an Austronesian marker (or even simply proto-Malagasy), the decrease in frequency that it reveals from east to west in the Mozambique Channel would confirm a movement from Madagascar towards the Comoros and eventually the African coast.

● The contemporaneous association of Bantu TIW pottery and shell-impression pottery of probably Austronesian (proto-Malagasy) influence seems possible in Mayotte between the fifth and eighth centuries. This interpretation would lend support to Simon's linguistic hypothesis and his concept of the creolization of the Malagasy language. This composite may then have been overlaid from the fourteenth century onwards by a push of African Swahili.

● Arab and Persian genetic markers have been detected in the Comoros, but the southeastern coast of Madagascar has been insufficiently studied. Indian genetic traces are abnormally absent, whether they be from the north of the subcontinent (Gujerati, for example) or from the south (Dravidian).

● The direct migration of already established Austronesian families contradicts the historical narratives of Flacourt,[8] who rather favoured a concept of waves of migration.

● The Austronesian influx comes from the southern part of Sulawesi (Buginese) and from Kalimantan, Borneo (Maanyan). Resemblances in characteristics of cultural anthropology and religion, such as the belief in child–animal twinning, but also the practice of double burial (found in the Philippines), corroborate genetic and linguistic indicators.

● The trans-Indian Ocean migration probably occurred around the seventh century. Both linguistics (Dahl and Adelaar) and archaeology support this hypothesis.

In the light of these considerations centred on the Indian Ocean, it should be noted that the migration concept, studied on four levels (genetic, archaeo-technological, cultural and botanical),[9] may not necessarily allow for the same results with regard to determining the ethnic composition of these voyagers.

Only genetics will be able to provide definite information on the origin of the human vector involved. All the other factors can appropriate a human vector which is not necessarily their inventor: technology, plants, language, cultural inputs and religion can all be carried by a third party.

Examples of this are numerous: we have only to think of the Vikings/Norsemen who introduced the French language into England.

Only genetic analysis may be considered a secure source of evidence, but this only under certain strict conditions, involving significant numbers (the practice of percentages), undertaken with the greatest vigilance, and with corroborative comparisons made with other disciplines (genealogical anthropology, history, etc). The ideal situation, something we would all hope to discover, would be the following: a necropolis containing numerous skeletons, permitting a comparison of DNA readings with carbon-14 dating from one of the earliest possible periods. Something like a Vohemar site,[10] more than a thousand years older and more carefully excavated.

# References

Adelaar, S. 1995. L'importance du samihim (Bornéo du Sud) pour l'étymologie malgache. *L'Etranger intime*. Mélanges offerts à Paul Ottino, Université de la Réunion, Saint-Denis de la Réunion: Océan/Université de la Réunion, pp. 47–59.

Allibert, C. 1991. Wakwak: végétal, minéral ou humain? Reconsidération du problème. *Etudes Océan Indien* 12: 171–89. Also published in *L'Arbre anthropogène du Waqwaq, les Femmes-fruits et les Iles des Femmes*, 2007, (ed. J.-L. Bacqué-Grammont en collaboration avec M. Bernardini and L. Berardi), Napoli, Universita Degli Studi di Napoli 'l'Orientale' and Institut Français d'Etudes Anatoliennes, pp. 225–41.

Allibert, C. 1992. Le monde austronésien et la civilisation du bambou; Une plume qui pèse lourd: l'oiseau Rokh des auteurs arabes. *Taloha* 11: 167–81.

Allibert, C. 1996, unpublished. Quelques notes sur la terminologie comparée des bateaux dans l'Ouest de l'océan Indien. Paper presented at the Colloque Communautés maritimes de l'océan Indien (IVe siècle avant J-C–XIVe siècle après J-C), June – July 1996, CNRS-Lyon II/ Maison de l'Orient méditerranéen.

Allibert, C. 2002. L'interdépendance de l'archéologie et de l'anthropologie culturelle dans l'océan Indien occidental. L'exemple de Mayotte. *Etudes Océan Indien* 33–4: 11–31.

Allibert, C. forthcoming. Les secondes funérailles: un marqueur austronésien majeur. Son rôle à Madagascar. Paris: *Etudes Océan Indien*, Inalco.

Aujas, L. 1927. Les rites du sacrifice à Madagascar. Tananarive: Mémoires de l'Académie Malgache, Pitot, fasc. II.

Beaujard, Ph. 2003. Les arrivées austronésiennes à Madagascar: vagues ou continuum. *Etudes Océan Indien* 35–36: 59–128.

Beaujard, Ph. unpublished. Voyage et histoire des plantes cultivées à Madagascar avant l'arrivée des Européens.

Bernard-Thierry, S. 1959. A propos des emprunts sanskrits en malgache. *Journal Asiatique* 247(3): 311–48.

Chami, F.A. and Msemwa, P.I. 1997. A new look at culture trade on the Azanian Coast. *Current Anthropology* 38(4): 673–77.

Coedès, G. 1931. Les inscriptions malaises de Çrivijaya. *BEFEO* 30: 29–80.

Dahl, O.C. 1951. *Malgache et Maanyan, une comparaison linguistique*. Oslo: Egede Instituttet.

Dahl, O.C. 1988. Bantu substratum in Malagasy. *Etudes Océan Indien* 9: 91–132.

Dahl, O.C. 1991. *Migration from Kalimantan to Madagascar*. Oslo: Institute for Comparative Research in Human Culture, Norwegian University Press.

Deschamps, H. 1960. *Histoire de Madagascar*. Paris: Berger-Levrault.

Dick-Read, R. 2005. *The Phantom Voyagers: evidence of Indonesian settlement*. Winchester: Thurlton.

Ducourneau, A., Boesch, G., Mitchell, M.J., Chiaroni, J. forthcoming. *The Y Chromosome in the Comoros Islands: a Middle Eastern and an Austronesian influence in Sub-Saharan East Africa*.

Ferrand, G. 1908. L'origine africaine des Malgaches. *Journal Asiatique* 11: 353–500.

Ferrand, G. 1913–14. *Relation des voyages et textes géographiques arabes, persans et turcs relatifs à l'Extrême-Orient du VIIIe au XVIIIe siècles*. Paris: Leroux.

Ferrand, G. 1932. Quatre textes épigraphiques malayo-sanskrits de Sumatra et de Banka. *Journal Asiatique*, Oct.– Dec.: 271–326.

Flacourt de, E. 1995. *Histoire de la Grande Isle Madagascar*. (ed.) C. Allibert. Paris: Karthala-INALCO.

Gosden, Ch. 1992. Dynamic traditionalism: Lapita as a long term social structure. J. Ch. Galipaud (ed.) *Poterie Lapita et peuplement*. Actes du colloque Lapita, Noumea: ORSTOM, pp. 21–26.

Grandidier, A. and Grandidier, G. 1908. *Histoire physique, naturelle et politique de Madagascar*, Vol. IV: Ethnographie, t. 1: Les habitants de Madagascar. Paris: Imprimerie nationale.

Hamonic, G. 1987. *Le langage des Dieux. Cultes et pouvoirs préislamiques en pays bugis*, Célèbes-Sud, Indonésie. Paris: Editions du CNRS.

Hébert, J-C. forthcoming. La proto-histoire de Komr (Madagascar et l'archipel des Comores).

Hurles, M.E., Sykes, B.C., Jobling, M.A., Forster, P. 2005. The dual origin of the Malagasy in Island Southeast Asia and East Africa: evidence from maternal and paternal lineages. *American Journal of Human Genetics* 76: 894–901.

Jones, A.M. 1971. *Africa and Indonesia*. Leiden: Brill.

Kent, R. 1970. *Early Kingdoms in Madagascar: 1500–1700*. New York: Holt, Rinehart and Winston.

Luquin, E. 2004. Abondance des ancêtres, abondance du riz: les relations socio-économiques des Mangyan Patag, île de Mindoro, Philippines. PhD Dissertation. Paris: Ecole des Hautes Etudes en Sciences Sociales.

Simon, P. 2006. *La langue des ancêtres. Ny Fitenin-dRazana. Une périodisation du malgache de l'origine au XVe siècle*. Paris: L'Harmattan.

Soodyall, H., Jenkins, H., Hewitt, T., Krause, R., Stoneking, A., Stoneking, M. 1996. The Peopling of Madagascar. A.J. Boyce, C.G.N. Mascie-Taylor (eds) *Molecular Biology and Human Diversity*, Cambridge: Cambridge University Press, pp. 157–70.

Vérin, P. 1980. Les apports culturels et la contribution africaine au peuplement de Madagascar. *Histoire générale de l'Afrique*. Relations historiques à travers l'océan Indien, Paris: UNESCO, pp. 103–23.

# Endnotes

1   Essay first published by SAGE-UNESCO (in French and English) in *Diogène*, 2008, 218, pp. 6–17, and *Diogenes*, 2008, 218, Vol. 55, No. 2, pp. 7–16.

2   Other researchers rather see it as an adstratum.

3   I pass over the incidence of Persian which is real but of relatively minor significance, often interspersed in the Arabic which used it.

4   A term which is credited to Horton.

5   Unnamed in this case; moreover, it is doubtful whether one might still attribute a sense to this concept in the local environment, in view of the numerous migrations over the centuries towards the island's interior.

6   Following this method I have been able to follow the diffusion of the coconut palm from East to West through the Austronesian terms *buahniu* (Bali) / *voanio* (Madagascar), not to mention *vanu* in the Loyalty Islands, but also from *narikela* (Sanskrit) / *nargil* (Arabic, Persian) / *mnadzi* (Bantu). This represents a double linguistic pathway for the same tree, one path directly across the Indian Ocean, the other via the north of the same ocean.

7   Which goes against the theories of Jones (1971), recently taken up by Dick-Read (2005).

8   One declarative, identified as from 500 years before the presence of the governor, that is in 1150; the other contextual, supposing Ramini as having been contemporary with Mahomet, hence in the seventh century.

9   Associations can be made between the diffusion zone of Southeast Asian plants: for example, *Barringtonia asiatica* and the distribution zone of the single or double outrigger canoe.

10   Necropolis from north-east Madagascar (thirteenth to eighteenth centuries).

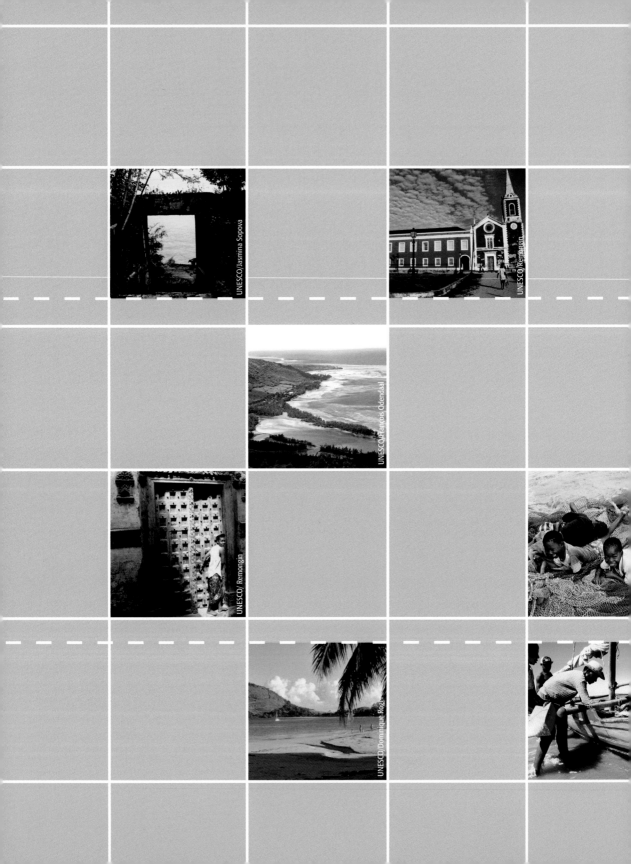

UNESCO/Jasmina Sopova

UNESCO/Remongin

UNESCO/François Odendaal

UNESCO/ Remongin

UNESCO/ Dominique Roger

# MEMORY AND CULTURAL DIVERSITY IN THE SMALL ISLANDS OF THE WESTERN INDIAN OCEAN

## The case of the Mascarene Islands and the Seychelles

Sudel Fuma, *Université de la Réunion, Saint Denis, Ile de la Réunion, France*

From the outset, it is important to set forth the following prerequisite: the situation of the Mascarene Islands and the Seychelles present such specificities that they represent a case which may be said, without exaggeration, to be unique in the world (Poirier and Fuma, 1998). In fact, nowhere else do the following three key elements exist. Firstly, we are in the presence of a history that begins from a *terminus a quo*. We know with relative precision the conditions of the first settlements on the island – at least the first which left traces – and which unfolded without interruption up to the present day, notwithstanding the occasional visits of migratory Arabs. Secondly, the island societies of the Indian Ocean were born out of the co-existence and interactions, to different degrees, of three fundamental matrices: the Afro-Malagasy matrix, the European matrix and the Hindu matrix. Onto these were grafted adventitious elements of less importance – Chinese, Indo-Melanesian and Gujarat contributions – which exercised very different influences with regard to the physical and cultural mixings specific to each island. Thirdly, this geographic ensemble, which was essentially disparate at the beginning

of its colonial history, has developed new forms of solidarity in spite of the different forms of political evolution (independence in 1968 for Mauritius and the Seychelles and 'departmentalization' and integration in the French national ensemble for the island of Reunion in 1946). The result of this process has been the birth of an original Creole society marked by its cultural diversity.

This chapter formulates questions that address the cultural diversity found in these small islands, relying on research undertaken over the past thirty years with ethnologist Jean Poirier,[1] within the framework of a multi-disciplinary programme dedicated to oral history.

The ethnic components of the Creole societies of the Indian Ocean are quite dissimilar when compared in terms of their demographic importance, historic age, value systems, and also according to the relations that they have entered into, or not, with each other. Three facts merit emphasis.

First of all, it seems that during the eighteenth century the African contribution was not strong.

It derives, as is well understood, from colonial slavery, which developed after the application of the *Code Noir* in the French islands Île de France and Bourbon in 1724.[2] The lists of slave traders exist in the port archives (Deschamps, 1972; Deveau, 1990; Roman, 2001). The boats that arrived in the Mascarene islands loaded their complement on the Malagasy coasts in western Madagascar (Maintirano, Majunga and Morondava) or to the north-east (Baie d'Antongil, Foulpointe and Tamatave), which were considered the most valued ports during the slave trade (Institut de civilisation-Musée d'Art et d'Archéologie, 1997). From the eighteenth century onwards, some slaves were taken from the east coast of Africa (the blacks of 'Mozambique') and others were taken from the Atlantic coast (Senegal); however, these constituted the exception. Moreover, the demand for slaves from Guinea was reduced by the nearby presence of the Great Island, Madagascar, whose proximity reduced the total cost of the slave.

Secondly, it appears on the contrary that slaves originating from Madagascar – although less appreciated by Western colonizers on account of being physically weaker than the Africans – were more numerous. The Malagasy elements on Mauritius, as on Reunion, were present from the beginning and constituted the majority of the labour force.[3] On Bourbon during the eighteenth century, 58 per cent of the slave population originated from Madagascar. The proportion of Malagasies on Île de France was as high as on Bourbon, the two islands being governed by the same French administration. Catholicism was the

only authorized religion under colonial law, but animism was practised clandestinely by the slaves. It would be useful, in this regard, to undertake a precise inventory of all the elements of a Malagasy origin present in Reunion, Mauritius and the Seychelles. Athough anthroponomy is of little help since names were given by slave owners (until the abolition of slavery), on Reunion, toponymy illustrates in a most clear manner the importance of the Malagasy peopling. Almost all of the sites and villages of the highlands on Reunion – the domain controlled by the *maroon* slaves during the first half of the eighteenth century – have names with Malagasy origins: *Cilaos, Maffate, Salazie, Bélouve, Bérive, Cimendef, Tapcal,* and so on. Similarly, analysis of animist worship practices such as the 'servis malgas' or the 'servis Kaf', relating to orature, cuisine and music helped to identify the importance of references to the Great Island.[4]

The African contribution dates primarily from the end of the eighteenth century and the beginning of the nineteenth with the development of the sugar industry on Île de Bourbon and Île de France. Confronted with the difficulties of obtaining slaves from Madagascar after the expansion of the 'Merina' kingdom, the French returned to Africa and negotiated with the Arab sultans of Zanzibar and the Portuguese authorities of Mozambique. Millions of African slaves left from Kilwa, Pemba, Zanzibar, the Ilha da Mozambica and the region of Inhambane, destined for the Mascarene islands. They carried with them their values, oral traditions and religion, which in spite of colonial pressure, permitted the

African cultural model to survive clandestinely on the Île de France and Île de Bourbon.

Thirdly, the Asian cultural influence manifested itself in the nineteenth century with the arrival of Indian 'indentured labourers'. These were newcomers in the service of a colonial system that invented the concept of 'indentured labour' to justify manual labour. They came primarily from southern India to replace slaves after their manumission in 1835 on Mauritius – which became a British territory in 1810 – and in 1848 on Reunion, a French colony (Carter, 1998; Fuma, 1999). The number of Indian workers, designated by the pejorative term 'Coolies', grew rapidly on Mauritius and surpassed the number of former slaves.[5] Unlike the African and Malagasy populations who endured slavery with its consequential prohibition of their cultural and worship practices, the Indians benefited from judicial protection of their cultural and religious practices. On Bourbon, the decree of 3 July 1829 accorded the first Indian indentured labourers the right to religion and the use of a site for religious practices on the sugar estates. Similarly, on Mauritius, British legislation recognized the right of Indian labourers to their culture and their religion.

The European contribution – in particular that of France – began with the colonization and peopling of the islands of the Indian Ocean. The Dutch were present on Mauritius from 1638 to 1698, but abandoned the island leaving behind few traces of their cultural influence. In general, however, the arrival of European colonists has had a primordial cultural influence, whether in Île de Bourbon in 1663 (Barrassin, 1989: 15–23), Île de France in 1721 (Toussaint, 1974: 36), the Seychelles in 1770 (Ministry of Education, 1983: 60), or Rodrigues in 1735 (Berthelot, 2002: 2). On Bourbon, cultural mixing occurred from the beginnings of settlement as a result of intermarriage between European colonizers and Malagasy women – a consequence, in effect, of the lack of white women on the island (Barrassin 1989: 104–05). If European cultural values were imposed on the Malagasy and Indo-Portuguese wives of the colonizers, as well as on their children who received a French education, some Malagasy or Indian cultural elements – carried by the women – penetrated the official education system and participated in the Creolization of the original European environment.

Finally, two other communities, established more recently on Mauritius and Reunion, but numerically less important than the others, lived in a particular situation with regard to cultural mixing: the Indo-Muslims, originally from the Northwest of India and called 'Zarab' on Reunion, and the Chinese, many of whom came from the regions of Canton and Fou-Kien. Both these populations had long practised endogamy as a matter of fact, although this went unrecorded by any officially recognized model. This behaviour was accompanied by a type of cultural self-centeredness – an observation quantifiable on the basis of matrimonial statistics.

Despite a difference in the treatment of cultural models by the colonial administrations of Mauritius and Reunion – a result of the breaks in their colonial history in 1815 (Mauritius becoming British and Reunion, French) – it is clear that slavery and indentured labour, the founding systems of Creole societies of the Indian Ocean, fashioned these societies through mixing and Creolization, without erasing the cultural diversity inherited from the people's countries of origin (Fuma and Poirier, 1990: 49–66).

The cultural mixing that expresses itself through Creole, the common language of the islands, as well as other assets including music and culinary practices, constitutes one piece of evidence; however, it should be noted that the reality of mixing has been obscured over a long period of time. To take the example of Reunion, we could say that all 'Reunionese' are genetically mixed, comprising three key components: European, Afro-Malagasy and Indian. The white Creoles include among their ancestors Malagasies and Indians; the blacks of Africa are mixed with Malagasies, Indians and Europeans – a biological mix also experienced by the Tamil Indians. The fact that the people of Reunion, as well as those of Mauritius and the Seychelles, represent a cultural and genetic mix is today widely recognized, supplanting the previous belief that the populations were of 'local stock'. This in itself has become an occasion for a new 'reunion'.

Until the end of the twentieth century, the cultural and physical mixing of peoples was de-valorized as a consequence of a colonial history marked by the unspoken and the suppression of cultural diversity. The mixed Mauritian became the 'mulatto' under the colonial typology of groups identified by the colour of their skin. It is important here to define two constants that exist filigreed across the social fabric, and which have not been verbalized by Creole societies until very recently: the first concerns the scars of slavery; the second, the latent forms now taken by racist prejudices.

One must understand that the cultural field of Creole societies is crossed by a few important themes, situated either at the level of the collective unconscious (these would be the mnemonic traces analogous to those that Jung thought to identify), or at the level of the individual consciousness. The essential theme which marks its presence everywhere is slavery. If taken into consideration as a means to understand cultural diversity, it serves, in a certain manner, as an interlocutory condition for the validity of research in the Indian Ocean countries. Whether the topic concerns slavery, strictly speaking, or what is called indentured labour – this last concept was designated the 'coolie-trade' on Mauritius and 'servitude' on Reunion – what counts is that we designate enslavement, in other words, the reification of subject become object, as the total negation of human rights (Fuma, 2001b: 54–62). Such was the situation of the 'Indoceanese' on both the level of individual psychology and the level of the collective unconscious.[6] Enslavement has become the inexpiable crime, and the collective unconscious of the descendants of slaves and indentured labourers still guards the stigmas of yesterday's enslavement. This original sin affects all components of the population, as much the descendants of slaves as the descendants of masters: the first because they share in the infamous status which deprived the slave of all human dignity, the second because they share in the fault. Everything happens as if each part of the population has interiorized the same feeling of rejection, manifested by a negative attitude: enslavement is condemned by all parties, by some for having suffered through their ancestors, by others for having inflicted the suffering.

Today, this double heritage is in the process of being acknowledged – the necessary condition for its passing. In the twentieth century, this double heritage generated a series of difficulties and formed the basis of conflicted relations, establishing themselves on the basis of the unspoken and the implicit.[7] We are now in the presence of an irreversible change, capable of transforming the conditions of the 'reunion' of the various cultural components of Creole societies within an interdependent community. The concept of a *Maison des Civilisations et de l'Unité Réunionnaise* (Reunion House of Civilizations and Unity)[8] perfectly illustrates this change at the cultural level, in other words, the recognition of the diversity at the heart of the union of a Creole island (Vergès, 2002: 170–74). As of the moment that the mnemonic traces of servitude are recognized and a critical attitude applied to their re-evaluation, a new arrangement will be put into place which will permit the transformation of yesterday's antagonisms into complementarities and cultural wealth.

Among the latent antagonisms that still remain on the islands of Mauritius, the Seychelles and Reunion, we can predict the progressive disappearance of racist prejudices inherited from slavery (Bissoondoyal and Servansing, 1989; Cangy et al, 2002; Low, 2003: 325–37; Scarr, 2000). Such prejudices are still a reality in the domain of the unspoken and should not be denied. In the islands, the problem of racism is not generally as marked as is found elsewhere in the West or in the developing world. On the contrary, it is pleasing to be able to note the absence of all manifestations of race-related violence, and to recognize that the co-existence of 'ethnic' and cultural communities unfolds against a peaceful landscape of tolerance and reciprocal recognition. But it should be recognized that there exist, not just one, but many latent racisms that situate themselves at the level of daily life, in a manner that is tacit, cushioned, embryonic, and in some ways, self-ashamed. These prejudices express themselves within the framework of a network of complex interrelations between communities: between Creoles mixed in the strict sense, Creole 'Kaf' or 'Mazambik', 'Malbar' or Hindu, Chinese, white of European origin, Indo-Muslim or 'Zarab'.[9] The data regarding these problems should therefore be nuanced according to each island. Nevertheless, the feeling of common residential belonging increasingly works as a unifying factor, reducing disparities and according each cultural group the right to diversity within unity. Herein, there exists a truly 'Creole miracle' that derives from the process of Creolization and from the system of slavery.[10]

Indeed, the 'Creole miracle', when situated within the field of culture, is a concept that requires consideration in order to understand Creole societies. It concerns an unexpected situation that was largely unforeseeable. In the Creole islands, the descendents of slaves have succeeded in establishing re-composed societies, possessing their own logic and signification (Fuma, 2004). The result is surprising: the Creole societies of the Indian Ocean have engendered from their history a paradoxical masterpiece that in its manner testifies to the possibilities of human ingenuity. Indeed, the situation at the beginning comprised very diverse cultural elements: it was a waste-basket of exiled individuals, cut off definitively from their families, ancestors, symbols and from all that constituted their reasons to live. Even the African slave, deprived of liberty, could locate his or her bearings in the motherland. The situation was different for the same individual deported to the islands of the Indian Ocean. It is necessary to understand the parameters of the problem: the ethnic groups were strangers to each other, the languages were different, as were the traditions and social architecture. There were disparities between councils of elders and monarchies, matrilineal and patrilineal systems, economies of hunter gatherers, farmers, fishermen, or of peasants, and polygamous or monogamous societies!

Under these circumstances, the performance of former slaves was completely surprising: people that were truly wrecks, de-socialized, deprived of culture, potentially dehumanized, lacking a common language, crushed by arduous work, constantly controlled by masters to prevent re-grouping, and victims of an institutionalized, permanent racism, were able to reconstitute – to fabricate – a new society and a new culture. After having evaluated this performance, which is truly unique in the world, it remains for researchers in human sciences to apply themselves to understanding how this social surgery was conducted in a little over three centuries, and how the process of Creolization was established, giving fruition to the Indian Ocean societies. Here, then, are a few central points for reflection.

Certain negative factors are evident at the beginning of this social mutation; however, there are also positive factors, which are so strange as to seem almost impossible. The negative factors, though, are more numerous, the following of which seem key:

- Although not often cited, the 'pulverization' of the African population is a key factor. In the eighteenth and nineteenth century, a significant number of slaves originated from Africa, coming from a variety of ethnic groups – the Yao, Makondé, Makuas, and so on. This was in spite of the fact that the slave trade to the islands of the Indian Ocean also dealt in slaves from Madagascar. In terms of the maritime slave trade, the zones for departure to the islands ran north of today's Tanzania and south of Mozambique. This strongly indicates significant differences between languages and even cultures – not just between the Shona or the Ndebele of Zimbabwe, or the different ethnic Bantu groups of Tanzania (in particular, the Makondés, Makuas, Yao and Ngoni, who fed the Arab and Western slave ships), but also between the different ethnic groups of Mozambique (Sheriff, 1987). We can only imagine the communication difficulties among slaves who travelled from the interior of the continent to be loaded at Zanzibar, Bagamoyo, Kilwa, Pemba, Ilha da Mozambica and Quelimane.[11]

● This 'pulverization' was reinforced by a deliberate policy of diversification of recruitment areas, and by precautions the masters took in most regions to separate slaves with the same origins on island plantations. It is important to remind ourselves of the harsh living conditions of slaves on colonial plantations with regards to housing, nourishment and health, which understandably permanently weakened them.

In such a negative context, the slaves truly excelled themselves (Police, 1999). It should not be forgotten that the fundamental slave condition translates into a destruction of the self, in other words, de-socialization, de-culturation and de-humanization. De-socialization brutally removed all social memberships; indeed, the African slave lived only by reference to the many groups who conferred his identity. These are not abstract terms; on the contrary, this issue concretely concerns very precise processes as indicated by three key structures:

● The *group* defined by marriage, lineage and kinship, which gathers together actual relatives of the extended family, united by blood and by alliance, and members of other clans, with whom existed more or less close relations.

● The *clan* in which either the lineage or the lineage segment theoretically groups the descendents of the same ancestor (for a clan, mythic; for a lineage, historical, with a genealogy that can be traced). The clans, lineages or extended families only exist through propitiation of the ancestors: their life in the beyond is strengthened through the consecration of ritual forms of worship and, in return, the ancestors assume the protection of their descendants. Without ancestors, a person would not exist. This was precisely the case of the slave in the Indian Ocean islands. We can only imagine the anguish and trauma of the Malagasy slaves, deprived of their sacred ancestral worship (Ravaosolo, 2000a and b).

● The *ethnicity* or ethnic group, which combines these many components. The importance of this entity, which was formerly debated, is real. Although colonization reinforced ethnic groups in certain cases, these were not a by-product of colonization, as the narratives of the first explorers show that ethnic groups existed prior to colonial times.

De-culturation took place through the loss of all moral, ethical and religious points of reference: participation in cultural heritage, beliefs and sacred practices (symbols, rituals and taboos); and symbiosis with invisible entities (spirits, chthonians, totems and gods). This was combined with a complete break with the whole system of values expressed by orature (myths, fables and proverbs). The entire symbolic capital of the African or the Malagasy was destroyed with arrival in the colony.

De-humanization occurred because the slave was either 'animalized' or 'reified' by the racist prejudices which negated all their rights to humanity. The descendants of Africans and Malagasies could no longer refer to their culture of origin under threat of ridicule and even humiliation by their own group (Campebort, 2000).[12] These same prejudices survived the abolition of slavery. During the 1970s, a famous *séga* singer of African descent, a 'Kaf' from Reunion, was ridiculed by a racist rumour taken up under the guise of a 'pleasantry' by the conservative society of the island: the joke was that a monkey from the zoo had called the singer and asked him how he had managed to escape from his cage. More than a century after the abolition of slavery, African descendents in the islands were still being 'animalized' in the unconscious of one segment of the population of Reunion. However, with such handicaps, this 'sub-human' population succeeded in a few centuries in creating authentic societies, with their own values, specific features, concepts, language, sacred practices, aesthetics, and a system of mental protection against a destructive 'elsewhere' peopled by malevolent spirits.[13] How this occurred is a puzzle that occupies historians and ethnologists. Considering the road taken, it

is difficult not to speak of some type of 'miracle'? But a miracle should be explained. This will be the work of social scientists who must work to understand the intervening transformations in two great periods: the first prior to the abolition of slavery (2 February 1835 for Mauritius, the Seychelles and Rodrigues; 20 December 1848 for Reunion), and the second from the latter half of the twentieth century – a period in which the judicial, economic and political conditions changed, giving birth to new societies.

It is possible to locate the beginnings of an explanation in identifying, after the negative factors which are too easily enumerated, the existence of positive factors – elements that were favourable to this metamorphosis. These are fewer in number and the following are among the most significant:

● The first fact seems indisputable, however paradoxical: it was amid the extreme severity of slavery that those slaves who survived were able to dominate their situation, from the period of capture and deportation to the centuries of exploitation that followed. This resulted partially from a choice: of the slaves offered to traders, only the youngest, the most vigorous and the healthiest were sold. The frightful conditions of the journey by slave ship provided, what must be called a second process of selection: only the strongest – physically and morally – survived. Having arrived in the colonies, a third selection process, spread out over time, served the same role: the harsh conditions which influenced child mortality, as is attested by demographic and historical research, allowed only the most resistant to survive (Eve, 1999a).

• Secondly, demographic growth enabled the formation of populations that imposed themselves through their very weight. Moreover, these populations found that their importance increased tenfold as a result of recognition, accompanied by the implementation of a political plan based on the democratic ideals of colonial capitals following the abolition of slavery, even if the descendents of slaves continued to be politically used and manipulated by the descendents of masters.

• Finally, a whole series of elements have played a role in the spheres of psychology and sociology, especially after the abolition of slavery. Indeed, a 'Westerners with a bad conscience' psychology was progressively put into place, with, in compensation, a re-evaluation of the rights acquired by the victims of slavery. Simultaneous with this, slaves were 'Creolized' or 'Mauritius-ized' and took possession of their land, even if it was only a patch of ground.[14] The African and Malagasy dream of former slaves, and the Indian dream for the descendents of Indian indentured labourers, resides as a cultural referent for the part of the population that has kept contact with its culture of origin through music or religion. But the true country where these populations reside is

that of cultural diversity, of the recognition and sharing of original cultures. The concept of residential identity is fundamental to island societies in the Indian Ocean.

## Conclusion

The research undertaken on island societies in the Indian Ocean led to the following finding: the specificity of a memory and a shared cultural diversity founded on slavery and indentured servitude. The interrelations between groups of different origins on Mauritius, Rodrigues, in the Seychelles or on Reunion, would all merit further in-depth study. In December 1998, at the end of the conference 'Slavery and Abolition in the Indian Ocean' organized by the University of Reunion, a wish was expressed for the creation of a 'Creology' laboratory. The 2007 event organized by UNESCO in the Seychelles, 'Islands as Crossroads: Cultural Diversities in Small Island Developing States', permitted the researchers to re-affirm the urgency of this wish, the implementation of which would protect the rich and diverse cultural heritage of the small islands of the Indian Ocean. In particular, it is necessary to organize interdisciplinary research to improve understanding of the mechanisms and dynamics of 'Creolizations'. On the basis of which objective indicators can we define Creolization? What were the principle factors at the emergence of this movement, and which factors have affected its evolution over time? One objective of a Creology laboratory would be to conduct a historical analysis of the Creolization journey, examining, for example, the consequences of policies enacted in the colonial capitals, in particular the differences and permanent effects of the Anglo-Saxon versus the Latin approach on the current evolution of the islands. It would be equally advisable to focus research on situations, which in their early stages could have led to the birth to a Creole society, but ultimately took other paths.[15] It would also be of interest to research the criteria for 'Creole-ness', both with regard to the spheres of history and anthropology. Within the framework of this type of research, great attention should be given on the one hand to demographic evolution, and on the other to the history of material culture and techniques. It should be possible to more precisely define data by developing a better understanding of the various technical and cultural contributions. By identifying all the givens, we would undoubtedly arrive at the truth concerning the origins of Creolization, and thereby obtain a better understanding of the functioning of Creole societies and their ability to integrate unity and cultural diversity. At a time when identity crises threaten the cohesion of ancient European countries, the Creole models of the small islands provide new approaches worthy of consideration.[16]

# References

Barrassin, J. 1989. *La vie quotidienne des colons de l'Ile Bourbon à la fin du règne de Louis XIV, 1700–1715*. Réunion: Académie de La Réunion, VID.

Berthelot, L. 2002. *La Petite Mascareigne: aspect de l'histoire de Rodrigue*. Réunion: Government publication, Centre Nelson Mandela.

Bissoondoyal, U. and Servansing, S.B.C. (eds). 1989. *Slavery in West Indian Ocean*. Mauritius: Mahatma Gandhi Institute.

Bollée, A. and Rosalie, M. 1994. *Parol ek Memwar, récits de vie des Seychelles*. Hamburg: Buske.

Bunwaree, S. 2003. Politics of identity – recognitions, representations and reparations: articulating Afro Mauritian, Mauritius and Africa. S. Fuma (ed.) *Regards sur l'Afrique et l'océan Indien*. Paris: Sedes, Le Publieur.

Campebort, J.P. 2000. Handicap et éducation à La réunion: socio-histoire et psychogénèse. *Kabaro, revue internationale sciences de l'homme*, Dec. Mauritius/Paris: Université de La Réunion/l'Harmattan, pp. 92–108.

Cangy, J.C., Chan Low, J. and Paroomal, M. (eds). 2002. *L'esclavage et ses séquelles: Mémoire et Vécu d'hier et d'aujourd'hui*. Papers of the international conference organized by UNESCO. Mauritius: UNESCO.

Carter, M. (ed.) 1998. *Colouring the Rainbow, Mauritian Society in the Making*. Port Louis, Mauritius: Centre for Research on Indian Societies.

Chan Low, J. 2003. De l'Afrique rejetée à l'Afrique retrouvée. S. Fuma (ed.) *Regards sur l'Afrique et l'océan Indien*. Paris: Sedes, Le Publieur.

Chazan-Gillig, S. 2003. Diasporas et créolisation de la société mauricienne contemporaine. S. Fuma (ed.) *Regards sur l'Afrique et l'océan Indien*. Paris: Sedes, Le Publieur, pp. 337–51.

Deschamps, H. 1972. *Histoire de la Traite des Noirs de l'antiquité à nos jours.* Paris: Fayard.

Deveau, J.M. 1990. *La Traite Rochelaise.* Paris: Karthala, CNRS.

Eve, P. 1999a. *Naître et mourir à l'Ile de La Réunion: Bourbon à l'époque de l'esclavage.* Paris/ Université de La Réunion: l'Harmattan.

Eve, P. 1999b. *Variations sur le thème de l'amour à Bourbon à l'époque de l'esclavage.* Reunion, Saint-André: Océan éditions.

Filliot, J.M. 1974. *La traite des esclaves vers les Mascareignes au XVIIIe siècle.* Paris: ORMSTOM.

Franck, R.P.D. 1995. *Journal d'un exorciste.* Introduction by Raymond Eches, April. Reunion, Saint-André: Océans Editions.

Fuma, S. 1999. *De l'Inde du sud à l'Ile de La Réunion, les réunionnais d'origine indienne d'après le rapport Mackenzie.* Saint-Denis de La Réunion: Université de la Réunion and GRAHTER.

Fuma, S. 2001a. *Aux origines ethno-historiques du maloya réunionnais ou le maloya, expression d'une interculturalité indocéanique.* International conference on 'Diversité et spécificités des musiques traditionnelles, ethnomusicologie de l'Océan Indien Occidental.' Université de La Réunion, 29– 30 October 2001. Rpt in Kabaro.

Fuma, S. 2001b. Le servilisme: statut des travailleurs immigrés ou affranchis dans les colonies françaises. *Revue Tarehi.* Dec. Comores, Moroni: INYA.

Fuma, S. 2004. Savoir-faire, inventivité et richesse culturelles des esclaves des Iles créoles de l'océan Indien. *Courrier de l'UNESCO,* Oct., Paris: UNESCO Publishing.

Fuma, S. (ed.) 2005. *L'Afrique et l'océan Indien.* Paris: SEDES-CRESOI.

Fuma, S. and Poirier, J. 1990. Métissages, hétéroculture et identité réunionnaise, le défi réunionnais. J.L. Alber, C. Bavoux and M. Watin (eds) *Métissages: Linguistique et Anthropologie.* Paris/Université de La Réunion: l'Harmattan.

Gerbeau, H. 1979. Les esclaves et la mer à Bourbon au XIXe siècle. *Etudes et Documents.* Table ronde de Sénanque sur l'océan Indien, IPHOM, Aix en Provence, pp. 10–51.

Gerbeau, H. 1980. Quelques aspects de la traite illégale des esclaves à Bourbon au XIXe siècle. *Mouvement de populations dans l'océan Indien.* Paris: Champion.

Gunputh, V.D. 1984. *Indians overseas, the Mauritian experience.* Mauritius: Mahatma Gandhi Institute.

Institut de civilisation-Musée d'Art et d'Archéologie. 1997. *L'esclavage à Madagascar, Aspects historiques et résurgences contemporaines.* Papers presented at the international conference on slavery in Madagascar. Antananarivo: Institut de civilisation-Musée d'Art et d'Archéologie.

Ministère de l'Education et de l'Information, République des Seychelles. 1983. *Histoire des Seychelles.* Paris, Jouve: ORMSTOM.

Poirier, J. and Fuma, S. 1998. *Esclavage et condition servile dans les processus de colonisation.* International conference on 'Emancipation, citoyenneté, droits de l'homme.' April. Paris: UNESCO.

Police, D. 1999. Les pratiques musicales de la population servile et affranchie dans les écrits francophones des XVIIIe et XIXe siècles. V. Teelock and E.A. Alsper (eds) *History, Memory and Identity.* Mauritius: University of Mauritius, pp. 81–110.

Ravaosolo, J. 2000a. Apprentissage formelle et informelle dans le rituel Hazomanga du sud de Madagascar. *Kabaro, revue Internationale des sciences de l'homme et des sociétés*. Dec. Mauritius/Paris: Université de La Réunion/ l'Harmattan, pp. 22–40.

Ravaosolo, J. 2000b. Transmission culturelle chez les Masikoro de Madagascar. *Kabaro, revue Internationale des sciences de l'homme et des sociétés*, Dec. Mauritius/Paris: Université de La Réunion/l'Harmattan, pp. 41–54.

Roman, A. 2001. *Saint-Malo au temps des Négriers*. Paris: Karthala.

Scarr, D. 2000. *Seychelles since 1770: History of a slave and post slavery society*. London: Hurst Company.

Sheriff, A. 1987. *Slaves, Spices and Ivory in Zanzibar*. London: James Currey.

Toussaint, A. 1974. *Histoire de l'Ile Maurice*. Paris: Presse Universitaire de France, Collection Que sais-je.

Vergès, P. (président de La Région Réunion). 2002. *Speech rpt Diversité culturelle et identité réunionnaise*, Nov. Maison des Civilisations et de l'Unité Réunionnaise, Graphica.

# Endnotes

1   Jean Poirier was a professor emeritus at the University of Nice. He died in July, 2009.

2   Île de France retook the name of Mauritius in 1810 following the conquest of the island by the British, and Bourbon took that of La Réunion in 1848 with the abolition of slavery. See the work of Auguste Toussaint (1974).

3   The Malagasy slaves were deported to Mauritius by the Dutch in 1638, and would remain on the island after the departure of the colonists in 1698. They can be considered as the first permanent inhabitants of the island of Mauritius. On Bourbon, the Malagasies arrived in 1663. Pierre Pau and Louis Payen (two Frenchmen) and ten Malagasies (three women and seven men) settled on the island. These last were the first permanent inhabitants of the island.

4   The 'servis malgas' was an animist worship practice originating in Madagascar. The 'servis Kaf' is originally from Africa. Among the musical practices, one must emphasize the 'Maloya', traditional music with sacred origins, although today secular and strongly marked by Malagasy and African influences. On Mauritius, is found the 'Séga ravane', on Rodrigues the 'Séga tambour', and in the Seychelles the 'Moutya' (Bollée and Rosalie, 1994). Similarly the 'Moring', a martial art practised by the slaves, has Afro-Malagasy origins (Fuma, 2001).

5   On the day after the abolition of slavery, the slave population of Mauritius consisted of 66,051 individuals. In 1851, there were 86,000 Indians on Mauritius and 259,700 in 1901 (Gunputh, 1984: 214).

6   The 'Indoceanese' are for us the inhabitants of the Creole islands of the Indian Ocean.

7   From 1982 on Reunion and from 1995 on Mauritius, the authorities celebrated the commemoration of the abolition of slavery. A project by the *Maison des Civilisations et de l'Unité Réunionnaise* is currently being undertaken in Reunion.

8   The *Maison des Civilisations et de l'Unité Réunionnaise* being created on Reunion is designed to promote the cultures of origin through the unity of the Creole culture, inherited from colonial history.

9   The designations of different communities differ according to the island: on Mauritius, those who originate from the north-west of India are called 'Indo-Muslims' and on Reunion they are called 'Zarab'. Similarly, the Reunionese who originate from Africa are called 'Kaf' on Reunion and 'Mazambik' or 'Nations' on Mauritius and Rodrigues (Chazan-Gillig, 2003; Bunwaree, 2003).

10  The concept of the 'Creole Miracle' was born in discussions with Jean Poirier, the result of our research since 1976 on oral history and slavery in the Indian Ocean.

11  Many works have been published on the slave trade in the Indian Ocean. We are interested by the research of Jean Marie Filliot (1974) and that of Hubert Gerbeau (1979, 1980). See also the work *L'Afrique et l'océan Indien*, edited by Sudel Fuma (2005).

12  In his study, Campebort (2000) presents the sociological consequences of the inheritance of a colonial system that partitioned the population groups born of plantation societies.

13  To protect themselves from spirits, the common people used 'guaranties' or 'body-guards', ritual objects that are worn continually to chase away evil spirits (see Franck, 1995).

14  The definitions for the term 'Creole' are not the same among the islands. On Mauritius a 'Creole' is a descendent of a person of mixed race. On Reunion the definition is much wider, referring to former slaves, those of mixed-race, and the descendents of indentured labourers and Europeans.

15  The Portuguese of Macao are a notable example of this. Although today of mixed race, in five centuries they have not succeeded in creating either a Creole society or a Creole language.

16  While campaigning in Reunion on the occasion of the presidential campaign of 2007, both candidates for the right (Nicolas Sarkozy and Francois Bayrou) and the left (Ségolène Royal) emphasized the Reunion model as an answer to the problems of French integration resulting from immigration.

UNESCO/François Odendaal

UNESCO/Bernard Jacquier

UNESCO/J. Foy

UNESCO/J. Foy

UNESCO/François Odendaal

# MEMORY, IDENTITY AND HERITAGE IN A MULTI-ETHNIC ISLAND
## The case of Mauritius

Jocelyn Chan Low, *University of Mauritius, Reduit, Mauritius*

As a result of its geographic position, Mauritius, like other island states, found itself situated on trade and migration routes in the middle of a large ocean. Mauritius itself is the fruit of interaction between Europe and the Indian Ocean. As a port of providential refuge, an obligatory stop-over, or a fortress island-strategic naval base, it has simultaneously known Dutch, French and British colonization. Due to the lack of an indigenous population, Mauritian society over the years has comprised successive populations: European colonizers; slaves torn from Mozambique, Guinea and other parts of the African continent, Madagascar, the great Indian peninsula, and the islands of south-eastern Asia; indentured labourers for the sugar plantations coming principally from various regions of India, but also Madagascar and the Comoros; and Gujarat, Tamil and Chinese traders, and so on (Durand and Durand, 1978; de L'Estrac, 2004). These populations organized themselves according to various circumstances into distinct ethnic groups, often exclusive despite the mixture and inevitable cultural creolization. All this occurred within a society criss-crossed by socio-economic, religious and cultural fissures.

Located at the crossroads of the former 'coolie' and slave routes, the island republic of Mauritius today is in possession of a rich human melting pot, as is the case of many other island states. It also boasts an extensive palette of cultures and ancestral traditions, some of which have remained intact, but have more often been reworked and modified, influencing one other in ways both confrontational and harmonious.

In this way, a rich cultural heritage has developed over the years, side-by-side with a very particular natural heritage. It reflects the necessity of physical adaptation to an insular environment of uprooted immigrants; it also reflects the various re-constituted ways of life and quests for spirituality and identity pursued by the various population groups that constitute Mauritian society.

This cultural heritage can be divided and subdivided into numerous categories: intangible heritage, movable tangible heritage and fixed tangible heritage. This last category includes colonial structures and underwater heritage, notably the numerous wrecks around the island: the East Indiamen of the United Dutch East Asia Company (VOC) and the French Company of the East

Indies, pirate or privateer ships, and slave ships such as the recently discovered presumed wreck of the *Coureur*, at present the object of archaeological excavation.[1]

Intangible and movable forms of heritage include traditional forms of expression found in many domains: various idioms and proverbs; dances, chants and other musical forms; musical instruments; religious practices and beliefs; domestic arts including cooking (the *dholls puris*, the Chinese *poutou*), clothing; crafts; traditional technology (i.e. fishing with weirs); oral traditions, often comprising the historical memory of various population groups; literary and iconographic works; and plastic as well as other elite arts.

Fixed tangible heritage includes, notably, architecture, comprising traditional housing, ranging from the *lakaz la pay* and the *maray* (huts made of thatch and cow dung respectively), to sugar camps, fishing villages, Creole houses, places of worship and business assets such as old factories and furnaces, and finally colonial structures such as fortifications (the Martellos towers, the Citadel, and so on), civil buildings, cemeteries, public gardens and historic monuments (La Hausse, 1998; Mahadeo, 1989).

It is on the basis of this cultural heritage that the identity and many personalities of Mauritius, Rodrigues and Agaléga rest. But today, a large part of this heritage runs the great risk of disappearing as a result of globalization and the fundamental transformations currently underway. The old plantation society based on the single crop of sugar cane is transforming into a newly industrialized country, with a free manufacturing zone, tourism and services as its new economic pillars. Today, this society is attempting to make the great leap forward into post-industrialization, consolidating its status as a duty free, cyber island (Bertile, 2008; Dinan, 2005). These transformations bring with them profound structural changes visible and tangible at both the level of space management (acceleration of urbanization, creation of a cybercity at Ebéne and plans for a new city/administrative centre at Highlands), and at the social level (growth of the middle classes, emergence of a consumer society, transformations in family structure, evolving status for Mauritian women, and changes in values with the triumph of hedonistic individualism). To this list should also be added the end of insularity, not only as a consequence of the revolution in air travel and the arrival of tourists, but also with the development of audiovisual media and information and communications technology.

To give an example, the island of Rodrigues, until very recently, was visited by ship once every three months (Barat, 1985: 13). Today, there are five flights a day. Moreover, the evolution of internet and satellite communications ensures that the island is linked to the rest of the world.

The acceleration of economic development has completely upturned the quality and style of local life, with notable repercussions in the social processes that create intangible heritage. While it is true that intangible heritage is bound to evolve, fast food such as pizzas, Kentucky Fried Chicken and McDonald's are rapidly replacing traditional dishes. One only has to measure the evolution of *séga* (the country's traditional music and dance) over the past thirty years to realize the extent of the situation, with authentic forms having ceded ground to commercial interpretations in response to pressure from the tourist sector. This reached such a point that one of contemporary Mauritius' most creative singers, the late Kaya, remarked, with good reason, that *séga* performances were intended for tourists: *séga Lev Zip, sa na pa mo kiltir.*[2]

Similarly, urbanization and new spatial planning on Mauritius inevitably brings with it extensive disruption of the architectural landscape, with profound repercussions for fixed tangible heritage. For example, Port Louis' China Town has been completely transformed over the last ten years. At one point, a proposal was even put forward to transform a nineteenth-century pagoda into a modern mall.

Faced with these threats, there is an urgent need to identify, inventory, safeguard and promote this rich island heritage. The authorities, however, have been slow in reacting. Nevertheless, as of 1996, following more than twenty years of inertia at the level of heritage management, an institutional and legal framework for new laws covering archives was enacted through parliamentary vote, taking the form of the National Archives Act, the National Library Act, the Mauritius Museums Council Act and the National Heritage Trust Fund Act

(Martial, 2002: 163–64). New institutions have since been created including cultural centres for Tamils, the Telegu, the Marathis and Mauritians in general, among many other trusts. These add to the cultural institutions already in existence, which include the Mahatma Gandhi Institute, the Nelson Mandela Cultural Centre for African Culture and the Islamic Cultural Centre. To such a list, we must add the subsequent creation of the Morne Heritage Trust Fund and the Appavasi Ghat Trust Fund – the result of applications for nomination of these sites to the World Heritage List. There have been other initiatives, notably at the level of the Ministry of the Environment: for example, no development project can be initiated without an Environmental Impact Assessment Certificate, which takes into account both natural and cultural heritage, and can be contested by civil society. To this, must also be added the new restrictions imposed by the Ministry of Housing and local collectives. The point of departure for this new heritage policy was the Forum on Arts and Culture in February 1996.

For the Ministry of Arts and Culture, the objective of this exercise was to reach an agreement among stakeholders – artists, intellectuals and civil servants responsible for culture – concerning the formulation of a cultural strategy to address the challenges of cultural plurality in Mauritius, which would then be presented in a Comprehensive Policy Paper. To a great extent, the vision elaborated in 1996 has remained unchanged, despite a few corrections due to changes in political administrations through the democratic process.

# Heritage and memory

This newly orientated Mauritian cultural policy took effect at the end of the twentieth century. This period was marked – as was the case worldwide – by a fever for commemoration and an unprecedented wave of interest in heritage, articulated around the concept of 'the responsibility of memory' as relating to public spaces.

Historians such as Prost attribute this wave to the failure of great ideologies, leading to disempowerment: 'The cult of the past thus responds to the uncertainty of the future and to the absence of a collective project' (translated from the French) (1996: 305).

Others attributed it to globalization giving rise to a world in perpetual movement – one which is constantly looking for its bearings. From this derived a perspective on cultural heritage that focuses increasingly on identity. As Prost noted, 'our "Memory society" thinks that without history it will lose its identity' (translated from the French) (ibid).

However, in Mauritius in the 1980s and 1990s, this 'time of remembering' also coincided with the institutionalization of the concept of 'multiculturalism'. This was achieved through promotion of the idea of a rainbow nation, in which each person was expected to find his or her own 'colour', and was symbolized by the 'Composite Shows' (Eriksen, 1990: 80). Specific cultural centres were created as a result of this movement.

It is possible to argue that the colonial state, loyal to the British tradition, acknowledged to a certain degree the ethnic diversity of the country. For example, the constitution of 1947 indirectly recognized the existence of nine spoken languages in the country, including Créole. Furthermore the 'best loser' electoral system, which was developed hastily in 1967 and then included in the constitution of 1968, divided the country into four religious or ethnic communities.[3] Similarly, the 1956 report[4] led to the granting of subsidies to religious organizations grouped on a linguistic and cultural basis.

In the 1970s, the Mahatma Gandhi Institute was established with the mission to study Mauritian history and culture in *all* its diversity. However, over the years various distinct cultural institutes such as the African, Islamic, Tamil, Telegus, and other centres, as well as 'Speaking Unions' for Urdu, Hindi and English have been created. Almost all of these institutions have as their objective the preservation and promotion of so-called ancestral cultures through research on genealogy, memory, and tangible and intangible heritage.

Thus, the state promotes true cultural activism with regard to the intangible heritage of various population groups, while also establishing, for balance, institutions that are more global in scope, such as the Mauritian Cultural Centre, the National Heritage Trust Fund and the Mauritius Museums Council.

One could argue that this policy inscribes itself directly within a framework of institutional recognition of the cultural diversity of Mauritian society, according to a logic of reparation for true injustices perpetuated during the colonial period. In other words, this policy inscribes itself within a perspective of decolonization.

In effect, the state for too long confused cultural heritage with the cultural production of an elite minority that, until the Second World War, exercised a truly hegemonic political, economic, social, cultural and perhaps even religious control over the colony. From an institutional point of view, the notion of cultural heritage was directly linked to a vision and discourse of the past that was tied to a system of power.

The colonial and traditional historiography of Mauritius, on which rests the traditional vision of heritage, is primarily characterized by profound gaps in memory: entire portions of the country's history are missing. This historiography was the fruit of a small colonial elite, primarily French in origin, which sought to affirm its identity – *vieille france* – when faced with the English onslaught and Anglicization of the colony in the nineteenth century following the British conquest of 1810. It should also be emphasized that this oligarchy, characterized by race and ethnicity, needed to legitimize its social, economic, cultural and even religious hegemony in a society that was amid a demographic transformation (the massive arrival of Asian immigrants at the end of slavery). This need led to the emergence of a discourse and a distinct historical tradition which focused its research on the Île de France,[5] with emphasis duly placed on

the role of French colonists in the construction of Mauritius. In short, this historiography does its best to demonstrate that Mauritius was constructed by colonists of French origin to whom, as a result of this fact, the island belongs. This historical tradition was accompanied by the notion of a civilizing cultural mission, and reoccurs in texts from those of Hervé de Rauville (1909) to those of Noel Marrier d'Unienville (1949). It was institutionalized in place names, memorials, museums and even scholarly manuals through the collaboration of so-called learned societies, and continues to haunt the nation's tangible and intangible heritage.

However, the national elite's need to create and legitimize itself led to distortions in traditional historiography and, by extension, of recognized and institutionalized heritage. These distortions were formed through silences and elements censured or forgotten. For example, the contributions of African, Malagasy and Indian slaves were elided for a long time from the narration of history. Likewise, a monument dedicated to the introduction of the stag was inaugurated on Mauritius almost fifty years (1939) before one commemorating the abolition of slavery (1985), hunting being the favourite sport of colonial high society.

Nevertheless, as might be expected, this institutionalized history was quickly contested by a counter history produced through multiple mediums including novels, theatre and journalism. This counter history was directly linked to the construction of ethnic identities by the intellectual elite of various population groups in Mauritius.

As situationalists indicate, ethnic identities are shaped by the context in which particular groups find themselves. When these groups perceive themselves to be caught in a dangerous situation, faced with a dominant order, they react by regrouping within a new form of ethnic or community identity. Memory, culture, heritage and so on, are manipulated and reworked in order to erect ethnic barriers to serve the needs of socio-political mobilization (Brown, 1989). On Mauritius, we can postulate that there were 'defining moments' in the construction of different ethnic identities during different periods of the country's history. Each time, the writing of history, memory, culture and heritage was annexed to this process (Chan Low, 2008). As M. Ferro emphasizes, the counter history generated is primarily a political project, an action. This counter history is thus often controlled by the bearer of the project and can therefore also be manipulated (1985: 77).

Thus, one can speak of a counter history born of 'people of colour' (Hitié, 1897), a counter history developed by the Indo-Mauritian intelligentsia starting in the 1930s (Beejadhur, 1935; Emrith, 1967; Hazareesingh, 1973; Sooriamoorthy, 1977), and recently, a counter history linked to the process of identity construction among the 'Creole' group who identify themselves as the descendants of Afro-Malagasy slaves (Moutou, 1996), and this latter in the wake of the emergence of the 'malaise créole' discourse (essentially a demand for reparation for slavery) (Chan Low, 2004).

There have been attempts to re-appropriate the history of slavery, and to transform the day commemorating the abolition of slavery (1 February) into an identity festival and a day of demands. In this context, elements of intangible, national and cultural heritage such as the Créole language and *séga* become languages of identity and ethnicity. Similarly, one can note the rediscovery of roots and the invention of an African-ness to the exclusion of actual Indian-ness in a group particularly composed of mixed people, but primarily defined in relation to Mauritians of Indian ancestry (Chan Low, 2005).

This society still sadly functions on an operational modality of negative consensus. The introduction of the 'malaise créole' into this public space, recalling the memory of slavery, has a consequent impact on the identity quest of other groups in Mauritian society also engaged in the same search for origins.

The political debate shifts, therefore, through the national narrative, the control and production of signifiers and social symbols, and the semiosphere of values.

It is true that the counter history discourse has not been solely ethnocentric. During the 1970s, in a post-colonial context and in a country tortured by a truly acute crisis of underdevelopment, the emergence of the Militant Mauritian Movement ushered in a true paradigm shift. The new left, advocating Marxism and resolutely third world in its approach, wanted to root the revolutionary fight in the history of the country, and in resistance to slavery, racism and other forms of exploitation (Oodiah, 1989: 13). They made a genuine plea for a new reading of the country's history, for a 'history from below', which would take into account class struggle and form a new approach with regard to national heritage, the Créole language and Mauritian culture. It envisaged the creation of a revolutionary Mauritianism which would put an end to 'neo-colonialist' ways of thinking (ibid). These preoccupations were to join those of post-colonial academic history which, at the time, was establishing itself with the development of tertiary institutions.

Nevertheless, during the 1980s, with the decline of this ideology and the return of 'ethnic politics', those positions that were judged too radical in their support of the revolutionary *Créole* culture were abandoned (Eriksen, 1992: 82) and multiculturalism was adopted. It is within this context that the debate and work on intangible and tangible heritage is moving forward today.

It is true that multiculturalism implies the acceptance of cultural diversity, which is perceived, for example, by the economist Stephen Marglin as key to the survival of the human race (cited in Mason, 2000). The need for diversity justifies itself from both an ecological and a political point of view. In addition, post-colonial arguments insist on the need for diverse cultures to confront the homogenizing and repressive might of the dominant Western culture.

It is also true that the policy of recognizing cultural specificities tends to promote differences within a multi-ethnic island society. It is thus legitimate to question the danger posed by the invasion, institutionally speaking, of a proliferating heritage that no longer constitutes the common identity of a young nation, but on the contrary, would fragment into a multitude of particular ethnic identities, each of which would require respect and development in community museums of a strong ethnic character. The national historic narrative would cede space to a mosaic of particular memories that would feed ethnic chauvinists, or worse, cultural fundamentalists.

This could occur at a time when indications are emerging of a post-ethnic society, as emphasized by analysts like Thomas Hylland Eriksen (1990): a workplace less ethnically segregated, the definition of the Mauritian in relation to outsiders and, in particular, convergences in ways of life. The following cases illustrate current difficulties.

In 2001, two holidays were granted to commemorate the abolition of slavery and the arrival of Indian immigrants. That 1 February be decreed a holiday was a long-standing demand of socio-cultural Créole associations militating for reparations for slavery. To avoid other demands and in consideration of economic imperatives, the government first contemplated commemorating, in a manner both unified and national, the end of slavery and indentured labour on the same day, both being forms of servitude. A postage stamp to such effect was even launched.

However, in response to pressure on all sides, the authorities felt constrained to grant two separate holidays – 1 February for the end of slavery and 2 November for the arrival of Indian immigrants in the nineteenth century – with the risks to ethnic exploitation that this decision might involve. However, the date chosen to mark the arrival of Indian immigrants created disputes along ethnic lines: some within the Tamil community felt wronged since the Tamil presence dates back to the eighteenth century. The debate also leant itself to the question of commemorating the arrival of the first French colonizers.

A similar situation occurred around the nomination of sites to the World Heritage List. Although Mauritius had been a signatory to the Convention concerning the Protection of the World Cultural and Natural Heritage since its adoption in 1972, it wasn't until the end of the 1990s that the authorities began to seriously consider registering a site on the list. This begged the following question: what would be the focus of the first nomination? One option could have been the Pamplemousses Botanical Gardens. Dating from the period of Mahé de Labourdonnais and Pierre Poivre in the eighteenth century, these gardens were directly associated, as Richard Grove emphasizes in his work *Green Imperialism* (1995), with the emergence on a world scale of one of the first environmentalist philosophies. This option, however, was not chosen. In the recent past the place had been perceived as a source of pride and a marker of national identity similar to 'the earth of seven colours' at Chamarel.[6] However,

within the framework created by the ethnic reconstruction of heritage, some people had begun to associate the gardens with the heritage of the descendants of Franco-Mauritian colonizers. It was thus decided to submit, at the same time, for reasons of ethnic balance, the candidatures of the Coolie Ghat and the Montagne du Morne. The Coolie Ghat had recently been re-baptized the Appravasi Ghat, and is unfortunately and erroneously associated in the collective memory with the arrival of Indian immigrants of the Hindu faith. Meanwhile, the *Montagne du Morne* is claimed as a sacred site of pilgrimage by socio-cultural *Créole* associations because it holds the memory of *maroon* slaves of Malagasy and African origin. Although these sites remain national, even universal, symbols, they were warped to fit identity objectives, and perceived by some as competing for nomination to the World Heritage List (Carmiagni, 2006).

In this way, the equation of cultural heritage and ethnic identity has given an emotional and even dangerous dimension to the debates over heritage management. For example, in 1998 the authorities decided to reverse the respective places of Hindi and Tamil languages on bank notes. As a result, there were noisy demonstrations and threats of public immolations. Faced with an explosive situation, the authorities felt constrained to retract from circulation the new bills, which had been printed at great cost. More recently, at the beginning of 2007 the Supreme Court decided that the *azaan*, the Muslim call to prayer, which had been amplified and broadcast for years, could be defined as noise pollution and should therefore be forbidden. This provoked an explosive situation; the Muslims argued that the call of the *muezzin* was a given right and an immutable heritage.

Therefore, the right to diversity in a multi-ethnic society also implies the need to put in place strategies to ensure that this diversity creates a durable conviviality, a true acceptance of the other, and a common identity in a context of multiple identities. There is a need to develop strategies to erect bridges between the various cultures and to focus on the recognition of 'commonalities'.

From this arises the need to create institutions that favour such meetings of cultures and encourage the various specific centres in their attempts to making overtures, and de-compartmentalize to facilitate the emergence and consolidation of a Mauritian culture that is both plural and intercultural.

## History and memory

In this context, the duty of history prevails over the duty of memory (Prost, 1996: 306). Despite the post-modernist critique and 'linguistic turn' with regard to the scientific quality of history, described as an author' invention (Noiriel, 2005: 154–76), history responds to the need to organize the past 'in order to prevent it from weighing too heavily on our shoulders' (Febvre, 1949) (translated from the French).

An objective and critical history would help, in fact, to deconstruct the particular ethnic memories that too often, unfortunately, serve as a reference in the symbolic construction of heritage in the public space. As Pierre Nora emphasizes, everything opposes history to memory (1984). History, because it is an intellectual and secular operation, demands analysis and a critical discourse. But memory is a phenomenon which is manifested in the present, is carried by living groups (who are unaware of its successive mutations), and is vulnerable to being manipulated and used as an instrument. Indeed, at the heart of history works a criticism which destroys spontaneous memory (ibid).

On the other hand, history is a secular activity and does not present a collection of isolated facts from which people 'pick and choose' to construct identities. History organizes the facts, explains them, and to explain them, creates classifications of unequal value. As a result, because history contextualizes and explains, it helps to mourn certain past events, which, when we carry them in the present with their emotional burden, make it more difficult to live together in a plural society.

The work of the historian is not restricted to reconciliation with a memory to which he or she is merely the servant. The work is to produce a history that is critical of memory (Prost, 1996: 306).

The announcement of the creation of a Truth and Justice Commission, meant to study the key events of the country's history, must be situated within this context. The parameters of this commission are still ill defined, but it will clearly help to mourn and bring closure to the past. This is because, in effect, a national history that is post-ethnocentric will deconstruct both the stereotypes and the erroneous myths present in popular memory that surround the origins of ethnic groups. Such a history would testify that not all slaves were African, that not all masters were whites, and that not all indentured labourers on sugar plantations were Indians, much less Hindus (Carter, 1998).

This history would demonstrate, for example, that because of the widespread racial mixing that occurred during the nineteenth century, and because of the gender imbalance among immigrants, those who today describe themselves as Afro-Mauritians and who claim their African-ness as a result of being descended from slaves are, to a large extent, Indian in origin. This history would also reveal that the Muslim community derives its culture from Indian and Urdu culture, not just from Arabic culture as the pro-Arabs argue.

In the same way, this history would demonstrate that, in addition to the conflicts and isolated confrontations, the history of island society has also and especially been a history of true cohabitation and intercultural exchange, even in the most painful of moments. For example, slavery was a crucible out of which was born a rich, vibrant and creative créoleness. In fact, although the elements of cultural heritage derived from different geographic origins, they hardly existed in seclusion. Could it be otherwise in the case of

an island? A critical cultural history would reveal the extent and persistence of interactions between cultures and the cultural mixing that contributed to the emergence of a new and authentic Mauritian culture, adapted to the needs of an insular environment (Chaudenson, 1992).

This critical history would be a foundation for the symbolic representation of sites of memory and heritage, eliminating exclusive ethnic significations by representing sites in their national and even universal dimensions. Institutions that manage heritage should rise to this challenge, and some such as the Appravasi Ghat Trust Fund do so admirably.

In this context, the creation of institutions such as the Mauritian Cultural Centre is notable. Its objectives include the promotion of intercultural exchange and the assistance of various centres which are specific in their founding missions, thereby supporting the emergence and consolidation of a plural and intercultural Mauritian culture. Indeed, intercultural dialogue cannot be prescribed. However, it is imperative for creating the necessary framework in order to give rise to and encourage 'the will to surmount the obstacles of communication that result from cultural difference in order to profit, on the contrary, from the wealth of each culture' (Verbunt, 2001: 90) (translated from the French), for interculturalism should not exist only in the realm of discourse.

The Mauritian Cultural Centre celebrated the day of music by creating a musical village where the public was invited to immerse itself in the various musical traditions of the country, and appreciate both their commonalities and diversity. Similarly, the Centre conceived a musical show, 'Tambours en Liberté' (Free Drums), which melded the various percussion instruments present on the island. To commemorate the abolition of slavery, the Centre worked together with both the Nelson Mandela Centre and the Mahatma Gandhi Institute.

Also of note are the efforts underway to create an international institute for intercultural dialogue and peace, with the support of UNESCO. However, a more appropriate project would be the establishment of an observatory of cultural diversity in island states, with a rotating headquarters, to federate the academic institutions engaged in research.

Such an intercultural encounter would help to construct a durable and legitimate form of cultural diversity – one that would be more productive and creative of cultural goods, serving to mark national identities and counter the dangers of homogenization posed by globalization. These same cultural goods would serve as a starting point for the emergence of a culture industry strongly rooted in the country.

## Tourism and a cultural industry

However, promoting intercultural approaches and multiculturalism, taking stock, restoring and valuing heritage, and casting the bases for culture industry, are all expensive exercises. Even though the central and regional authorities constitute in themselves a market for cultural productions, there are clearly limits to the financial capacity of the state. From this derives the necessity to collaborate with civil society and the private sector.

On Mauritius, this issue revolves, in particular, around collaboration between the tourism and culture sectors. At first glance, there is great potential for development. Tourism is one of the pillars of the Mauritian economy and will be called upon to develop even further over both the short and long term, especially as the number of arrivals is predicted to grow by 400 per cent by 2010, increasing from 500,000 to 2 million tourists annually.

To date, no in-depth studies have been undertaken on this issue. Nevertheless, it is possible to foresee serious obstacles to the development of cultural tourism, given the minefield presented by the country's culture and the structure of the Mauritian tourism industry.

Cultural tourism has been described by the World Tourism Organization as an immersion in natural history, human heritage, the arts, philosophy and the institutions of another region (Beuze, 1996). In order for it to be the bearer of sustainable development, it is essential that local people be involved and contribute to the various projects.

The tourism sector in Mauritius is particular in that it has been built and sustained by local capital.

This local capital, as numerous studies have demonstrated, derives almost exclusively from sugar profits. Thus, the descendants of the Franco-Mauritian colonial elite constitute the biggest tourism operators (Paratian, 1991). The sector is very integrated, the tourist being taken care of by hotel groups and their subsidiaries from arrival to departure. In addition, the form of tourism practised is essentially of the coastal resort variety (Fontaine, 2008).

It is in this context that the stakes of culture tourism must be situated. According to certain studies, cultural tourism could contribute strongly to reinforcing and preserving the cultural heritage of the country (La Hausse de la Louvière, 2007; Martial 2002: 121–26), while supporting the development of a cultural industry.

First, however, it is important, to remind ourselves that the priority of corporate interests in the tourist sector remains the marketing of entertainment. In addition, Mauritius is increasingly positioning itself as a 'high-end' destination. The typical tourist is a mid to upper-level executive, frequently of European origin, who has decided to take a long-distance flight, generally with family, and with the objective of staying for five nights in a luxurious coastal hotel. Therefore, tourist companies sell the natural setting, enchanting and sunlit. The principle objective of 'postcard references' to the lives of Mauritians is to strongly emphasize the hospitality of the people and the idyllic setting of an island without conflict.

It is for this reason that tourism (or culture) developers have a tendency to use nostalgic and romantic images of the past, to the exclusion of images that are crueler and whose truth is confirmed by history. As a result, they focus primarily on colonial historiography, with its emphasis on great men, governors, and the acts and doings of the colonial elite. In performances and other shows, the ocean is marketed in terms of escape – as a theatre for the adventures of Robert Surcouf and other corsairs – rather than as a prison for the millions of men and women brought as slaves in the bottom of ship's holds to toil for colonial enterprises. Similarly, one could note the eagerness with which developers in search of this aesthetic restore old colonial buildings and Créole houses, former homes of the colonial elite.

There is a risk, therefore, that such colonial representations of history, today long disregarded, will return with vigour, having been strengthened by economic activity. In the inter-ethnic minefield of Mauritius this possibility has real significance.

Secondly, the tourist sector is well integrated. The tourist is almost completely taken care of from arrival to departure by the same operators. Moreover, the nature of the tourist sector makes involvement by the wider population difficult, despite attempts to establish 'les tables d'hote', and so on.

With regard to intangible and movable tangible heritage, culture tourism can effectively become a source of revenue for the peoples of Rodrigues and Mauritius, through the valorization and commercialization of this heritage (Jauze, 1998: 204–06).

Nevertheless, threats of deterioration and loss of authenticity remain, since the way of life that generates these forms of heritage is in perpetual change. There is also the question of whether a concept of development that views cultural heritage only as a source of benefits for the tourism industry is viable in a complex and multi-ethnic society. This question is particularly important, given the fact that the cultural heritage has been re-appropriated with the objective of constituting the fundamental substance of the identities of the various groups in the country.

It is true, however, that the tourism sector offers possibilities for marketing and employment, and constitutes a source of revenue for artists and other cultural actors. Moreover, hotel entertainment constitutes an important economic activity.

Increase in the number of hotels on an island with limited space could also endanger the authenticity of natural and historical heritage. During the 1980s, it was found necessary to move a cemetery in order to develop a hotel at Grand Gaube; yet this was one of the first ex-slave villages. In addition, the links between sugar producers and tourism developers mean that controversies surrounding tourist projects on heritage sites inevitably and unfortunately have the tendency to revive old wounds. Examples include the disagreements surrounding the cableway projects or the opening of 'Integrated Resort Schemes' within the perimeter of Morne Brabant.[7]

There is, nevertheless, an urgent need to construct an interface between policies regarding culture and strategies for tourism, given the weight of the sector in the country's economy. Within this context, it should be emphasized that responsibility for the organization of the annual Créole festival was given to the Ministry of Tourism in 2006. The festival is now a cultural and tourism event with a significant budget.

Others emphasize the need to create a cultural industry that will constitute yet another pillar of the country's economy. To such effect, following the Budget discussions of 2008–2009, a fund has been created by the state to help, in part, with the promotion of Mauritian artists living abroad.

Recent communications with Keith Nurse and Hopeton Dunn on the subject of cultural industries, lend credence to the belief that Mauritius will likely use its assets for the better to give birth to a solid cultural industry. Firstly, the essential infrastructure at the level of information technology and other new technologies is now present, with Mauritius positioning itself as a cyber-island. Secondly, the 'business infrastructure' is well developed and sophisticated. Moreover, modern legislation with regard to author's rights and a specialized police unit trained in counterfeit prevention exist. The provision of capital necessary for the development of new sectors has not lacked in former cases, and it should be noted that the Mauritian Diaspora is present throughout the world, but especially in some of the large European metropoles.

Even so, while the textile industry has become one of the most important in the world, a fashion industry has not been able to emerge. If there is a printing industry, it principally prints the works of international authors. At the level of film, the country seems satisfied with offering the framework and logistics for shooting full-length films by big names from Bollywood. In brief, Mauritius is, to use Hopeton Dunn's terms, a 'downloader' and not an 'uploader' of cultural products at the international level. The reasons for this situation derive not only from its limited territory and heavy restrictions on the size of its population, but also, without doubt, from a vision of culture. Mauritius belongs to the ancient world of the Indian Ocean. As a crucible of Europe, Africa and Asia, Mauritius possesses diverse so-called ancestral traditions that often constitute the basis of the ethnic groups constructed within its plural society. Culture is thus most often perceived through the prism of an attachment to the past and ethnicity, and not through that of creativity. This vision gives rise to the need to promote de-compartmentalization for fear of seeing the emergence of a free zone of cultural products, completely disconnected from the local cultural scene.

There is also a need to establish a network with the other island states in the region. This would help move beyond the limits of a restricted market, which slows the development of cultural industries. The mixing of cultures and peoples in the Indian Ocean has, in effect, created a heritage wherein are found many convergences. There exists the possibility of working together to promote these cultures at a global level. We could look, for example, at *seggae*. Although created in Mauritius, the Seychelles and Réunion have also been quick to accept this blend of *reggae* and *séga*. But such types of promotion require large investment – hence the role of regional organizations such as the Commission for the Indian Ocean, which, through the expedient of a festival touring the Indian Ocean, recently attempted to promote the cultural heritage of the region. The Créole Festival of the Indian Ocean could also become an important asset in such forms of promotion.

However, there is first a need for a genuine paradigm shift in the cultural policy of the authorities. In short, there is a need to create a new vision of culture at the service of sustainable development, not one held captive by the inertia of ethnic identities.

# References

Barat, C., Carayol, M. and Chaudenson, R. 1985. *Rodrigues: La Cendrillon des Mascareignes*. St. André: Université de la Réunion, Presses de Graphica.

Beejadhur, A. 1935. *Les Indiens à l'île Maurice*. Port Louis: Typographie Moderne.

Bertile, W. 2008. De la colonisation à l'indépendance. Une économie ouverte. J.M. Jauze (ed.) *L'île Maurice face à ses nouveaux defis*. Paris: Université de la Réunion/L'Harmattan.

Beuze, L. 1996. *Tourisme culturel et musées dans la Caraïbe (trois examples: Barbade, Martinique et Porto Rico)*. Patrimoine Francophone:

Développement, Tourisme et Protection du Patrimoine Culturel. Alexandria: Senghor University.

Brown, D. 1989. Ethnic Revival. Perspectives on State and Society. *Third World Quarterly.* II(4): 1–17.

Carmiagni, S. 2006. Figures identitaires créoles et patrimoine à l'île Maurice: une montagne en jeu. *Journal des anthropologues.* 104–05: 265–85.

Carter, M. (ed.) 1998. *Colouring the rainbow: Mauritian society in the making.* Port Louis: CRIOS.

Chan Low, J. 2004. Les enjeux des débats actuels sur la Mémoire et la Réparation pour l'esclavage à l'île Maurice. *Cahiers d'études Africaines.* XLIV: 173–74. Rpt. EHSS. 401–08.

Chan Low, J. 2005. 'De l'Afrique rejetée à l'Afrique retrouvée? Les Créoles de l'île Maurice et l'africanité.' S. Fuma (ed.) *Regards sur l'Afrique et l'Océan Indien.* Paris: Sedes, Le Publieur.

Chan Low, J. 2008. Une perspective historique du processus de construction identitaire à l'île Maurice. *Kabaro, Revue Internationale des Sciences de l'Homme et des Sociétés.* IV(4–5): 13–26. Paris/Réunion: L'Harmattan/Université de la Réunion.

Chaudenson, R. 1992. *Des îles, des hommes, des langues. Essai sur la créolisation linguistique et culturelle.* Paris: L'Harmattan.

Dinan, P. 2005. *La République de Maurice en marche.* 1980–2030. Port Louis: Best Graphics.

Durand, J.P. and Durand, J. 1978. *L'île Maurice et ses populations.* Paris: Editions Complexe.

Emrith, M. 1967. *The Muslims in Mauritius.* Port Louis: Regent Press.

Eriksen, T.H. 1990. Communicating cultural difference and identity. *Oslo occasional papers in anthropology.* 16: 215–32.

Eriksen, T.H. 1992. *Us and them in modern societies: ethnicity and nationalism in Mauritius, Trinidad and Beyond.* Oslo: Scandinavian University Press.

de L'Estrac, J.C. 2004. *Mauriciens: enfants de mille races.* Port Louis: Graphics Press.

Febvre, L. 1949. Vers une autre histoire. *Revue de Métaphysique et de Morale,* LVIII. (Cited in A. Prost. (eds) 1996. *Douze leçons sur l'Histoire.* Paris: Seuil, p. 300.)

Ferro M. 1985. *L'Histoire sous surveillance.* Paris: Gallimard.

Fontaine, G. 2008. Approche du système touristique mauricien. (Cited in J.M. Jauze (ed.) 2008 *L'île Maurice face à ses nouveaux défis.* Paris: Université de la Réunion/L'Harmattan, p. 186.)

Grove, R. 1995. *Green imperialism.* Cambridge: Cambridge University Press.

La Hausse de la Louvière, P. (ed.) 1998. *Coastal fortifications.* Tamarin: Heritage.

La Hausse de la Louvière, P. 2007. Preserving Heritage in 21st Century Mauritius and the Cimetière de l'Enfoncement Heritage Site. P. La Hausse de la Louvière (ed.) *Les bâtisseurs de l'île Maurice. Pierre et Patrimoine de Port Louis.* Tamarin: Heritage.

Hazareesingh, K. 1973. *Histoire des Indiens à l'Ile Maurice.* Paris: Librairie d'Amérique et d'Orient.

Hitié, E. 1897. *Histoire de Maurice.* Tome 1. Port Louis: Engelbrecht and Cie.

Jauze, J.M. 1998. Rodrigues: La troisième île des Mascareignes. J.M. Jauze (ed.) *L'île Maurice face à ses nouveaux défis.* (2008). Paris: Université de la Réunion/L'Harmattan.

Mahadeo, P. 1989. *Mauritius Cultural Heritage.* Port Louis: Gold Hill Publication.

Martial, D. 2002. *Identité et politique culturelle à l'île Maurice. Regards sur une société plurielle.* Paris: L'Harmattan.

Mason R. and M. De la Torre. 2000. La conservation et les valeurs du patrimoine dans les sociétés en voie de mondialisation. *Rapport mondial sur la culture 2000. Diversité culturelle, conflit et pluralisme.* Paris: UNESCO Publishing.

Moutou, B. 1996. *Les Chrétiens de l'île Maurice.* Port Louis: Best Graphics.

Nora, P. 1984. Entre Mémoire et Histoire. La problématique des lieux. P. Nora (ed.) *Les lieux de Mémoire.* Paris: La République, Gallimard.

Noiriel, G. 2005. *Sur la crise de l'histoire.* Paris: Gallimard.

Oodiah, M.D. 1989. *Mouvement militant mauricien: 20 ans d'histoire (1969–1989).* Port Louis: Electronic Graphic Systems.

Paratian, R. 1991. L'évolution du secteur des services à l'île Maurice. *Annuaire des Pays de l'Océan Indien. Aix-Marseille XI 1986–1989:* 237–64.

Prost, A. 1996. *Douze leçons sur l'Histoire.* Paris: Seuil.

de Rauville, H. 1909. *L'île de France Contemporaine.* Paris: Nouvelle Librairie Nationale.

Sooriamoorthy, R. 1977. *Les Tamouls à l'île Maurice.* Port Louis: Olympic Printing.

d'Unienville, N.M. 1949. *L'île Maurice et sa civilisation.* Paris: G. Durassié and Co.

Verbunt, G. 2001. *La société Interculturelle: vivre la diversité humaine.* Paris: Seuil.

# Endnotes

1  The *Coureur*, a vessel engaged in illegal trade, was wrecked near the Pointe aux Feuilles on 3 March, 1821.

2  'The *séga* in which we raise the skirts, that is not my culture.'

3  Therefore, for reasons of ethnic representation in Parliament, the Constitution divides the population into distinct communities according to variable criteria of religion (Hindu and Muslim), of race (Chinese), or of way of life (General Population).

4  Since the early days of European colonization only Christian churches were subsidized by the state. In 1956, a select committee set up by the Legislative Council voted in favour of government subsidies for all recognized religious bodies on the island.

5  *Île de France* was the colonial French name for Mauritius.

6  Chamarel is a popular tourist spot famous for its variety of coloured volcanic soil.

7  The great scenic beauty of the cultural and natural landscape of Le Morne Brabant has recently led some wealthy Franco-Mauritian promoters to develop highly speculative land development projects built around either cableways, hotels and restaurants or high-class villas and golf-courses, mainly for foreign nationals in the area. This was seen by socio-cultural associations of the creole population as an insult to the memory of their slave ancestors.

UNESCO/Claude Van Engeland

UNESCO/Fubomichi Kudo

UNESCO/Wagner Horst

UNESCO/Cécile Mirrengarten

UNESCO/Ariane Bailey

# 'A SIMPLE COLONIAL PHILISTINE SOCIETY'
## Cultural complexity and identity politics in small islands

Thomas Hylland Eriksen, *University of Oslo, Norway*

Oceanic islands have been cultural cross-roads[1] for centuries, in some cases for millennia. They have served as intermediate ports for colonial vessels, which often brought with them populations of diverse origins. Notions of cultural mixing and pluralism are familiar in many of these societies, in spite of their small size and geographical isolation. Indeed, the concept of the *Creole*, in linguistic as well as in cultural terms, has been developed both locally and by scholars undertaking research in islands such as Jamaica, Martinique and Mauritius (see Stewart, 2007). Moreover, although the term creolization is associated with plantation societies in the Indian Ocean and the Caribbean, a group of scholars on the Pacific recently published a book about creolization in the Pacific islands (Willis, 2002). In fact, the concept of the 'plural society', in which the constituent groups are distinctly culturally different, yet share a political system and an economy, largely grew out of research on island plantation societies (Smith, 1965). This chapter consists of an attempt to compare and discuss social and cultural features of small islands in general, and to suggest some theoretical tools which may be appropriate for an analysis of their current challenges.

The Canary Islands aptly illustrate the continued role of islands as crossroads. In early colonial times, European vessels routinely stopped in the archipelago to replenish their stocks. Much later, the islands became a stepping-stone for Spaniards who, oppressed by the fascist regime, fled to Latin America. Later still, the Canary Islands became a favoured holiday destination for North Europeans craving sun and sand. Today, thousands of North Europeans are settling semi-permanently in the islands, while the tourist industry continues to grow. At the same time, boat refugees from West Africa have been arriving since the mid-1990s, reaching a record 30,000 in 2006. The contrast between these worlds – the North European world of affluence and boredom, and the African world of poverty and dreams – is painfully visible in places like Gran Canaria.

There is some continuity with the past: in a small Canarian fishing port, a monument has been erected, commemorating the Spaniards who fled from Fascism. It depicts a man carrying a suitcase, facing the sea. However, where his heart should have be there is a hole. He is departing *malgré lui*, leaving something of himself behind. This person still exists in the Canary Islands, only the colour has changed.

The man or woman with a hole where the heart used to be is a familiar person in many small island societies that have been populated partly or wholly through successive waves of migration. This is as true of Hawaii as it is of St Lucia. Whether enforced, voluntary or somewhere in-between, migration creates conditions for many kinds of identity projects and identity politics. Some try to recreate the culture or identity of the homeland as faithfully as possible, which sometimes results in a frozen, museum-like form. Others try to assimilate to the best of their abilities. Yet others develop entirely new identities – unique, localized and mixed. As generations pass, the identity projects of the migrants' children and grandchildren change, but not always in the ways anticipated. Quite often, the yearning for an ancestral culture is strongest among those who have never known it – this used to be known in the United States as 'the problem of the third generation'. Sometimes it is necessary to lose one's culture before one can begin to save it from oblivion.

This is true of all culturally complex situations, but in island societies, projects of identity take on a particular character. The physical isolation of island states, although it has never resulted in cultural isolation (the sea being effectively a highway), creates a set of problems, or vulnerabilities if one prefers. By virtue of their small populations, they depend, more than other societies, on trade for subsistence and services; they are expensive to govern, prone to political inbreeding or dominance by a few individuals or families, and usually economically vulnerable in their dependence on one or a few

marketable goods. As pointed out by the anthropologist Burton Benedict many years ago:

> *A strike at an industrial plant in Britain has little immediate effect on most Englishmen; a strike at a sugar mill in Mauritius has very serious effects throughout the island, not only economically but politically. Not just a few but nearly everyone would be affected.*

> (Benedict, 1966: 28)

Their extreme vulnerability to the effects of contemporary climate change is also, sadly, becoming increasingly felt, and not only in the case of low-lying coral islands.

Questions to do with cultural identity and social cohesion have rarely been addressed in this context. Although it has to be conceded that, in the following, I have chiefly the proverbially complex or 'plural' island states of Mauritius, Trinidad and Tobago and Fiji in mind (cf. Eriksen, 1992a, 1998, 2001), my aim is to make some observations with relevance to other island states as well.

In the current era of intensified globalization, ideas travel faster than ever before, leading to an increased volatility in the ideologies and identity politics of these societies. Given their small scale and the dominance of often tiny political and intellectual elites, small islands are especially prone to social epidemics, that is, processes of change that are both fast and highly consequential (see e.g. Gladwell, 2000).

As far as culture is concerned, both centrifugal processes of fragmentation and centripetal processes of integration are at work simultaneously: people become more similar by sharing the same (limited) space and by being exposed to the same transnational trends, yet there is a tendency for some to become intensely preoccupied with demarcating their uniqueness vis-a-vis other groups. Varying groups may be culturally similar (with respect to language, habits etc.), but different at the level of identification. However, there may also be important cultural differences which contribute to explaining the prevalence of social boundaries. Distinguishing between *cultural content* and *social identity* thus becomes crucially important.

With these initial reflections in mind, two themes seem especially interesting in the context of the present UNESCO project on SIDS:

- the form of cultural complexity characteristic of small island states, and the peculiar challenges faced by decision-makers and civil society in these countries; and

- the potential of social epidemics to shape politics and collective identities in these societies.

Beginning with complexity, it should be noted at the outset that the term is often used but rarely defined. 'Cultural complexity' could refer to anything from fundamental differences in worldviews or social segregation along ethnic lines, to the presence of 'ethnic' restaurants or religious pluralism. When the young V.S. Naipaul wrote bitterly of his native Trinidad that, 'Superficially, because of the multitude of races, Trinidad may seem complex, but to anyone who knows it, it is a simple colonial philistine society' (Naipaul, 1979 [1958]), he focused on the emergent similarities, not the differences. However, by neglecting the differences, Naipaul (and many others) at the same time ignored the continued functioning of ethnically based networks and local associations, the continuation of endogamy, religious segregation and ethnically dominated politics at work in Trinidad. The idea that people come to develop a shared collective identity simply because they develop cultural similarities has been proven wrong again and again – indeed, it can be argued that the more similar people become, the more different they strive to appear. Or at least some of them do. Also, it helps little to share cultural values, or to praise the rainbow society, if the division of labour and the distribution of resources are uneven and follow ethnic lines.

The kind of society in which Naipaul grew up is socially complex in the sense of there being a number of distinctive, more or less endogamous groups and their anomalous permutations (people of 'mixed' origins, often even 'mixed' identities), but can be described as culturally simple in the sense of not harbouring a wide range of value systems and distinctive cosmologies. In Naipaul's view, Trinidad was basically permeated by a petit-bourgeois morality. Be this as it may – to my mind, Naipaul underestimates the cultural complexity of Trinidad in the 1940s – the point is that such a society, which combines social diversity with cultural uniformity, is perfectly conceivable.

Vice versa, one can also imagine a society with considerable cultural variation but a high degree of social cohesion (Eriksen, 1992b). The *social* is about relationships and interaction; the *cultural* about ideas, values and notions. Two groups can thus be culturally similar without interacting much (think of Serbs and Croats during and after the Yugoslav civil war), but there can also be considerable cultural variation within a social group, whose members share an identity and interact frequently.

When talking about culturally complex societies, it is necessary to reflect on the implications of our choice of vocabulary. There have been many debates around the concept of culture in the last twenty years, but no similar examination of complexity.

In his eponymous book, the anthropologist Ulf Hannerz (1992) avoids defining cultural complexity – 'it is about as intellectually attractive as the word "messy"' (Hannerz, 1992: 6) – but instead, uses it as a means to talk about culture as something which cannot be characterized 'in terms of some single essence' (ibid.). Hannerz then distinguishes between three dimensions of culture: ideas and modes of thought, their forms of externalization (public communication), and their social distribution. In this way, both the symbolic realm and its social correlates can be studied simultaneously. This text, like most of Hannerz' work, is concerned with the *organization of diversity* rather than the *replication of uniformity* (Anthony Wallace's terms), and argues against classical perspectives in cultural anthropology, which held that cultures must be coherent, or which, as in the case of Edward Sapir,

made a distinction between 'real' and 'spurious' culture, where the latter was more superficial and more poorly integrated than the former. In Hannerz' analysis of contemporary cultural flows, their 'moving interconnectedness' (1992: 167) does not at any point lead to anything resembling a fixed form. In a later contribution, Hannerz (1996) argues in a friendly critique of Ernest Gellner (1983) that the homogenizing processes associated with industrial-society nationalism were counteracted in the late twentieth century by the dissipating and heterogenizing forces of globalization. While Gellner had spoken, metaphorically, about the replacement of Kokoschka's complex, colourful mosaics with Modigliani's calm, monochrome surfaces, Hannerz argues that the world of Kokoschka seems to have been given a second chance with the fluxes and flows, juxtapositions and creolizations of the global era. However, it needs to be added that whereas the new cultural complexity resulting from migration and hybridity results in increased and enhanced contact, the earlier mosaic characterizing a less connected world represented a cultural diversity of another kind. In the famous words of Clifford Geertz, difference 'will doubtless remain – the French will never eat salted butter. But the good old days of widow burning and cannibalism are gone forever' (Geertz, 1986: 105). Cultural differences, in this sense, can be deep or superficial, ontological or cosmetic.

Many other anthropologists have had their say about complexity, but few have tried to operationalize it. One who has is Fredrik Barth, who once (Barth, 1972) proposed a generative model of societies based on the degree of complexity in task allocation and social statuses. But it is in his later studies from Oman (1983) and Bali (1989, 1993), in particular, that Barth tries to specify how different cultural 'streams', which impinge on and intermingle in cultural universes and life-worlds, relate to one another. In the case of Bali, Barth identifies five such streams: Balinese Hinduism, Islam, Bali Aga culture (indigenous, pre-Hindu villages), the modern sector of education and politics, and 'a sorcery-focused construction of social relations' which appears to operate fairly independently of the other traditions or streams (Barth, 1989: 131). While noting that this kind of cultural complexity cannot and should not be conflated in homogenizing statements about 'the Balinese', Barth also acknowledges that there are certain templates for thought and behaviour which are shared by most Balinese. However, neither in his monograph (1993), which includes a generative model that generates plurality, nor in his articles about Bali, does Barth explore hybridity: he describes the streams, in relation to each other, but not their mixing. Nor does he try to specify conditions for social cohesion, an issue which I believe to be of central importance.

In a similar but not identical vein, the sociologist David Byrne shows, in his book about complexity and the social sciences, the limitations of mono-causal accounts. In an attempt to make chaos and complexity theory from physics relevant in the social sciences, he shows through examples how 'small things make for big differences, and lots of thing are out to play, together' (1998: 18).

Applying technical terms like attractors, bifurcation and fractals to topics in the social sciences, Byrne makes a good case for complexity theory in urban studies. Recognizing that a disease like tuberculosis (TB) is a result of the interaction of several causal factors – diet, housing conditions, ethnic relations, class – he then goes on to argue the necessity of moving beyond mere complex causation and look at the interaction of different systemic levels. TB, then, is 'a disease of societies which are in the attractor state for societies of being relatively highly unequal' (1998: 118), which means that urban planning, welfare systems or the lack thereof, and the overall class structure of a society need to be taken into account, and – this is where the term 'attractor' comes into its own – that there is no simple determinism involved.

The need to understand not only the interaction of a great number of major and minor causal factors, but also the relationship between systemic levels (such as group versus greater society) is far from absent even in the study of societies with less than a hundred thousand individuals. Indeed, the networks connecting people are, if anything, denser and thicker there than in larger societies where centripetal forces are stronger in social life.

If we now move to considering group identities, a main implication of the above view of complexity is not merely that each of us have 'many roles' and thus belong to different groups (a trivial fact, which nevertheless bears repeating), but also that different kinds of groups or collectivities can be constituted on various grounds or principles.

Thus researchers on ethnic and cultural diversity who place their bets on both horses – parsimony and richness – often oscillate in their writings between dividing their field of study into ethnic or religious groups, and denying or at least relativizing the significance of ethnic or religious divisions. Groups exist from certain points of view, but from another point of view they vanish. From a perspective accepting the complexity of social life, both descriptions may in fact be true, but should not be allowed to stand alone. As Gregory Bateson entitled a chapter in his *Mind and Nature* (Bateson 1979: 67): 'Two descriptions are better than one'.

The cultural complexity of postcolonial island societies is often commented upon in academic debates and research, but has rarely been seriously discussed at the conceptual level. This is a serious omission in so far as many of the debates – academic as well as non-academic – gravitate around the old and discredited notion of 'cultural pluralism'. These societies are assumed to be 'plural', but as there are important differences between the adaptations of individuals as well as of ethnic and religious groups, some clarification is needed. What exactly is it that we are talking about, then, when we say 'cultural complexity'?

Although cultural complexity is perfectly possible with little or no ethnic variation, the problems of complexity are usually raised in the context of ethnically plural societies: how much, or how little, can people have in common at the cultural level and still retain a sense of solidarity, equality before the law and a sufficient degree of equal

opportunity to remain loyal to a common cause? Since secession is not an option in small islands, there is no alternative to raising and dealing with this question.

To be even more specific: *What are the criteria of exclusion and inclusion in a limited social environment?* This question, which takes complexity as a premise not an answer, must initially be asked at two societal levels and from two analytical angles.

First, we need to ask which forms of exclusion are practised in society, and what are the requirements for inclusion. Are people of different cultural identities treated differently or discriminated against on the basis of colour, language, religion, and so on – and does exclusion primarily take place in the labour market, in the housing market or in the educational system? In some island states, politics and parts of public services are notoriously dominated by one ethnic group, with consequences for career opportunities and, ultimately, political stability.

Conversely, it is necessary to investigate the criteria of inclusion into the groups in question. Who is a member, and on what grounds? Is it possible to change group membership or to relinquish it altogether? What are the resources associated with group membership, and what are the prospects for shared national identities?

Raising these questions may enable us to find out to what extent it is possible for members of minorities to satisfy some or most of their needs within the community – in other words, without being fully 'assimilated' – and to what extent the majority/minority boundary is fixed or more like a semi-permeable membrane. This is crucial in order to understand the limits of pluralism in a well-functioning society.

The next set of questions following logically from this pertains to the kind of group identities that emerge following these dynamics of inclusion and exclusion at the societal and group levels. The kinds of groups that become strongly incorporated need to be feasible and either beneficial to their members, beneficial to some of them (e.g. community leaders), or enforced by greater society. Class-based organization is widely and probably correctly perceived as chosen and beneficial to the members, whether it is a case of working-class trade unions or informal elite organizations. An ethnic or religious organization, be it formal or informal, is more difficult to classify. It may be enforced (as in South Africa under apartheid, or indeed in societies with a positive attitude towards multiculturalism), but it may also arise from an opportunity situation where ethnic or religious solidarity may channel resources towards and within the group. With ethnic elites (Chua; 2003; see also Cohen, 1999, Chapter 4, on Lebanese and Chinese diasporas), the benefits of tight ethnic incorporation are easy to see, but even members of relatively underprivileged groups may for complex motivations, including self-esteem, opt for ethnic incorporation. This has been the case with the indigenous Sami in northern Scandinavia, although there are many Sami, or people who could have chosen a Sami identity, who decide to let other kinds of group membership (regional, gender, class, occupation) overrule their ethnic identity; who would rather be known as engineers or schoolteachers than as Sami.

It is a sociological truism that social groups are closed and open in different ways, and that the degree of group incorporation varies. No group or collectivity is entirely closed, but no group is completely open; in a complex society, no group offers its members everything they need, but it is equally true that no group offers its members nothing. Yet, it is important to understand why it is that some groups or other kinds of collectivities are more open to new recruits than others.

This cannot be put down merely to 'cultural differences' codified as ethnic differences. Indeed, one of the most complex and controversial aspects of ethnicity concerns its relationship to culture. I have already noted that it is necessary to take the cultural dimension of ethnic identity seriously. Of course, its significance varies, but systematic differences often exist between the groups that make up a society, relating to language, forms of socialization, and not least, microeconomic history. In this context, an island state such as Fiji is clearly different from, for example, Trinidad and Tobago. In Fiji, about half the population are indigenous Fijians, while the rest are descendants of indentured Indian labourers. Trinidad and Tobago, by contrast, have no indigenous population. In Fiji, deep-seated cultural differences have an impact on politics and identity, while it could be argued that the sub-populations of Trinidad have been strongly creolized over the years and are much less different in cultural terms than one might expect, given that they look so different from each other.

If cultural resources are granted importance in studies of ethnic entrepreneurship and social mobility, then arguments about 'cultures of poverty', frequently dismissed as victim-blaming, also need to be taken seriously. If cultural resources can help an ethnic group economically, then it goes without saying that cultural resources can equally well limit the performance of its members. Whether they do or not, is a matter of empirical enquiry, and one of the enduring insights from studies in ethnic complexity is that the significance of a particular cultural universe varies from context to context. People from the same castes and from the same parts of India, who migrated at the same time under the same circumstances, eventually became smallplanters in Trinidad, politicians in Mauritius and businessmen in Fiji.

To distinguish between different sets of factors at work, following the discussion above, I propose the following table:

The dimensions depicted in the figure represent general features of complexity. Some of the unique aspects of small island states with composite/plural populations in an ethnic, religious and/or linguistic sense, include the widespread contact between groups (due to the small space) and the potential significance of a few key persons. Social epidemics may spread very quickly under such cirumstances, given the right kind of charismatic leadership, and may die down equally fast. One could mention the virtually overnight switch from French to English in the creole population of Trinidad in the early twentieth century and the phenomenal success of the socialist MMM party in Mauritius after its formation by a handful of students in 1969. Closer to our own time, the attempted coup-d'etat in Trinidad and Tobago in 1990, led by a small group of militant converts to Islam, illustrates the vulnerability of central institutions in small-scale states. Similarly, the violent riots which erupted in Mauritius in 1999, following the death of a popular Creole singer at the hands of the (Hindu-dominated) police, brought the entire country to the brink of chaos, only to die down within a few days, showing how a relatively minor event taking place in a small island state can have serious repercussions throughout the society, because of its modest scale (cf. Benedict, 1966).

| | Culturally open | Culturally closed | Socially open | Socially closed |
|---|---|---|---|---|
| Internal factors | Ambitions of mobility Elite status | Religious zeal Cultural estate | Competitive individualism Meritocracy | Hierarchy Gender inequality Elite status |
| External factors | Pressure from mass culture and state | Stigmatizing ideology Discrimination | Inclusive labour market | Segregated labour market and housing |

The checks and balances limiting the impact of social epidemics in larger societies, cannot be counted upon in small island states. Events with modest effects in a larger country may be devastating in a small one. At the same time, the impact of transnational processes on local identity politics is growing and leads to increased vulnerability regarding societal cohesion. On the one hand, long-distance nationalism engaged in by exiles (who need not be accountable for their actions, since they do not live 'at home'), can have important effects locally. On the other hand, transnational networks engaged in by locals with political ambitions, can also be both enriching and disruptive. *Hindutva* (Hindu nationalism), for example, would take on a very different character in Mauritius, Fiji or Trinidad than in India. Finally, I should like to point out that the 'spectre of comparisons' originally described by the nineteenth-century Filipino author and freedom fighter José Rizal (see Anderson, 2002) adds a further cause for concern: whatever is beautiful or impressive at home is immediately dwarfed when compared to the achievements of larger, metropolitan countries. The challenges are thus threefold: securing social cohesion and equality without obliterating cultural diversity – one could say promoting social equality without demanding cultural similarity; developing a pride in the local as something unique, not as an inferior copy of the metropolitan; and finally, developing a local politics which grows out of domestic concerns proper, not of political projects developed overseas.

# References

Anderson, B. 1998. *The Spectre of Comparisons*. London: Verso.

Barth, F. 1972. Analytical dimensions in the comparison of social organizations. *American Anthropologist*, 74: 207–20.

Barth, F. 1983. *Sohar: culture and society in an Omani town*. Baltimore: Johns Hopkins Press.

Barth, F. 1989. The analysis of culture in complex societies. *Ethnos*, 54: 120–42.

Barth, F. 1993. *Balinese Worlds*. Chicago: University of Chicago Press.

Bateson, G. 1979. *Mind and Nature: a necessary unity*. Glasgow: Fontana.

Benedict, B. 1966. Sociological characteristics of small territories and their implications for economic development. M. Banton (ed.) *The Social Anthropology of Complex Societies*. London: Tavistock, pp. 23–36.

Byrne, D. 1998. *Complexity Theory and the Social Sciences*. London: Routledge.

Chua, A. 2003. *World on Fire: how exporting free market democracy breeds ethnic hatred and global instability*. London: Heinemann.

Cohen, R. 1999. *Global Diasporas*. London: Routledge.

Eriksen, T.H. 1992a. *Us and Them in Modern Societies: ethnicity and nationalism in Trinidad, Mauritius and beyond*. Oslo: Scandinavian University Press.

Eriksen, T.H. 1992b. Multiple traditions and the problem of cultural integration. *Ethnos*, 57(1–2), pp. 5–30.

Eriksen, T.H. 1998. *Common Denominators: politics, deology and compromise in Mauritius*. Oxford: Berg.

Eriksen, T.H. 2001. Ethnic identity, national identity and intergroup conflict: the significance of personal experiences. R.D. Ashmore, L. Jussim and D. Wilder (eds) *Social Identity, Intergroup Conflict, and Conflict Reduction*. Oxford: Oxford University Press, pp. 42–70.

Geertz, C. (1986) The uses of diversity. *Michigan Quarterly Review* 25(1): 105–23.

Gellner, E. 1983. *Nations and Nationalism*. Oxford: Blackwell.

Gladwell, M. 2000. *The Tipping Point: how little things can make a big difference*. London: Abacus.

Hannerz, U. 1992. *Cultural Complexity: studies in the social organization of meaning*. New York: Columbia University Press.

Hannerz, U. 1996. *Transnational Connections*. London: Routledge.

Naipaul, V.S. 1979 (195879) London. In R.D. Hamner, (ed.) *Critical Perspectives on V. S. Naipaul*. London: Heinemann 1979 (originally published in the *Times Literary Supplement*, August 1958.)

Smith, M.G. 1965. *The Plural Society of The British West Indies*. London: Sangster's.

Stewart, C. (ed.) 2007. *Creolization: history, ethnography, theory*. Berkeley: Left Coast Press.

Willis, D. (ed.) 2002. *The Age of Creolization in the Pacific: in search of emerging cultures and shared values in the Japan-America borderlands*. Hiroshima: Keisuisha.

# Endnotes

*1*   Some years ago, I published a collection of essays entitled 'Cultural Crossroads' in which I attempted to develop a view of culture as something characterized by mixing and communication rather than sharing and a common past. The main essays in the book discussed Trinidad, Mauritius, Brussels, Bombay (or Mumbai), the internet and the encounter between Robinson Crusoe and Friday, seen through the eyes of the present. Since Robinson was definitely stranded on an island (possibly Tobago), three out of the six essays concern islands. This is no coincidence.

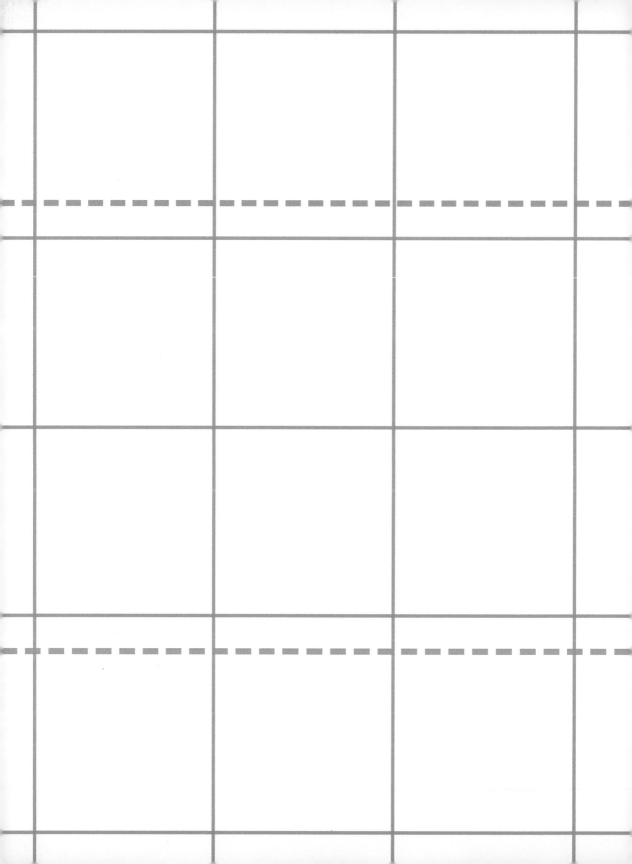

# PART 2

## CONTEMPORARY CROSSROADS

UNESCO/Jens

UNESCO/Daniel Martin

UNESCO/Jens Boel

UNESCO/Cécile Nirrengarten

UNESCO/Jens Boel

# PRESERVING CARIBBEAN CULTURAL IDENTITY IN THE FACE OF GLOBALIZATION

Gordon Rohlehr, *University of the West Indies, St. Augustine, Trinidad and Tobago*

The subject of this chapter has preoccupied Caribbean thinkers for more than five decades now, surfacing as a concern of nationalist movements throughout the region since the 1920s and 1930s, and becoming a central feature of the early post-Independence years, at a time when new Caribbean nations were faced with the necessity of either defining national identities, or identifying foundational values upon which such identities needed to be constructed. This process of identifying the features of and laying the groundwork for identity-construction, went hand-in-hand with the drive to create space between the familiar subaltern identities of the colonial period and the emerging and supposedly different national identities of the reconstructive post-independence period.

During the 1970s, UNESCO's first decade of cultural development, these preoccupations of new Caribbean nations were given focus in the seminal UNESCO 'Intergovernmental Conference on Cultural Policies in Latin America and the Caribbean', held in Bogota between 10 and 20 January 1978. Although Antigua, St. Kitts, Anguilla, St. Lucia and St. Vincent were not represented, Barbados, Grenada, Guyana and Trinidad and Tobago each sent two delegates, while Jamaica and Cuba were represented by three and twelve delegates respectively. Bogota was the fifth in a series of conferences held throughout the seventies – Venice (1970) Helsinki (1972), Yogyakarta (1973), Accra (1975) and Bogota (1978) – culminating in a General Conference in Belgrade (Mondiacult) 1980, and the World Conference on Cultural Policies held in Mexico City from 26 July to 6 August, 1982.

With the possible exception of Venice and Helsinki, both minor cities, not one of these conferences was held in any of the major Western European countries, or in the United States or the USSR – the major centres of both world economic and political power and prominent battlefields of old world and Cold War issues. UNESCO's decade of cultural development was an important element in the organization's efforts to redefine the relationship between developed and developing (or undeveloped), and the centre and the periphery. The proposed New World Information Order and New World Economic Order formed the two other ideological pillars upon which UNESCO's 'New World' was to be erected.

The seven conferences on cultural policy brought peripheral subaltern voices close to the centre of international discourse, Cuban and Latin American initiatives to redefine and promote the concept of 'cultural sovereignty', as well as to the identification of the most powerful nations in the world as the ugly purveyors of 'cultural imperialism'. Cold War protagonists and representatives of the old world order resented this profound change in the rhetoric, direction and imagery of international discourse. UNESCO would find itself under attack in the 1980s from the United States and Great Britain, two of its major donors, both of whom eventually withdrew their membership and support from the organization. Imperialism felt that if it was paying the piper, it must also call the tune, and the most persistent tune of all those seven conferences did not harmonize with the familiar melody of imperialism: its right to invade, penetrate, violate and misappropriate.

Resolutions of the World Conference in Mexico 1982, for example, included 'the promotion of cultural identities, recognized as fundamental for the liberation of peoples and for the self-reliance of individuals' (UNESCO, 1983). The World Conference spelt out what was involved in the protection of cultural heritage. Proposals such as the recognition of the cultural rights of minorities and the restitution of cultural property did not and could not find favour with imperialist agendas for the erosion or suppression of subaltern cultures, or the traditional pillaging of the cultural artifacts of conquered civilizations for the museums of the conquerors. Proposals such as the promotion of national languages and the fostering of intercultural studies, assumed the rights of children of the ten thousand lesser gods of the world, to both

cultural autonomy and participation on a basis of equality in any other cultures that might suit their fancy. Such proposals would be unthinkable to the dominant world powers who routinely suppressed minority languages, religious practices and cultural identities within the subject nations of their empires.

Delegates to the Bogota Conferences of 1978 were provided by UNESCO with fifty booklets of studies and documents on cultural policies, and over the ten days of the conference wrestled with the large objectives of defining cultural identity, cultural development and cultural cooperation, in ways that would take into account the historical, social and political realities of the Caribbean and Latin American regions. Emerging from and related to these broad concerns were the specific objectives of clarifying what was meant by the following:

1.  the cultural dimension of development

2.  cultural pluralism and its relations to national and regional unity

3.  cultural research, inventory, cataloguing and preservation

4.  cultural training, the transmission of values via education and cultural dissemination, and

5.  the fostering and facilitating of the expansion of culture and the cultural product (UNESCO, 1978).

By far the deepest and most difficult issues contested at Bogota 1978 concerned the paradoxical nature of Caribbean and Latin American cultural identities, the contradictory forces that had brought those identities into being, the tensions between the separate (and at times separatist) agendas of antagonistic ethnic communities, and the overriding national objectives of the state. Wrestling with the ethnic and cultural pluralism of the region, the delegates concluded that cultural identity lay in the interface of 'several mutually enriched differences' (UNESCO, 1978: 7, para 24). The Final Report concluded that 'the countries in the region were seeking a culture of synthesis, one of a universal nature that would respect and fully assume the plurality of differences' (ibid, para 25).

Delegates of the Conference more than once envisioned the region as being at a 'crossroads', and certainly this notion of a crossroads is a natural product of the paradox inherent in Caribbean cultural identity and the dilemma of having to choose between 'a culture of synthesis' and 'the plurality of differences'. Rex Nettleford, who represented Jamaica at the Bogota Conference, was fascinated by the crossroads concept, and would in 1991 give a keynote address to the International Social Studies Conference held in Florida on 'The Caribbean: Crossroads of the Americas'. Since the title of Nettleford's address was also the theme of the Florida Conference, and since that theme closely resembles the theme of this publication, I thought it might be useful to summarize Nettleford's ideas about the crossroads concept as it applies to

the islands of the Caribbean Archipelago, sandwiched between the two massive continents of North and South America.

Such a geographical location has resulted in the Caribbean becoming a natural point of intersection for languages, ideologies, cultures and ethnicities as its citizens endure 'a halfway house existence' and learn to describe themselves as 'Afro-this, Indo-, Franco- or Hispanico- that, like their more powerful hyphenated overlords of North America'. 'Crossroads', then, is a signifier of ethnic duality, double identities, or a sense of only partial belonging to one category or another: a notion of transitional or oscillating identities. Nettleford (1993: 3) speaks of the Caribbean as 'a region of options' but notes that:

> Variety at the crossroads at worst spells confusion, periodically inviting self-doubt and equivocation. At best it engenders among individuals the capacity to operate on two or more levels, sequentially or simultaneously, in dealing with the quixotic, multi-faceted social phenomena characteristic of the crossroads where disparate elements meet, contend and have their being.

Nettleford describes the Caribbean as 'creative and disintegrative', a microcosm of planet Earth and 'a laboratory for all the tensions [...] of the human condition as we have come to know them'. He sums up thus:

> The Caribbean, as crossroads, meeting place, and centre of encounters of myriad cultural elements, as well as crucible in which new forms of human

*expression have been forged over this past half a
millennium and are still being forged, deserves closer
study and investigation by those in the Americas
who are preparing the new generation for the
next half a millennium.*

(1993: 5)

The paradox of insular multi-ethnic societies
that function as crossroads intensifies when such
societies undertake the perilous but necessary
journey from being colonies to becoming independent nation states. By the 1960s, in places
such as Guyana and Trinidad in particular, the
contestation of mutually militant ethnic entities seeking their separate self-interest and visibility had become a dominant feature of social
existence. In such fragmented societies, it was difficult for the leadership to allay rooted fears that
synthesis – the supposedly higher ideal of unity
– would not require the destruction of 'the plurality of differences'. 'A culture of synthesis' might
involve more of the same old erasure, engulfment,
alienation and marginalization of peripheralized
ethnic communities, that had been characteristic
of former colonizing regimes, and today constitute
the most dreaded attributes of the neo-imperial-
ism now euphemistically termed 'globalization'.

The Caribbean, and perhaps Latin America, are
possibly more afraid of erasure and cultural and
economic absorption taking place within the microcosm of nation or region than the threat of oblit-
eration by globalization. Just as Afro-Guyanese and
Indo-Trinidadians of the 1980s and 1990s used
to accuse their respective governments – Indo-
Guyanese in the case of Guyana, predominantly

Afro-Creole in the case of Trinidad – of practising
'ethnic cleansing', so I have heard Caribbean citizens
complain against the threat of their particular island
cultures becoming engulfed by the aggressive and
itinerant global outreach of Trinidad and Jamaican
cultural forms and styles. Similarly, member countries of the Organization of East Caribbean States
(OECS) have been more sensitive to the reality of
economic domination from larger and more industrialized Caribbean Community (CARICOM)
states, than to the fear – as underlined by the first
Prime Minister of Trinidad and Tobago, Eric Wil-
liams – of recolonization of the entire region by
Venezuela and/or Cuba (or the United States, the
most powerful and best loved of these colonizers).

This is curious: we are more afraid of ourselves and
either the authoritarianism tendencies of our leaders within our island microcosms or the globalizing
tendencies of the larger and more fortunate richer
territories in the region, than the threat posed by
the greater systems of global marketing, communications, indoctrination and manipulation in which
we are all entrammelled. Why is this so? Perhaps because we unconsciously recognize that today's 'globalization' is just the contemporary version of multi-
national imperialist colonization that the region has
known for the 515 years since Columbus. Caribbean
cultural identity has long been the product of Caribbean peoples' wrestle with, resistance and total or
partial surrender to, or compromise with imperialism and colonization in all their aspects.

The ambiguous results of Caribbean resistance
to, and compromise with, imperialism on the

economic plane have been societies of complacent exploitative and well-fed ruling élites and mendicant turbulent proles. On the political plane it has settled for authoritarian leaders or cliques and subservient or sagacious clients. On the social plane, Caribbean territories have evolved from hierachies based on blood and land, as with the old Caucasian plutocracy, then to blood, money and property as with the old merchant class. Of course, it might be argued that both planters and merchants lived off the blood money generated by the exploitation of first forced, then free labour. Class was also traditionally based on money, education and 'broughtupsy': what used to be termed 'culture' up to two or three generations ago. Next there was education, which in the emerging professional and skilled artisan castes led eventually to greater or lesser money, and with money, property and lifestyles that soared several realms above the survivalism at which these groups might well have started. Next there was and is money, with or without education or cultural nurturing. Such money has become the predominant determinant of all sorts of significance in the latter half and certainly the last quarter of the twentieth century, when most people have come to the realization that money talks and absolute money talks absolutely.

Beneath these layers and liars of the hierarchy, there have been blood, sweat and tears, the perennial markers of the working class; and beneath this are those who either through their own most grievous fault or through fixity within 'the unalterable groove of grinding poverty' (Walcott,

1986: 88) don't fit into or tangibly benefit from the system that sits on their heads. These are the ultimate products and victims of erosion: empty within, reduced without. Their markers are blood and sand. The secret desire and hope of many is that these elements, abandoned to their own devices, will eventually destroy each other and cancel themselves out of the social equation.

Now when we consider preserving Caribbean cultural identity in or out of the face of globalization, we need to be clear in our minds whether we are also talking about preserving Caribbean social structures such as I have just, in an unorthodox but I trust accurate manner, outlined them; those hierarchies of class based originally, on blood, property, race colour and caste, but tempered over time by the gradual intellectual and commercial transcendence of new (and equally malignant) meritocracies.

The delegates at Bogota did not explore this dimension of the paradox of Caribbean and Latin American societies: that these societies require not preservation, but a transformation that must radically undermine both the mindsets and lifestyles of the old 'validating élites', who have the greatest vested interests in preserving the nostalgically remembered structures of the past. Thus the Final Report tended to waver between appeasement and apprehension as the delegates – all of them members of the validating élite – recognized the crossroads at which the region had arrived. The following two quotations from the Final Report, respectively illustrate the rhetoric of sentimental optimism and that of contemplative omen.

> *The cultural identity of the region was the product of an intense blending of indigenous, European, African and Asian cultures, and even of Hindu and Moslem cultures in the case of certain countries. They had given rise to an extraordinary cultural and human structure in the region in which a varied and extremely wealthy cultural mosaic was perceptible at the local and regional levels.*
>
> (UNESCO, 1978: 7, para 31)

> *Several delegates believed that the region had reached a crucial point in its history. One delegate stated that it was a question of a dual society, seeking integration in the midst of ferment without knowing which paths to follow – whether economic change and the restructuring of society, the grouping of countries with different characteristics but similar strengths; new political experiments based on none of the traditional patterns, an attempt to combine humanism and nationalism, or a dialectical contention between tradition and revolution.*
>
> (ibid: 8, para 34)

The first quotation seems, with words like 'extraordinary', 'extremely wealthy' and 'cultural mosaic', to accept and celebrate the cultural heritage bequeathed to the region by its grim history. This conventionally hopeful and acquiescent rhetoric, notwithstanding the perspective of many that the fragments of the Caribbean mosaic represent not wealth at all, but mutual violation and degradation, has for generations sustained the faith of multitudes of affirmative Caribbean patriots. For such adherents, the collision and contestation of cultures has been an enrichening experience and the resultant synthesis has led to the formation of an 'extraordinary' society. I have heard this society described as marvelous, magical, something both rich and strange and 'torn and new' (Brathwaite: 270). This marvelous new world bears within its viscerals the power to withstand, live through and transcend today's globalization. It is tough, flexible, creative, imaginative and innovatory and capable of adapting itself to almost any circumstance.

The second quotation suggests a region at the crossroads, faced with the necessity for radical choice and paralysed. It locates cultural change squarely within the challenge of radical, indigenous and original politics, but recognizes that paralysis has undermined the region's ability to choose and to restructure society. It speaks of a 'dual', that is, a divided society, that seeks 'integration in the midst of ferment', although it does not define the characteristics of this duality or identify the nature of the ferment in the society. Of course, both the duality and the ferment may vary from place to place, and territory to territory. One is led to assume that the division and turmoil of Caribbean societies result in situations where the strengths of contesting interest groups are pitted against each other, and the warring factions cancel each other and stymie the ability of these societies, paralysed at the crossroads of possibility, to make the kinds of daring, radical and revolutionary choices that will be necessary if the traditional blood and land/blood and sand dichotomy is to be courageously addressed.

The region, paralysed in 1978 at what that anonymous delegate to the Bogota Conference recognized as a 'crucial point in its history' certainly did not choose a radical departure from inherited colonial tradition. What followed 1978 was the annihilation in Suriname of a substantial part of its political opposition; the assassinations of Walter Rodney and Maurice Bishop; the deradicalization of both Michael Manley and Cheddi Jagan following the systematic destruction in India and Africa of the non-aligned movement by means of the strategic killings of its leaders; the rising tide of bloodshed in Jamaica, Trinidad, Guyana and Haiti; and the almost universal expansion throughout the Caribbean, of the international narcotics trade – one of the illegitimate and most extreme aspects of globalization – and its ancillary culture of gun-violence and gangsterism. Of all the above, the devastating combination of drug-trading and gun violence has had the most damaging impact on the cultural identity of the contemporary Caribbean, engendering lifestyles that no one should ever want to see preserved.

Thirteen years ago, in an address entitled 'Folk Research: Fossil or Living Bone' (Rohlehr, 1994: 383–94), delivered on the occasion of the inauguration of the Folk Research Centre in St. Lucia, I termed these developments in Caribbean culture and society an evolving 'culture of terminality'. I did not then anticipate how much worse things would get, although I did get a hint in the mid-1990s when one calypsonian responding to the then incredible murder and rape rate in Trinidad, sang a calypso that sought to capture the spirit of the time. He called it *Murder Calendar,* and walking on stage armed with a calendar he had designed, suggested we should start telling time and dating events by the more spectacular murders being committed each month. One decade later, he would need to abandon the idea, murders having outstripped days of the month in Trinidad. Meanwhile, in Jamaica between January and August 2006, there was a significant 25 per cent reduction in the murder rate from over 1,000 for the same period in 2005 to approximately 750 for 2006.

Some have blamed globalization for these negative changes in Caribbean lifestyles, pointing out that the New World Economic Order never came into being; instead, the Empire struck back and by the 1990s the word 'sovereignty' virtually disappeared from the discourse, the new nations having learnt betimes to bow down in silence to the reality of things and accept the status and stasis of subalternity. Even the phrase 'sustainable development', which for some time replaced discarded clichés such as 'cultural sovereignty', suggested the uncertainty of the new nations that such development as they had sought and in which they might have heavily invested, was genuine or could last. To cap it all, during the 1990s 'nationalism' became a dirty word, the 'nation' only an 'imagined community' – at least until 9/11 when plane bombings of the World Trade Centre and the Pentagon led to the resuscitation from sea to shining sea of nationalist rituals of mourning and deeply sworn cowboy gunslinger revenge.

The New World Information Order also went the way of globalization. Meant by UNESCO as an instrument or at least a concept to establish balance and multi-directional flow in the worldwide exchange of information, the New World Information Order simply died under the weight of global media. Meanwhile, the free flow of information has meant for the Caribbean and most other places in the world first the satellite dish, then cable television, video, DVD and the information highway, followed by massively advertised commercial and cultural commodities of the so-called global market place including drugs, such as Viagra alternatives and generously proffered strategies for penile enlargement which, one guesses, constitute another kind of sustainable development. Multiple channels allow viewers to revel in various world religions, the dead or living music of the metropole, violence, fake sexuality, and endlessly breaking and heart-breaking news along with directions on how to interpret it: everything is a commodity in the global marketplace.

The question then is whether Caribbean identity, itself a product of earlier versions of what is now being called globalization, can avoid being constantly shaped and reshaped, shattered and transformed by the various instruments of the global market. Is there a Caribbean cultural identity left to preserve – one that is different from and immune to either expropriation by or erosion through the influences of globalization?

The Guyanese poet, Martin Carter, described identity as being 'a process and a becoming' (Carter, 1971), and although he was talking about individual identity, his observation is applicable to a community, nation or region such as the Caribbean, where in each island multiple forces have always been at play in the shaping of cultural identities.

The Bogota Conference, while acknowledging culture to be 'the total expression of all the people' of a country, also noted (as Martin Carter had observed of identity) that culture is not an established system, but a process in which new forms are constantly being born out of the death, destruction, choice or rejection of old ones. Change, transformation and flux are aspects of cultures. Accepting this assertion as true, one recognizes that Caribbean countries, because of their very histories of violent inter-cultural confrontation – the fracturing and emptying-out of the govis, gourds and sacred calabashes within which, as the Haitians once believed, our truest and most precious souls and selves were contained – have been perennially forced to create new selves, new identities and cultures out of the ruins of the old.

Thus, while today's urgent need seems to require a sort of freeze-drying and preservation of 'cultural identity', a sort of solidification and ossification of remembered or imagined past selves together with the forms and styles through which those selves were made manifest, it may be more important for Caribbean people to recognize, develop and enhance their mechanisms for self-renewal, via a complex blend of absorption of and resistance and adaptation to the forces that constantly challenge and threaten to annihilate them. Preserving the cultural identity of the Caribbean must, therefore, involve both a concern for the past and a capacity to encounter present challenges and create towards the future. Caribbean societies are indeed at a crossroads, where they are required to explore several pathways at the same time.

The Bogota Conference established a web of guidelines for both preserving and developing culture and cultural heritage in the region. Of particular concern was the problem of how far the state should intervene in culture: how to establish cultural policies without imposing such cultural forms as might serve only to advance the socio-political agenda of the regime in power at any given time. This dilemma was of particular importance in ex-plantation societies, where cultures had often developed and sustained themselves underground or in maroonage at the peripheries of power and in open or covert defiance of the state.

Cautious about the state, the conference nevertheless accorded it the role of honest broker between competitive ethnicities and interest groups in the multi-ethnic nations of the Caribbean and Latin America. This role would prove problematic in Trinidad and Tobago where the state itself has for decades been the product of democratic processes rooted in ethnic particularity. The state has had serious problems convincing the various factions and fractions of society that it can function as an honest broker. Yet the conference viewed

the state as the main player in the implementation of cultural policy. The responsibility accorded the state was huge and included:

1. protection of cultural heritage(s)

2. support and promotion of artistic creativity

3. dissemination of culture via libraries, technology, mass media and education

4. the fostering of arts and human resources training for cultural development

5. the improvement of legislation relating to cultural development

6. the design and implementation of cultural financing policies

7. support for research related to cultural development, and

8. training for cultural administrators (UNESCO, 1978: 14).

If, twenty-eight years after 1978, we are still concerned with the crisis of protecting Caribbean cultural identities in or from the face of globalization, it must be because Caribbean governments have been delinquent in shouldering the admittedly onerous and complex responsibilities that were spelt out at Bogota. Trinidad and Tobago has on several occasions analysed and defined its cultural situation, and has also attempted over two decades to design a cultural policy, but has made little coherent effort to implement anything as comprehensive and holistic as the Bogota recommendations. This does not mean that nothing has happened since 1978. As I mean to show, a fair amount has occurred, although not necessarily through the direct agency of the state.

However, the question needs to be asked: why this reluctance to implement policies arrived at after much talk, intellectual headache and hard work? Non-implementation in Trinidad and Tobago and the wider Caribbean region amounts to a terrible wastage of intellectual capital, leading often to a loss of faith in both self and country. It is as if the precious containers of the nation's soul were being shattered all over again, this time not by any colonial system or globalizing agency, but by ourselves. We neglect, waste, then water down our intellectual resources to our own detriment.

Non-implementation in Trinidad and Tobago is partly the result of the inter-ethnic contestation that I described earlier. 'Culture' has become a major battleground upon which space, significance and visibility are won and lost, and the contribution of the ethnic group to national constructions is demonstrated and affirmed. The fierceness of contestation for state-financed and state-validated cultural space makes the state cautious about implementing anything on a grand scale because:

- Each attempt at implementation becomes a fresh source of contestation in which the ethnic competitors strive, openly or covertly, to gain the upper hand in the grand competition.

- Implementation, particularly in the context of post-colonial societies, often involves the creation of radical new structures from 'foundation to finish'. Implementation involves comprehensive and foundational change, whether we are talking about programmes for sport, arts education, the shape of a national festival such as the Carnival, or hardest of all, the change in attitudes that will be necessary if any other changes are to take place.

The non-implementation, except piecemeal, of cultural policy is also a result of the notion, even more powerfully believed and clung to in this era of globalization, that culture is, like everything else, a commodity for market sale. Cultural development is thus regarded as a mere subset of economic development. The state will therefore invest in only the most obviously and immediately marketable aspects of culture such as, for example, those areas in the performing arts that might enhance the tourist trade. Culture is viewed as a show ruthlessly geared for the entertainment of the foreign visitor, who is fed whatever might be the current clichés and stereotypes of exotic national self-representation that he or she has been pre-programmed through the package-deal brochure to expect.

Culture thus envisaged and fostered becomes the spearhead of an economic thrust – (Nettleford's 'outward reach' perhaps) – but can seldom serve as a transformative force in the inner lives of Caribbean people (Nettleford's 'inward stretch'). During the 1980s, Brother Mudada in his calypso *Tourist Jump*,[1] spoke out against what seemed to be a policy of asking local performers to 'jump for the tourist, wine for the tourist, do dis for the tourist, an dat for the tourist' and threatened to do nothing for the tourist until the state tangibly demonstrated its intention to foster and support both the artists and their art. It can, of course, be argued that bread is more immediately necessary for human existence than illumination; that, in the words of one political seer, one cannot eat culture.

Most of the objectives and high ideals of UNESCO's many declarations on cultural policy crumble against this rock. Another famous pronouncement, made by either a minister of one of the regional governments, or one of his senior advisors in the Civil Service stated simply: 'policy is politics'. And 'politics' is no more or less than doing whatever will every five years generate the vote necessary to keep a regime in powerless power. 'Culture', broadly or narrowly defined, usually has a low priority on the agenda of such regimes.

It is possible that private non-governmental agencies have done more than or as much as Caribbean governments to promote culture and preserve cultural identity. Throughout the 1960s and well into the 1970s, Derek Walcott, who was then the industrious and illuminating cultural reporter of the *Trinidad Guardian*, complained about the state's neglect of areas such as arts education and cultural training. Today, with the Centre for the Creative and Festival Arts UWI in its twentieth year, and another arts centre planned for the University of Trinidad and Tobago, things are or should be better than they were in the 1960s.

There are now over sixty clones of the T&T Carnival throughout the Caribbean and in North America and Britain. Carnival skills of designing and wire-bending and even the judging of *mas* have been marketable for decades. Regional performers find steady employment at those festivals, which are themselves illustrations of how one part of Caribbean identity has coped with exile and the metropolitan marketplace. The example of Carnival as an exportable and economically viable commodity hints at the strength of Caribbean identity, its flexibility and self-confidence. It is also illustrates the power of individual and collective enterprises, largely unencumbered by state assistance.

At home in the Caribbean, festivals have grown almost as rapidly as the escalating murder rates. There is substantial state investment in these events, which generate tourist dollars, prevent collapsing airlines from becoming collapsed ones, and fill hotels and guest houses. Festivals and the entertainment and hospitality industries fit easily into state initiatives for culture and development. Culture and development, however, are not exactly the same thing as developing culture, and the growth and adaptation of Carnival to the current needs of these times has been due to the masqueraders and *mas* designers themselves, rather than the state as fostering agency. This is not in itself a bad thing; it simply illustrates the point that the state is probably better at dealing with tangible externals than the interior spirit of culture.

It was the masqueraders – mainly the growing lower middle class – in alliance with the Port of Spain grassroots, who resuscitated the 'J'Ouvert' street party as a meaningful alternative to 'pretty mas'. In so doing, they also resuscitated and updated the jacket-man phenomenon of the early twentieth century.[2] The rumbling anger of South East Port of Spain against what had become 'a big-shot mas, pack up with commercials' was articulated by Black Stalin in *De Jam*[3] (1980). Chalkdust in *De Spirit Gone*[4] (1978) and Valentino in *King Carnival*[5] (mid-1970s) were equally clear about the loss of meaning and spirit as the festival made its outward commercial reach at the expense of any inward spiritual or emotional stretch. Fin de siècle J'Ouvert attempted a restoration of meaning as it reached back into the memory (largely imagined) of 1880s Canboulay. Along with the dynamic Laventille Rhythm Section and other musicians, it created a whole new genre of J'Ouvert songs, that are slower than the more commercially engendered and oriented Soca songs. J'Ouvert music represents a slowing down of tempo and a symbolic return in memory to an earlier age. It is both nostalgic and contemporary, and marks the emergence of old and new sensibilities.

The state has nothing to do with this sort of development, or with Soca-Parang, which like J'Ouvert is a reinvention and an innovation of old and new rhythms to suit this age. The startling and heart-warming resurgence of Mokojumbie *mas* is a result of cultural training undertaken by a private individual. The late Brian Honoré not only kept the Midnight Robber *mas* alive, he reinvented it by blending Robber rhetoric with the acrid satire of the social commentary calypso. State activity, by contrast, has been most evident in the financing of infrastructure such as stands and bleachers, and of rewards for performers in the various categories of *mas*. One frequent complaint concerns the length of time it takes the state via the NCC (National Carnival Commission) to produce the promised sums of money. Other and higher rewards come from sponsors, in particular, business firms, whose association with the festival has a long history.

UNESCO has for decades now been emphasizing the desirability of state facilitation of cultural research, documentation, education and dissemination, as the cornerstones of cultural policy. These activities are crucial for former colonies, where so much of past lifestyles, customs, modes of understanding and created forms has been eroded, abandoned or simply forgotten. But research is a hard, unglamorous and unrewarding activity which does not generate votes. It requires financing but promises few immediate or marketable returns. Research into Caribbean culture has, nonetheless, grown through the private enthusiasms of several Caribbean and non-Caribbean researchers. Often, the foreign researcher is more interested in the region's culture than the locals who live and create it. Much fruitful cooperation and mutual exchange has evolved between Caribbean and foreign cultural researchers – which suggests that not all globalization is bad.

Documentation of Caribbean music has improved considerably since the arrival of CD and DVD technology. Traditional calypsos are available on about twenty CDs and with the release of *West Indian Rhythm*,[6] a boxed set of Decca recordings (1938–1940), 270 more calypsos have become available, some for the first time. Not one of these CDs, crucial to any unlocking of Caribbean cultural heritage, has been the result of state investment in cultural archiving. Of course, the case may be different in other parts of the region: in Cuba say, or Jamaica with its famous Institute, or St. Lucia with its centre for folklore research. Nor is the situation in Trinidad a static one: there are always signals of official concern with regard to the archiving of cultural heritage, and there may be more going on than is immediately visible.

Yet, on the whole, the overall impression has been one of indifference at the elusive and invisible centre, the result of which has been the disconnection of contemporary from even recently ancestral culture, combined with the sense that many youths feel, of proceeding out of a void. One youth with whom I recently raised the issue of Caribbean cultural identity defined it as 'ex-slaves wearing blue denim jeans'. Accustomed to living without a sense of the past, many

contemporary Caribbean people may be quite at ease with the very globalization that seeks to make all faces one. Cultural research seeks the very opposite: to establish or restore the distinctness of each face; to accord each people, nation or ethnicity due recognition for whatever is unique in its contribution – small or large – to the total human heritage of knowing, understanding and creating meaning. Cultural research for the Caribbean should therefore aim at an unearthing of the narratives of both recent and distant ancestors, who have become dead or inert because they have been unacknowledged and unremembered.

A substantial element of social and psychic order in traditional African, Asian and European societies used to depend on both private and communal rituals of mourning the dead, where mourning involved not just lamentation, the wearing of sackcloth and ashes, or the pasting of mud on the body, but acknowledgement, reverence and remembering. To (re)member is to (re)collect the fragments of narrative that, reassembled like the scattered skeleton of Osiris, still have the power to restore and reanimate the ancestor as a living, active body of achievements and created meanings. Thus restored, the ancestors become accessible to the living as guides, as a code of admonitions and examples of how to act or refrain from acting in any given situation.

Our responsibility as people concerned about preserving Caribbean cultural identity is not only to research and archive the heritage, but to reanimate it through education. After we have, through enlightened research, identified, contemplated and defined the high or significant points of our making, we need to go further and teach, based on our understanding of the complexity of who we are and of what we have all been making in this time and place. We also need to teach the skills involved in our unending performance of ourselves. Our creative arts – literature, music, dance, painting, sculpture and drama – must continue to examine, interrogate and enact the seminal processes of interface, overlap, transgressive confrontation and resolution that have constituted our cultural history in the Caribbean, even when these processes have been apprehended by some only as chaos, crisis, violation and mutual defilement.

The task of cultural education, particularly of education in the arts, must be one of awakening and educating the imagination of our people, and of imparting the necessary skills, so that Caribbean people continue to develop not just ways of seeing, saying and understanding, but ways of doing, and of performance. If these two aspects of cultural education are fulfilled, Caribbean people will not only learn to respect their dreaming, but also to enhance their power to give shape and articulation to their dreams.

Bogota (1978) located the Caribbean and Latin America at 'a crossroads of civilization'. This suggests that we share both a need and a possibility to articulate alternatives to increasingly monolithic Western formulations that are being vigorously marketed to the rest of the world as 'global'. In order to articulate alternatives that are truer

to who we are as crossroads people, we Caribbean people will need to develop imaginative approaches to cultural research and education. Cultural research, as suggested above, can become a means of 're-narrating' the Caribbean, that is, reconnecting the Caribbean with its untold or forgotten stories, and thus reclaiming ancestral and contemporary wisdom and achievement towards the strengthening of cultural identity.

If we are indeed at the crossroads, where we go from here will depend on the choices we make. Wise selection of our pathway will require the cleverest, most dedicated and most carefully focused planning of which we are capable. We also will need help from those deities of the crossroads, Legba and Eshu, who according to whim may facilitate or hinder choice, and remove or erect the barriers to our passage. We also will need Anansi-like wisdom, subtlety and skill in implementation disproportionate to our size. If we really want to preserve Caribbean cultural identity in the face of so many ambiguous pressures and tensions, we will need courage, confidence, self-knowledge and caution as we approach the crossroads, where despite the rumoured demise of the ancestral gods, the issue is still Eshu.

# References

Brathwaite, K. 1973. *The Arrivants*. London: OUP, p. 270.

Carter, M. 1971. *Man and Making: victim and vehicle*, The Edgar Mittleholzer Memorial Lectures, October. Georgetown: National History and Arts Council.

Nettleford, R. 1993. The Caribbean: crossroads of the Americas. *Inward Stretch, Outward Reach: a voice from the Caribbean*, London: Macmillan, p. 3.

Rohlehr, G. 1994. Folk Research: Fossil or Living Bone? *The Massachusetts Review* XXXV, Nos 3/4, Autumn/Winter: 383–94.

UNESCO. 1978. *Final Report on Intergovernmental Conference on Cultural Policies in Latin America and the Caribbean*, Bogota, 10–12 January 1978. Paris: UNESCO.

UNESCO. 1983. *Cultures #33. Dialogue between Peoples of the World*. Paris: UNESCO.

Walcott, D. 1986. Laventille. *Derek Walcott: Collected Poems 1948–1984*. New York, Farrar, Straus & Giroux.

# Endnotes

1   Brother Mudada (Alan Fortune) *Tourist Jump*, New York, Oscar's Production Inc, OPI-0-002. 1988.

2   Historically, the connection between 'jammettes' and 'les hommes camisoles' signalled a tentative political alliance between bourgeois mulatto and black professionals and the rate payers, rent payers and proletariat of the time. Both classes of citizens shared a common need for political representation and autonomy, which found its cultural expression in the intrusion of the jacket men into popular J'Ouvert. The twentieth century and the start of the twenty-first has also seen a re-enactment of the Downtown versus Savannah controversy (between 1919 and 1957) become part of J'Ouvert.

3   Black Stalin (Leroy Calliste) 'De Jam' on *This Is It*, 33⅓ rpm LP, Brooklyn, Makossa International Records MD 9055, 1980.

4   Mighty Chalkdust, *De Spirit Gone*.

5   Brother Valentino, *King Carnival*.

6   *West Indian Rhythms*, Bear Family Records, Hamburg, LC05197 2006. Original Producers: Ralph Perez and Luis Sebok; Reissue Producers: Dick Spottswood and Richard Weize; Essays: John Cowley, Don Hill, Lise Winer, Dick Spottswood, Hollis Liverpool and Denis Malins-Smith.

UNESCO/Hans Thulstrup

UNESCO/D. Post

UNESCO/Peter Coles

UNESCO/Rocky Roe

UNESCO/Peter Coles

UN Photo/Yutaka Nagata

# Shifting cultures and emerging rites

## Kang Rom (chanting tales) as a way of building communities

Michael A. Mel, *University of Goroka, Papua New Guinea*

Small Islands Developing States (SIDS) have always been inhabited by unique cultural groups – each with its own language, history, knowledge and art practices – who have lived and made their homes on these islands. Today, cultures that were once relatively isolated and self-contained are exposed to ever-increasing contacts from within their regions and beyond. Cultural, political, economic and social shifts, as well as changes brought on by a history of migration have created landscapes full of tensions. Dominant cultures have exercized control over our peoples' ways of thinking and life through forms of knowledge relating to art, education and politics that have subjugated local bodies of knowledge. There is therefore a need to re-introduce our own ways into these contemporary contexts. Institutions in SIDS, including governments, need to counter this cultural hegemony by reasserting and placing local art, education and political processes alongside those from dominant contexts, contrasting and challenging in order to find meaningful and productive outcomes for local communities.

This chapter[1] focuses on the age-old traditions of story-telling as important and significant vehicles for building a sense of place and belonging in a community. The ways of story-telling found in *kang rom/tom yaya kange* in the Melpa and Ku Waru areas in Mt. Hagen, Papua New Guinea, form the basis of a small workshop, which started a couple of years ago. It marked the beginning of a journey to record these story-tellers, to transcribe and recount their stories, and to train story-tellers for tomorrow.

> *We cannot build a nation simply from technology; we cannot build a nation purely on the basis of the wheel and on the basis of the steam engine. We must build this country; we must build our civilization on values, which have been passed on to us from generation to generation. And I say this: that if we do not agree on common values, if it is not now the basis and the stem upon which we nurture and grow our children, then I say there will be no future for this country.*

Narakobi, 1991

## Introduction

Small Island Developing States, including Papua New Guinea (PNG), have been host to many social and cultural upheavals, experienced by people at all levels. Within these states, cultures that were once located in small and often isolated areas have had to come to terms with being a part of a nation and the wider world. This has created significant tension; however, this tension is not necessarily rooted in temperament or violence, but instead stems from the necessity for people to make choices about belonging. Where do I belong? What is important for me? This chapter, in part, attempts to explore this tension. Allow me to share a story.

> *Margaret sat in the corner, her head aching and confusion clouding her heart. Why couldn't she go out to the dance with her school friends? She pictured her friends enjoying their freedom while she obeyed her mother and stayed at home. She was lost between her culture and a modern perspective on life. To go out to dances, might mean finding a boyfriend, which would embarrass her parents in their traditional society. How could she make her people see that times are changing and so are values? Margaret fears being an outcast in her own society yet strongly believes in some of the changing perspectives on life. There she was – the pride of her parents, a top student at school, with a bright future, yet torn and confused inside. She looked around her and realized that nothing had changed in all those years: the same room, rules and lifestyle. Finally she went to bed and cried herself to sleep.*
>
> Gibbs, 2003: 61

Many of us have known the tension felt by Margaret. It is about subscribing our allegiance on the one hand to our small community and our heritage, and on the other about being drawn into the exciting new world of the nation state. Like Margaret, these thoughts and questions can be both confusing and disorientating – moments of schizophrenia. We are living in a time fraught with tensions that pull and push many of us between the communities we live in, the institutions we work in, and the nation state at large. What does this mean for the future of our own local communities, our tribal languages, histories, myths and experiences?

These and related questions can be examined by looking briefly at the different historical dimensions of membership of the various communities in SIDS. These dimensions are not separate entities and frequently overlap in our discussions and behaviour in numerous situations and circumstances. Hall's (1990) 'Cultural Identity and Diaspora', which approaches Caribbean identity from a historical perspective, has been helpful here.

## Pasin bilong tumbuna

In Papua New Guinea, prior to colonization, different cultural groups had their own ways of socializing their young within their communities. An intricate network of social and family relationships helped to ensure the survival of the group through interdependence and cooperation. People did not define themselves in terms of their individuality, but in terms of group affiliation. Basic to their thinking and knowing was mutuality, not separateness. Their actions stressed participation in activities with others and the establishment of meaningful relationships between people and the environment. These relationships formed part of an intricate and interconnected cosmos, where all cultural, social, spiritual and personal knowledge was seen as interrelated. *Pasin bilong tumbuna* refers to a sense of a shared culture through history, language, mythology and ancestry that is seemingly unchanging, and maintained to remind us, every now and again, of where we have come from.

## Taim bilong masta

Another aspect of the individual's connection to the community relates to our colonial history, the *taim bilong masta*. This second aspect of our sense of place is little talked about, but is significant. We were treated differently by the colonial masters because of our different language, behaviour, skin colour and customs. Compelled to work and serve, we learnt to become someone else's creation and internalized this sense of being different.

*Nelson Giraure, writing in 1976 makes for us a revealing confession when he describes his formal schooling experiences. He was taken away from his village early in life. His heathen name was replaced with a Christian name and then forced to speak and think in a foreign language. He recalls feeling confused and frightened initially and then becoming a vegetable in primary school because he had to think and do things in a completely foreign way. Gradually he acquired the skills and knowledge and managed to progress through the system and in doing so his language, dances, values and all that was about his people were abandoned.*

*When he went back to his village for holidays he felt like a stranger. He writes: 'By this time we looked with horror upon village life. To go back to the village was a fate worse than death.' The depth of his oppression hit home when he went fishing with an 'uneducated' Manus Islander. As Giraure fumbled and struggled with a fishing line, the Manus fisherman reeled in two other lines easily and came to help him laughing.*

Giraure, 1976 cited in Eyford n.d.

Giraure felt humiliated and frustrated, realizing he was becoming a stranger in his own place. This process of alienation relates to the machinations of colonization of the mind. Western education and knowledge are internalized and considered more important than local knowledge (Burnett, 1999). Papua New Guineans came to know and accept the introduced culture in all its forms, shapes and sizes as totally logical and meaningful. As a consequence, local culture became strange, foreign and even illogical and meaningless.

## Yumi iet

It is also important to mention here the sense of connection with the present time, the notion of *yumi iet*. The cultural shift in Papua New Guinea has created a context that is both impulsive and unpredictable. The situation has been made even more precarious by the emergence of a global economy and the transformations wrought by the World Wide Web, which have created an interconnected and effectively miniaturized world. Influences, both direct and indirect, brought about by new technologies (television, CD-ROMs, DVDs, virtual reality games), advertising, and other multimedia and mass media-related practices are dazzling and beguiling, especially for many communities in Melanesia that may be broadly innocent of such innovations. Communication and the dissemination of information through such technology have made the spoken and written word appear unwieldy and archaic. A new kind of literacy is needed in order to read and better organize and manage the meanings and influences brought about by these technologies. Where that literacy is lacking, these new technologies further compound the existing ideological situation relating to maintenance of power and control of the region.

Caught amid these tensions, our children – with our help – must decide which path to follow. What values and knowledge will form the basis of their choices? Educating and cultivating young minds is a significant process that must acknowledge their heritage and history, as well as elements important for themselves and their communities. The reform that we have engaged in is very much underpinned by this agenda and the belief that we need to continue to pursue these aspirations. The following project aims to address these issues in terms of cultural disruption and discontinuity, as described earlier, in order to research and store vital intangible cultural heritage for the future, thus ensuring recognition of what is truly our own sense of place.

# The Chanted Tales Project

This project brings together an interdisciplinary team from PNG and beyond to engage in research on the chanted tales of the region. The team comprises those who come from the region and grew up with the tradition of chanted tales, and have now been educated and trained in ways of the West. The team plans to collaborate on and develop digital recordings of the range of chanted epic tales performed in the Highlands of Papua New Guinea. These recordings will then be transcribed in the local languages and translated into *Tok Pisin* and English for Papua New Guineans and others. The material will then be made available for use by children in schools to provide them with access to this part of their heritage, and to help them to learn their language, knowledge and values.

# Background to chanted tales

Remarkable oral traditions concerning chanted tales exist in the Central Highlands of PNG, including the Southern and Western Highlands and Enga Provinces. These tales have functioned as poetic vehicles through which inhabitants of the region have maintained and shared with others their histories and knowledge of the land and people. They are also an enchanting means of community entertainment.

In many cases the tales were told indoors during the evenings. *Pikono* tales of the *Duna* area of the Southern Highlands would be told by a lone story-teller over some 7 to 10 hours. Conversely, the stories from the *Melpa/Ku Waru* areas of the Western Highlands last between 30 to 40 minutes. The pace of language used to tell the stories in the two regions also differed. In *pikono* tales, the pace was slower, more akin to normal speech, which partly accounted for the time it took to tell the stories. In contrast, the pace of language used by the *Melpa/Ku Waru* story-tellers was quite rapid. In both areas the language used was characterized by an inherent rhythmic pattern and a repetitive melodic structure.

The stories told ranged from boy-meets-girl love stories to conflicts between people and cannibals, ogres or giants, structured around universal themes of good and evil. They provided entertainment, but also constituted a record of history and a pictorial or image map of the home lands and folklore. Stock characters served to educate members of the communities on the 'dos' and 'don'ts' of their societies and other important knowledge and values binding them together.

The story-tellers were masters of their craft. Their chanting captured the attention of onlookers with images of heroes, heroines, journeys, places and deeds. Masters of oral imagery, they beguiled and bedeviled listeners as they juggled and juxtaposed words that were chanted in a seamless rhythmic pattern – an art form which would be new to many today, yet was deeply rooted in the Papua New Guinean context. The

art form of chanted tales formed a vital part of peoples' lives in terms of entertainment, history and knowledge of their communities.

## School and home cultures through chanted tales

Stories, legends and myths are elemental components of the folklore and mythology of our communities. They serve as windows into the deep and powerful store houses of history and knowledge. Reviving the tales of our past is a journey of discovery, as all kinds of knowledge and stories lie submerged. This process of discovery is a way to see, understand and appreciate the wisdom of our people. It also constitutes a challenge, as we compete with television screens that transmit value-laden stories and images from across the world, and with the world of science, where our stories and myths seem unscientific. However, while they may appear scientifically ridiculous, our stories represent the deeper recesses of spiritual reality that provide the basis for our livelihoods.

The experience recounted by Giraure described the difference between home and school cultures. The Chanted Tales Project is a way to help dismantle the separation of school and home and see both as extensions of the one context. This takes the form of the ways in which language, and the knowledge within it, are used in the home as well as at school. Efforts need to be made to reduce the gulf between school culture and home culture, in order for children to see the value and significance of what they learn at school and at home in helping to build and structure useful and meaningful knowledge and skills.

Language is a very important element of the Chanted Tales Project. Social and cultural context is very much identified by language and its use and maintenance is important in this regard. Specifically, the use of language in chanted tales transcends ordinary language: while some of the words and terms used resemble common everyday terms, others employing imagery and poetry are constructed by the story-teller during the chant. Onlookers are given the opportunity to listen, decipher and create images in their mind's eye from the rhythmic patterns the chanted words make. The construction of characters, events and the ebb and flow of the story are powerful processes; in addition, the chants provide clues and indications of familiar turf and terrain – land and creatures that are part of mythic and folkloric traditions of the community to which the listeners belong.

## Building strong communities

Chanted tales, like any good story, have within them a culture's sense of what is right, as well as a sense of beauty and perfection. Immersing children in the stories and chants and enveloping their minds and imagination in the events, characters and action, is a journey that will help them develop a sense of beauty and notions of right and wrong, as understood by their communities.

These processes transmit important and essential ingredients for building strong and solid communities, where members know what to do and how to go about their duties, and in which responsibilities are cultivated.

The telling of myths and folktales in our heritage constitute processes that emphasize the essential oneness of humanity and nature, particularly, with respect to the coherence of land, people, nature and time. Notions of living a meaningful life depend not only on the *quantity* of knowledge, but also on the *quality* of knowledge related to the *how* in living, and to human values essential to building and sustaining communities. The arts were seen as important conveyances that socialized the young to become articulate and responsible members of the community. Our indigenous communities regarded and practised education as a matter that concerned the hand, head and the heart. These were not seen as discrete entities, but interrelated components of an individual. Educating a person was about connecting these aspects within each person. This matter is discussed further in the following two examples.

Thaman (1995) describes the concepts of *ako*, *'ilo* and *poto* as they relate to the Tongan worldview of the education process: *ako* denotes teaching and learning; *'ilo* denotes knowledge and understanding; and *poto* relates to having a good mind or intelligence. The three concepts are interrelated and cannot be entirely separated from one another, although there has been some re-interpretation or 'misunderstanding' of the older sense of *poto*.

In contemporary education circles *poto* means a person's ability to read and write and do arithmetic, while the older meaning related to a person maintaining good relations, possessing wisdom, and having the ability and capacity to do something and do it well under difficult and trying circumstances.

The second example (Mel, 1995) provides the philosophical background to the Mogei people in PNG in terms of the three concepts of *Noman, Mbu Noman* and *Nuim. Noman* relates to knowledge and knowledge creation in an individual; it concerns thinking, feeling, doing and knowing. Learning and acquiring knowledge is understood as developing the *Noman.* The skill and dexterity of an individual in terms of speaking, knowledge of history and social relationships, and showing respect for others relates to *Mbu Noman.* Someone who is able to display *Mbu Noman* is said to have attained the quality of *Nuim. Nuim* is not necessarily intelligence alone, but an individual's capacity to work with others and for others in difficult and demanding situations. To have attained the quality of *Nuim* is really about the getting of wisdom.

In giving recognition to and realizing these three complimentary components of education, people understood that the process of education as a whole was really one of character building. Character related to ideas like humility, responsibility for actions, respect for authority, giving, caring for people and so on, as much as growth of the intellect and skills. Students in the villages of a bygone era were not only taught the skills and knowledge necessary to live, but also how to live. Chanting tales and stories were important vehicles, among others, through which history, social and moral character could be transmitted.

A report by the UNESCO International Commission on Education for the Twenty-first Century, entitled *Learning: the treasure within,* attempted to review, evaluate and map the future of education. Among a number of key ideas, the report placed emphasis on the importance of lifelong learning for effective education, a concept based around four main pillars (UNESCO, 1996: 22–23):

- learning to know
- learning to do
- learning to live together, and
- learning to be.

The types of education that have shaped much of the latter part of the last century have been built on the first two pillars. The last two have received very little attention in education circles although they are an inseparable part of living. They in fact constitute the deepest and most fundamental dimension to human actions.

Today, these aspects need to be included as part of school education. Western education should not consist entirely of intellectual knowledge (rational/cognition) and skills (practical/affective) alone, but must also include matters relating to the heart (emotional/sensibility). The community and its aspirations, its values and beliefs must find a place alongside the two dominant aspects of contemporary education. All three are attributes of being human. Focusing on only two aspects contributes to a person appearing knowledgeable and skilful, but lacking a certain capacity – the wisdom to recognize and live in a community. Chanted tales and story-telling are journeys into internalizing a sense of perfection and beauty, of what is good and right.

Here follows an example of a chanted tale:[2]

> *kang mel we mel kaniyl e*
> [Though the tinniest slip of a lad]
>
> *kang mai pup yaka nyirim e*
> [That boy strode from perch to perch]
>
> *kang komonga mong yaka nyirim e*
> [That boy strode from mountain to mountain]
>
> *ukuni yabu tobu midi nyirim e*
> [He wanted to slay the Ukuni]
>
> *kobulka yabu tobu midi nyirim*
> [He wanted to slay the Kobulka]
>
> *kang mel we mel kaniyl e*
> [Though the tinniest slip of a lad]
>
> *kang piditap mel kaniyl e*
> [Who'd been ignored since the day he was born]
>
> *pilyini kub nai-ko, nyirim e*
> [And who's ever heard such a tale?]
>
> *kanuni kub nai-ko nyirim e*
> [And who's ever seen such a thing?]

> *kang mai pup yaka nyirim e*
> [That boy strode from perch to perch]
>
> *kobulka yabu tokur midi nyirim e*
> [The Kombulka tribe he would slaughter]
>
> *minabi yabu toku midi nyirim e*
> [The Minyabi tribe he would slaughter]
>
> *kang mel we mel kaniyl e*
> [Though the tinniest slip of a lad]
>
> *pilyini kub nai-ko, nyirim e*
> [And who's ever heard such a tale?]
>
> *kanuni kub nai-ko nyirim e*
> [And who's ever seen such a thing?]

## Educating and contextualizing

In implementing this project our quest has been to begin the process of providing options and opportunities for our young, so that as they grow up in a competing world of meanings, they are grounded in some way to their place. This sense of being grounded is important and constitutes the closing part of this chapter.

This idea of being grounded relates to ideas that have been expressed eruditely by Peter Berger and Thomas Luckmann in *The Social Construction of Reality* (1967). Knowledge is not objective and value-free. In other words, knowledge is not independent of human beings and each individual has the capacity to see, experience and produce knowledge. The important point for us is that knowledge exists insofar as there are people who produce that knowledge. Knowledge, when institutionalized, sets out predefined patterns of conduct which people follow as routines; in this way the institution creates in us a sense of an objective reality that is meaningful. For example, when we in various circumstances play roles of being a parent, an uncle, a teacher, an aunt or a student, we participate in the social world. We learn routine behaviour patterns and gradually start to think as a teacher, student, parent and so on. We also begin to attach values to these roles. We accrue a body of knowledge that makes the role appropriate and acceptable to ourselves and to others. As we live out these roles they become real, subjectively real. We are grounded.

Now, imagine going through a sensation of 'unsettlement'. This is most often experienced when we travel to a new and strange place. We lose our bearings, and feel disorientated, vulnerable and insecure. We look for something or someone that may be familiar to help compose and place ourselves. If we know the language it may help. But suppose we allow ourselves some degree of opportunity to be open to what is there in the new and different. The strange can be frightening and scary. Which way to go? What are the priorities? In our efforts to reassert our own history and stories, this is a key element – to engender a sense of unsettlement into what seems settled. The dominant regimes have settled and are embedded in our ways of thinking and knowledge and how we feel and prioritize our lives. To bring back or even better, to bring ourselves back to our languages,

our knowledge, our myths and our values is really a quest to offer alternate ways of looking at and talking about the way things appear to be.

Stories are a journey to beginning the process of legitimizing our ways – a way of affirming that our ways are neither strange nor foreign, and that we do not have to experience a sense of being lost in our own land. In beginning the process of education our children should be grounded in their own world, so as to be able to engage with the world outside. If we can adapt Berger and Luckmann and their notions of levels of legitimizing knowledge and behaviour, our children should go through processes of enculturation that provide them with opportunities to:

- learn the stories by naming them, the characters and their deeds (pre-theoretical)

- learn the stories and the relationship of those stories to their place – for example, how a mountain came to be (rudimentary theoretical proposition)

- learn the stories, the relationship of the stories to place and their placement, ownership and care for the past as well as the future. These rules and knowledge of conduct are taught by specialized persons (explicit theories)

- understand that the stories are points of entry into a total picture of the community, in the way it sees the world and responds to it. As member of that community everything

I do has a consequence to that total picture (symbolic totalities).

It is interesting to note the juxtaposition of this process to Giraure's experiences of going to school, gradually legitimizing Western modes of education, and beginning to disown his own place and people.

If our language is to protect and maintain our heritage as we engage with what the twenty-first century has to offer, then our next generation needs to be engineered to be able to recognize and assimilate elements from our history – our own ancestral knowledge and our colonial history – as well as the ways of other cultures that pervade our shores.

# Conclusion

Small Island Developing States communities have become far more complex than the conventionally truncated voices of tribalism and cultural entities. The mythologized comforts of village life as serene locations away from the hubs of faster-paced town life, are imaginings of an 'elsewhere' that serve as rhetoric to gloss over the real images of rising ghettos, fringe dwellers, and the politically and economically marginalized. There are less and less tribally distinctive societies and even looming threats of cultural and tribal disintegration. These are the contemporary SIDS communities that have returned to pick up the pieces that colonialism left. State machineries advocate for greater conformity for purposes largely directed at economic wealth generation and nation building. It is a cosmopolitan admixture of highways and bi-ways, where people have left their homelands, hamlets and villages in search of work, education, marriage and in some cases as itinerant visitors and workers. But in the leaving we have brought with us an assorted luggage of languages, customs, stories myths – in part real and in part imagined – and memories of childhood. While we negotiate and forage in the modern cosmopolitan locations we find time to claim and cling to some authenticity. This is the location of creolized food, dances, songs, and costumes – the pot pourri of modern SIDS communities.

Reasserting our stories and our histories in the Small Island Developing States is a journey very much about revitalizing and even reinventing ourselves. It must be supported. If there are missteps let us talk about them and deal with them as best we can, because if we do not move forward the price we will pay is not worth contemplating.

As Freire (1970: 76) wrote:

> *Human existence cannot be silent, nor can it be*
> *nourished by false words, but only by true words,*
> *with which men transform the world.*
> *To exist, humanly, is to name the world,*
> *to change it.*

# References

Berger, P. and Luckmann, T. 1967. *The Social Construction of Reality: a treatise in the sociology of knowledge*. Harmondsworth: Penguin.

Burnett, G. 1999. Knowledge, schooling and post-school opportunities: an exploration of I-Kiribati parents' perceptions of secondary education. *Directions*, 21(2): 100–12, December. USP, Suva: Institute of Education.

Eyford, H. nd. *Relevant Curriculum: the cultural dimension*.

Freire, P. 1970. *Pedagogy of the Oppressed*. New York: Seabury Press.

Gibbs, P. 2003. Moral muddle? The missions and Enga traditional values. *Catalyst* 33(1): 61–91.

Giraure, N. 1976. *The need for a cultural education programme: personal reflections*. Paper presented at the Eighth Waigani Seminar, 'Education in Melanesia', UPNG, Waigani.

Hall, S. 1990. Cultural identity and diaspora. J. Rutherford (ed.) *Identity*. London: Lawrence and Wishart.

Mel, M.A. 1995. MBU: A culturally meaningful framework for education in Papua New Guinea. *Prospects: A quarterly review of comparative education*, 25(4): 683–94, December. Paris: UNESCO.

Narakobi, B. 1991. Education and development. B. Avalos and L. Neuendorf (eds) *Teaching in Papua New Guinea: a perspective for the nineties*. Port Moresby: UPNG Press, pp. 19–28.

Rumsey, A. 2001. Tom yaya kange: a metrical narrative genre from the New Guinea highlands. *Journal of Linguistic Anthropology* 11(2): 193–239, American Anthropological Association.

Thaman, K. 1995. Concepts of learning, knowledge and wisdom in Tonga, and their relevance to modern education. *Prospects: a quarterly review of comparative education* 25(4): 723–33, December. Paris: UNESCO.

UNESCO. 1996. *Learning: the treasure within*. Report to UNESCO of the International Commission on Education for the Twenty-first Century. Paris: UNESCO.

# Endnotes

1   The initial idea for this article was presented as the Keynote Address for the 2005 National Curriculum Reform Conference, July 12–15, 2005, in Port Moresby.

2   Translation of a *Tom Yaya* Performance by Kopia Noma, March 1997. (The full version of the *Tom Yaya* performance and prose summary of the tale can be found in the article by Alan Rumsey as indicated in the reference.) The CD recording of the performance was recorded and provided by Alan Rumsey.

# Of Poteau mitans, bedis, vèvè and things

## Caribbean Island identities and cultural production

Patricia Mohammed, *University of the West Indies, St. Augustine, Trinidad and Tobago*

The title of this chapter is an allusion to a line from Lewis Caroll's *The Hunting of the Snark*: 'The time has come the walrus said, to speak of many things, of ships and sails and sealing wax, of cabbages and kings'. The rhythm and metaphoric possibilities of the line resonated as I attempted to craft a central theme to pull together the disparate yet connected parts that represent island cultural identities. Perhaps most dominant was its quiet insistence that 'the time had come to speak of many things' in island cultural production. Island cultures have dealt with conflicting intersections of peoples, events, traditions, religions, belief systems, cuisine, sexualities and gender practices either through violations or mutual exchanges. Many of these processes have not yet found a voice in the global discourse of what constitutes the making of culture, or where they have, the narrative voice is a nostalgic, imaginary, prurient or at best, ill informed one.

Cultural production today cannot be understood in terms of simplicity and binaries, the stereotypes with which it was once viewed. Culture cannot be captured and harnessed unless it is approached with subtlety. New media and communication technologies make visuality a prime tool to be employed in the project of unwrapping culture. The roving television producer and documentary filmmaker have displaced the anthropologist and travel writer from the business of communication (although not completely). To speak of island cultural 'things', once elided, is not just to demonstrate the confidence of voice, but also to present the original interpretation of symbols, images and textual variations and the meanings they have taken on within a culture, not only as inherited products but as reinvented phenomena.

Having said this, it should not be assumed that only island peoples or insiders are privy to such meanings. Hidden meanings are and have always been accessible to those prepared to read beyond the clichés or received scripts. Perhaps it requires a particular state of mind to enter a culture and reserve value judgements or rules of aesthetics, particularly those created by others outside of the culture. A good example would be the work undertaken by Alan Lomax (1915–2002), the American folklorist and musicologist. Lomax was one of the twentieth century's great field collectors of folk music, recording thousands of songs in the United States, Great Britain, Ireland, the West Indies, Italy and Spain. He saw folk music and dance as art forms that evolved through centuries of experimentation and adaptation, each as irreplaceable as a biological species.[1]

# Intersections

This chapter introduces certain aspects of cultural production in the Caribbean, which have been either demonized into silence or separated into a space of *alterity* and have thus remained outside the notion of cultural production. The *Poteau mitan* is the central axis around which the Haitian voodoo rite is performed: a pole around which the *vèvè* or ground drawings representing Haitian divinities are drawn by priests or *houngans*. It resembles the *bedi* or altar in Hinduism; both are highly decorated, and used to invite and propitiate the gods.

These two fairly similar ritual spaces have been appropriated in different ways by cultural production. The Haitian *vèvè* has been mass-marketed both within and without Haiti, sold along with brightly decorated sequined flags and other voodoo apparatus, in particular to the United States, where links between New Orleans and southern US black culture have created a cult for consumption. The practice of Hinduism with its variations within the Caribbean has had a different reception. Perceived in the West as part of a continuity of Indian ritual and tradition, it has retained the aura of religiosity and deference which it admittedly deserves. For this reason it has not fully entered the arena of

what is viewed as cultural production, other than perhaps through the work of Derek Walcott. In his 1992 Nobel Lecture 'The Antilles: Fragments of Epic Memory', Walcott recognized and hinted at the depths of culture that remain outside the Trinidadian and certainly Caribbean mind, citing the creativity of *Ramleela*, the annual restaging of a passage from the *Ramayana* in a Trinidadian village.

In this chapter I also draw attention to the processes of artistic creation that take place around the *bedi* or prayer ground. As with the drawings that constitute the Haitian *vèvè*, these require a set of skills and formal values, which have been passed down and reinvented using new materials in new environments.

Islands can be transformed by waves of inward and outward migration. As such they are persistent sites for expanding diaspora and reinventions of culture, just as mainland territories also possess such characteristics. There is an assumption that smallness makes for provinciality, an insularity that denies other influences. However, this has not been the history of the Caribbean islands. For the last 500 years, the Caribbean has been a major crossroad for the old world and the new, for the east and the west, and the north and the south. Crossroads are meeting points, intersections of people, events, leisure traditions, religious belief systems, cuisine, sexualities, gender practices, violations and cultural exchanges. Such meeting points can barely be understood in their infinite complexity and as such they are configured around major narratives, such as colonization and post-colonization, plurality and assimilation, heterogeneity or hybridity, or the more contemporary concepts of displacement and adjustment. The condition of displacement, interpreted in different ways, has become a new dwelling place for the large majority of the world's people today. As such, it is no longer as fruitful a concept as it once was for exploration of cultural phenomena that are rich in their symbolisms and ripe with possibilities for visioning futures.

Throughout their evolution, Caribbean territories have consistently confronted displacement and adjustment, ever since the old world had to adjust to the newness of the new. This raises the question of what the new world has to say to the old, after 500 years, having previously listened with the awe demanded of the 'uncivilized'. More importantly, what might islands say to each other, drawing on the shared experience of islandness? One point common to all strategies of identity building is that culture is located in the memory banks of tradition. But culture is evanescent, highly charged in emotional memory and hotly debated in various forms of human exchange. Every culture can claim some kind of pain. The displacement of tradition provides ample ground for negotiating cultural space and dominance.

Cultural evolution and creativity depends, for better or worse, on the political conflicts within societies – those that play out either at national levels or at the individual or community level. These conflicts essentially revolve around people's claims to voice and visibility within any

geographic setting or historical period. Even among the same ethnic groups, conflicts exist between different classes or geographical separations, so no society or period can be said to be entirely exempt. Questions such as whose and which value systems should be imposed on different aspects of culture, and whether to observe tradition (as remembered) in its original form, or accept its reinterpretation by younger generations, all form part of the dynamic space within which culture evolves. In the midst of cultural diversity, these debates proceed with similarly highly charged political overtones: whose culture dominates, which ethnic group provides the dominant symbols and signifiers of heritage, and what forms might thus constitute a nation's culture?

Such questions have bedevilled Caribbean cultural evolution in differing ways in different territories. In Jamaica, the challenge has lain between a Eurocentric aesthetic and that claimed by a reinvented Caribbean vision of Africa as embodied in Rastafarian thought. Trinidad is the site of contestation between four continents: Europe, Africa and Asia and the Americas. Although Caribbean societies share similarities in terms of their history of colonial settlement and expansion from the fifteenth century onwards, there are variations between islands based on different language group colonizers, whether British, French, Hispanic or Dutch.

If culture is a resource that can be extracted not only from the mineral and material wealth of a nation, but also from its human populations, are the internecine battles waged around culture valuable or debilitating to its potential for transformation? On the one hand, we can argue that these struggles are a necessary part of its reinvention. On the other, post-colonial theory[2] offers a space for sovereignty and multi-culturalism, the illusion of co-existing differences. But post-colonial thought implicitly keeps the centre critical to the margin. The alliances of small island states perhaps offer possibilities for de-centering the centre, at least ideologically, for the marketplace still determines the rules of exchange. But to what extent? Symbolic resources may represent new ground for island identities at the present crossroads. Furthermore, it seems that the present historical juncture of political consciousness, economic globalization and technologies for sharing and popularizing new discourses offer possibilities that were not previously available to us.

The cultures of islands have been commodified in relation to centres or metropoles, and in the case of Caribbean territories, have had to create new identities in the absence of indigenous populations. Monotheism and scriptocentricity were privileged over polytheism, visuality and performance. In other words, cultures that had arrived at a concept of one god and which had written and published their histories and their theological doctrines were viewed as having attained higher aesthetic ground. By a theory of aesthetics, I refer to principles that form tastes, define what constitutes beautiful and desirable, and establish concepts of what is good versus bad or evil. In totality, the effect of the colonial

encounter on Caribbean territories was to keep those at the margin defined by the centre.

Let me use three religious images based upon this encounter to illustrate this effect. Each of these express the essential metaphors for aesthetics created during colonization. The Columbian encounter from 1492 established the first crossroads:[3] Christianity and the natives, with the cross as a signifier of redemption through suffering – a universal symbol that predated Christianity itself but here appropriated to mean separation of heaven and hell, earthly and heavenly, human beings and god. It is present alongside other binaries: the clothedness of the conqueror versus the nakedness of the early aboriginal populations with the assumption of ownership on sight. The European gaze of the encounter established the rules of engagement. The sword was as mighty as the pen.

From the sixteenth century onwards, the forced transportation of primarily West African peoples to the Caribbean grafted another layer onto a similar metaphor. African spiritualism proved disruptive to the monotheistic and binary system of thought embodied in the European *telos* of history, in which development and progress were dependent on science and mastery over nature. Thus, African peoples had to be converted, as the second image, 'The Ordinance of Baptism' (Figure 1), demonstrates in its depiction of Christianity: the purity of whiteness, baptism into a new faith by cleansing and expunging of the old, and the regimentation of the process overseen by mounted horsemen on the lower right of the painting. Few images are to be found of African-based religions and rituals from the sixteenth to nineteenth centuries in the archives of the region. Beliefs were observed in secrecy and disguise, and where recorded textually were deemed by the transcribers of culture to be without spiritual or aesthetic merit.

This is evident again in the image, 'Coolie Sacrificing' (Figure 2), and its interpretation by travel writer Charles Kingsley, writing on Trinidad. Let Kingsley speak for himself.

> *I leave it to those who know Hindu mythology*
> *better than I do, to interpret the meaning – or rather*
> *the past meaning, for I suspect it means very little*
> *now – of all this trumpery and nonsense, on which*
> *the poor folk seem to spend much money. [ … ]*
> *and all I could do on looking at these heathen idol*
> *chapels, in the midst of a Christian and civilized*
> *land, was to ponder, in sadness and astonishment,*
> *of a puzzle as yet to me inexplicably, [ … ]*
> *how humans got into their heads the vagary of*
> *worshipping images.*
>
> Charles Kingsley,
> *At Last a Christmas in the West Indies*, p. 300.

Kingsley, imbued with Church of England iconoclasm, is amnesiac about a parallel form of idol worship that is essential to an analysis of Western art and religion, and one might add, now even more vital to an understanding of contemporary capitalism. But that aside, it is the denial of the aesthetics of religions, a primary fount of cultural creativity, which is interesting at this point, especially as it relates to the bank of tradition and memory from which new interpretations of culture emerge.

**Figure 1**: *The Ordinance of Baptism*, circa eighteenth century (courtesy University of the West Indies library, Jamaica, Probyn Prints, West Indiana Collection).

**Figure 2**: Illustration 'Coolie Sacrificing' in Charles Kingsley, *At Last a Christmas in the West Indies*, London, Macmillan and Co, 1896 (courtesy, University of the West Indies Library, West Indiana Division, Trinidad).

## Crossroads in creativity

Crossroads present opportunities for new intersections and meeting points without the baggage of the past. Over the last 500 years, the Caribbean has been defined by iconic images and symbols, for example, the images found in the national flags and crests of various nations following independence. Embodied in many, although not all, of these flags are classic heraldic symbols, drawn from Western antiquity, which suggests that colonialism left a legacy of mind control over nation building. This intact symbolic language is used as a yardstick for measuring historical time, latched firmly to the Columbian encounter and European enlightenment discourses. However, many other cultural influences shaped the Caribbean over this period. How then may we allow for development of parallel ideas – for the introduction of other civilizations and their ongoing contribution to the constantly evolving identity of the region?

By inverting the demonized and paganized scripts of African and Asian religions, as defined above, it is possible to see a similar process at work in selective practices of Haitian voodoo and Hinduism, particularly in the artistry of the *vévé* and the *bedi* – the altars created by priests and *serviturs* to invite and propitiate the gods. Their capacity to provide a new aesthetic feel is still abundantly meaningful to people's ways of life in the islands, to the methods of how creativity itself evolves within and among individuals in a territory, and antidotal to the globalizing of culture itself. Nations are not built on Nike and Coca Cola symbols, even if people everywhere now run and quench their thirst with these products.

## The Haitian *vévé*

*Vévé* are symbolic drawings that represent the attribute of a *loa* or divinity. These drawings are traced on the ground with maize flour, ash, coffee grounds or brick dust by the *houngan* or voodoo priest and reveal the presence of the god in recognizable if symbolic form (see Figure 3). Voodoo has no formal theology or creed, no strictly defined organizational structure, and no credentialed clergy or ecclesiastical hierarchy. In this absence there are variations in beliefs and rituals from region to region and from temple to temple within Haiti.[4] The passing on of this visual memory from one priest or *houngan* to another permitted the evolution of a set of recognizable shared designs for each of the divinities, although these are numerous and can still vary from one region to the next. As importantly, the transmission of this skill by drawing – what I

Rex Dixon

**Figure 3**: Simulated drawing of the Haitian divinities represented in the *vévé* around a central axis (author, 2007).

refer to as a fingered memory – was essentially an informal school for what popularly became known as Haitian intuitive art.

Haiti has been so demonized and diminished in its evolution since the nineteenth century onwards, that despite the discourse of its revolutionary success in the new world, the country retains a space in the popular imagination as a poor, backward nation, unfit to rule itself, with a people steeped in magic and superstition. Caribbean islanders do not travel to Haiti for leisure, but may go for business or professional reasons. I am constantly surprised by comments from a range of Caribbean islanders

who still maintain this unhealthy perception. It is convenient for the West to sustain this view of a Haiti steeped in backwardness. It signals that a precocious nation will continue to pay a price.

The visual experience of Haiti is a stimulating one. Artistic production literally exudes from the cracks in the concrete and woodwork, including the sculptured heroes lining the Champs Mars, the

**Figure 6**: Highly sequined *vévé* flag to Legba made by *houngan* Joseph Silva.

**Figure 4**: Tap tap. Highly decorated buses such as these are to be found in Haiti (2001).

**Figure 7**: Paintings such as these are to be found by the thousands for sale in Haiti and other places in which a market for 'Haitian paintings' has been found. The artist is unknown.

**Figure 5**: Mural on sidewalk streets in Cap Haitien (2001).

yards and inches of repetitive Haitian canvases on sidewalks and open fields or the more kitsch examples filling many of the galleries of Petionville, the highly decorated tap taps or private buses in Port au Prince, the iron work studios of Croix des Bouquets, the painted murals which decorate rough and smooth public surfaces, and the sequined flags for sale in the home of *houngans* (Figures 4 to 7).

## The Hindu *bedi* and an East Indian aesthetic

The Asian[5] impact on the continuing evolution of the Caribbean remains unmapped. This is not to say that it has not been systematically examined through the disciplines of history, anthropology or increasingly in the fiction of the region. Travellers and visiting researchers, in particular during the late nineteenth century, differentiated the southern Caribbean territories of Trinidad, Guyana and Suriname as exhibiting features of the 'East'. This was largely owing to the presence and lifestyle of greater numbers of Asians, introduced into these societies as indentured migrants, and to a lesser extent as free labourers, throughout the nineteenth century. Architecturally distinctive mosques and temples throughout the landscape indicate the presence of Muslim[6] and Hindu populations, while other architectural or religious accoutrements signify in particular the practices of Hinduism. The influence of Asia on the landscape is plain to see. Between ten to fifteen temples and mosques are visible from the

highway in Trinidad as you drive north to south. Hindu households wave you by with *jhandis* or flags, planted to signify *puja* or prayers offered by the family. These constitute by far one of the most dominant iconic symbols of ethnic difference. The significance of these decorations as well as the use of organic and inorganic materials, shown in Figure 12, is known by adherents and practitioners. The constituent elements of the *bedi* include earth and pan leaves. Nine leaves are used representing nine seats for the deities involved; nine is also significant as it represents the nine orifices of the body and nine months for pregnancy. The pundit offers betel nut to represent food offerings to propitiate the gods. The colours of vermilion, saffron and white also have sacred meanings in this context (Figures 8 to 11).

Patricia Mohammed

**Figure 8**: *Jhandi* or prayer flags in a Hindu garden in Trinidad. At its base is a *shiva lingam*, an altar on which obeisance is made to the God Shiva and to other deities.

**Figure 9**: Named 'The Temple in the Sea' and consecrated in the 1990s as a national site, this temple on the coast of central Trinidad, Couva was built by an indentured immigrant in the early twentieth century.

**Figure 10**: *Deyas* or small clay pots made into delicate small lamps filled with coconut oil and cotton wicks are lit by the thousands in villages and homes throughout the island for the Hindu celebration of Divali. The light represents enlightenment or the celebration of light over dark, or good over evil.

**Figure 11**: The Hindu *bedi* or altar, like the Haitian *Poteau mitan*, is also decorated with drawings and organic material that represents the presence of gods and goddesses.

Why has the Indian aesthetic sensibility remained largely outside the realm of what is considered as Caribbean identity today? One reason relates to the demographic and geographic concentration of Indian populations in the southern Caribbean. The second factor is its distinct difference in aesthetic representation and sound: its music, language of prayer and the appurtenances of religion are vastly opposed in terms of colour, composition, detail, form, perspective and imagination from what is perceived as either 'Western' or 'African'. The third has to do with the negative values attached to what constitutes Indian-ness, that is, a group still viewed as relative newcomers and outsiders – a perception unfortunately internalized by many East Indians themselves who feel unrepresented in terms of visual culture.

Aspects of an Indian aesthetic may have persisted in ways that are not always apparent. Two examples practised over many years are the tradition of *kohbar* – drawings in coloured rice flour and multi-coloured powders around the area of a house or temple consecrated as a prayer ground, or on walls decorated for ceremonial wedding feasts – and the traditional decoration of the body itself. Renderings of traditional *kohbar* drawings were difficult to locate, although many people confirmed the existence of this tradition from memory. One such memory gave birth to a series of drawings by architect Glean Chase, who confirmed that his stylized and symmetrical paintings were influenced by the traditional *kohbar* he had seen in south Trinidad in the 1950s (Figure 12).

Patricia Mohammed

**Figure 12**: Painting by Glean Chase, influenced by Indian *kohbar* designs (used with the permission of the artist and CCA7).

This particular intricacy of detail and style of drawing has its roots in artistic expressions which travelled from India, becoming attenuated and simplified, perhaps, in the Caribbean. Courtly painters with highly developed skills were not found among the caste and workers recruited from India to become manual labourers in the plantations. Certain skills were passed on at first, as in the case of the *vévé*. For example, the practices of body art contained in the *goodhana* and *mehindi* require skill, precision and knowledge of materials. The *goodhana* or tattoo, was applied by a travelling male and female couple who carried out this art as a profession. The man would apply the tattoo while the woman sang, to ease the pain, and perhaps to chaperone the process. It was generally carried out on women who were about to be married, and the particular designs selected symbolized what was expected of the woman in marriage.

The *mehindi* is a less painful but more temporary form of traditional body art, in which henna

is used to decorate the hands and feet of those about to be married, or for other decorative purposes. The word *mehindi* is derived from the tree of the same name, whose leaves are powdered and mixed with water to form a semi-permanent dye. The dye is applied almost like a pen drawing on the body (see Figure 13). The process is both pleasurable to the eye and the skin – a pandering to the senses. The design is left to dry for at least two hours during which time it is absorbed by the skin, and when the blackened raised surface is peeled off, the colour changes to a reddish brown which lasts for a few days. The colour which it takes on is dependent on the body temperature of the individual, which suggests again that it blends with the shade of one's skin texture.

Rex Dixon

**Figure 13**: Nearly completed *mehindi* on hands of author by Jigna Patel.

In the crossroads of culture that now inhabit the region, a public Asian culture saturated with religious symbolism and lingering notions of paganism has been impressed on the awareness of Caribbean society, overshadowing the personal understanding of any who might have direct experience of this culture. In his 1992 Nobel Lecture, Derek Walcott conveyed the outsider status that this culture has been accorded in Caribbean society.

> *I had often thought of but never seen* Ramleela, *and had never seen this theatre, an open field, with village children as warriors, princes, and gods. I had no idea what the epic story was, who its hero was, what enemies he fought, yet I had recently adapted the* Odyssey *for a theatre in England, presuming that the audience knew the trials of Odysseus, hero of another Asia Minor epic, while nobody in Trinidad knew any more than I did about Rama, Kali, Shiva, Vishnu, apart from the Indians, a phrase I use pervertedly because that is the kind of remark you can still hear in Trinidad: 'apart from the Indians'.* [7]

In the context of the West, Haitian voodoo rituals that produce artistic forms such as the *vèvè* and altars, have been 'discovered' and claimed as recognizable artistic practice. A similar 'discovery' needs to take place in relation to Asian culture, where ritual artistic practice or performance is also recognized as the production of another aesthetic different but comparable to conventional Western forms. For example, just as Walcott recognizes the public performance of the *Ramleela* as epic theatre, so must we understand the decorated shrines and *bedis* or altars created for prayers as another artistic expression of Caribbean culture and society.

The Asian migrants are relative newcomers in cultural temporality. Music and aurality are far more insistent and dominant, and have already begin to enter the shared cultural milieu defined as Trinidadian with the emergence of Chutney Soca music and other variants. The visual remains submerged, perhaps necessarily so, in the private space of the home as against the world. While the Asian signature on the landscape is evident in the unfolding translation of visual culture in the region, it is interesting to see how this may infuse itself into another way of seeing and configuring what is defined as the Caribbean and thus of shaping culture itself.

## Conclusion: crossroads of cognition and recognition

Against the backdrop of post-9/11 events, which have ushered in a discourse of terror against multiculturalism, the complexities of modern political thought twinned with the sensationalism and immediacy of media technologies have created a certain scepticism with regard to the value of aesthetics. I am nonetheless convinced that the evolution of history, from antiquity to the present, represents the wisdom we have inherited from previous generations incarnated as the forms of beauty produced within cultures – whether this beauty emerges in song and musical instrumentation, dance movements, lyrical passages in writing, ideologies of national pride or, and in particular, in art with religion playing a primary role in the evolution of art itself. Five hundred years after its 'discovery', the Caribbean began to diminish gently in importance from the twentieth century onwards. However, it continues to offer itself up as a microcosm for artistic and sociological evolutions important to future worlds of multicultural and constantly migrating populations. It represents a place of meetings between East and West; meetings that took place after the old world and the new had collided and merged. Such collisions also occurred in the East itself, where long trails were blazed to find spices, goods and peoples. In this new modern incarnation of globalization, where the *realpolitik* of modernity is once again negotiated at many different levels, the artistic production and performance of people as they go about making sense of their daily lives, represents a valuable model for persistent interrogation, cognition and recognition.

# Endnotes

*1*   Details of Alan Lomax's life and work can be found, among other websites, on www.folkstreams.net/filmmaker.

*2*   See, for example, Edward Said, *Orientalism*, New York: Vintage Books, 1979; Homi K. Bhabha *The Location of Culture*, New York: Routledge, 1994; Gayatri Spivak, *The Post-Colonial critic: interviews, strategies, dialogues*, London: Routledge, 1990 and Stuart Hall, *Representation: cultural representations and signifying practices*. London, Sage/Open University, 1997.

*3*   The image being referred to is the painting of *Columbus landing on the Island of Guanahane (12 October 1492)* by John Vanderlyn. For copyright reasons the painting could not be reproduced here but can be viewed on the internet: www.wga.hu/frames-e.html?/html/v/vanderly/columbus.html

*4*   Voodoo practice in Haiti divides into two major traditions, or rites, which are also referred to as separate nations or tribes of spiritual beings: *Rada*, the more 'mainstream' version emphasizes the positive healing aspects of spirituality, and is closest to its African origins; the *Petro* rite, associated with more aggressive and often negative powers, is traced to runaway slaves in the mountains who initiated Haiti's revolution.

*5*   I use Asian in this context to refer to the populations drawn from the Asian sub-continent comprising Chinese, Indians and Indonesians who were brought to the region as indentured or other labourers and selected to remain in the Caribbean.

*6*   It must be recalled that the earliest influx of Muslim Asians were from India.

*7*   Derek Walcott, 'The Antilles: Fragments of Epic Memory', Nobel Lecture, 7 December 1992 http://nobelprize.org/nobel_prizes/literature/laureates/1992/walcott-lecture.html

*In Kiribati you know your parents love you if they help you to dance*

Teweiariki Teaero, 2006

Banaban children in a community displaced from Kiribati to Fiji in 1945, performing on 15 December 2007, Rabi Island

# CHOREOGRAPHING OCEANIA

Katerina Martina Teaiwa, *Australian National University, Canberra, Australia*

This chapter[1] focuses on dance and culture in relation to the Small Island Developing States (SIDS) concept in Oceania. Here, I situate the contemporary Pacific within an inter-regional and historical context, explore the significance of dance and performance to Pacific communities, reflect on the development of the Oceania Centre for Arts and Culture, and identify strategies for integrating dance into policies for supporting cultural industries in Oceania.[2]

The Pacific Islands represent about 20 per cent of the world's distinct languages amongst a population of over 12 million people (including New Zealand and PNG, excluding Australia) on 1 per cent of the world's land. As a region, the Pacific likely has the highest ratio of cultural and linguistic diversity per capita, and while the islands are small, the ocean covers one third of the globe. The term *'Océanique'* or 'Oceania' was once fairly inclusive but today primarily refers to Australia and the groups conceptually organized by French explorer Dumont d'Urville in 1832 as Polynesia ('many' islands) in the east and south, Micronesia ('small' islands) in the central and northwest, and Melanesia ('black' islands) in the western Pacific. Oceania, thus refers to all the Pacific Islands, but also includes Pacific diasporas within the region and communities extending from Australia and New Zealand to Canada, the US, the UK, the

Middle East and Europe. While d'Urville's terms have problematic origins they have been adopted by people in both the islands and diaspora as meaningful ways of describing wider and fluid cultural identities.

Dance is a fundamental vehicle of cultural expression throughout Oceania. As is the case for indigenous groups worldwide, Pacific peoples have carried and passed on their knowledge for millennia through oral, visual and embodied traditions. Performance arts embody spiritual, political, social, economic and aesthetic values and practices. As Adrienne Kaeppler writes,

> *... dance is not only important and worthy of study for its own sake, but is equally valuable for what it can tell us about social change and cultural history.*
>
> 1993: 96

While art is very low on the sustainable development agenda for most island countries, much can be learned about Pacific peoples, their histories and contemporary experiences by paying attention to indigenous dances and body movements, and how these change over time.

Dance, music, architecture and other arts have always functioned as primary vehicles for creating, recording, sharing and transforming knowledge.

These aesthetic forms reflect codes for conduct and responsibility, provide the glue for social cohesion, and mediate relations between the human, spiritual and ancestral realms. While the advent of colonialism, Christianity and written text – from as early as the sixteenth century in Guam, to as late as the twentieth century in the highlands of Papua New Guinea – altered the style and content of dance and music in some islands, these continued to function as the most visible markers of local and national identities. Today, in both the islands and the diaspora, cultural dances also build self-esteem and instil pride in performers and audiences, particularly in the younger generations, who exist at the nexus of competing local, national and global forces (Teaiwa, 2005).

Artistic practices in Oceania usually exist within state environments where culture and the arts reside on the lowest of priority scales due to their very 'lived' nature. Officially, culture is often present in rhetoric and adds colour to formal ceremonies; however, it does not always concretely or strategically manifest itself in national or regional economic and political policies and plans. But there are exceptions: the highly valued tourism sector in which island culture is perceived largely as service or entertainment for visitors; the Kingdom of Tonga, where 'culture' in the form of the monarchy dominates political and economic life; and where the *Fa'a Samoa* (the Samoan way), which shapes Samoan society both at home and abroad. For everyday people across the islands, dance, music, ceremonies and local languages are some of the primary ways in which they continue to express their highly valued heritage.

The Teaero epigraph to this chapter reflects the special relationship between dance and human society in the islands of Kiribati in the central Pacific. With the exception of the raised atoll of Banaba, these low-lying atolls are at the centre of current debates concerning the dangers of sea level rise in the Pacific. As environmental and other material resources are limited in Kiribati, artistic energies are often channelled into maritime skills, music and the art of the moving body (see Whincup, 2002). Kiribati dance is extremely difficult to master and there are well-understood grades of skill and virtuosity within a healthy and diverse environment of informal, traditional, contemporary and competitive dance. In Kiribati, all manner of movement is passionately performed, from the traditional sitting dance *te bino* to Bollywood dance (Teaiwa, 2007a).

Limited scholarship exists on music and dance in the Pacific, with the majority of work produced by ethnomusicologists focusing on traditional indigenous genres.[3] Study of the capacity of Pacific peoples to incorporate, re-fashion and re-produce introduced choreographies and sounds, is a limited but slowly growing field of research. There is also little appreciation of the fact that what we understand as 'traditional' is the result of exchanges and movements over hundreds of years of peoples, ideas, materials, sounds and choreographies across Oceania – a distance that covers almost one third of the planet's surface.[4] Even less is known or understood of the artistic forms of production of the Pacific communities in the diaspora, although museums such as Te Papa Tongarewa and popular journals such as *Spasifik* Magazine do strong work in this area for the New Zealand context.

The evolution of culture across the vast and diverse Pacific has been a core stream of the discipline of anthropology. Early scholarship was heavily shaped by a perception of Pacific peoples as rooted and static, with each island providing a perfect laboratory for analysis. Pacific dance practices often archive historical and cultural information through the moving, and sometimes travelling body, and the process can be difficult to document if scholars themselves do not possess the literary, musical or choreographic background to grasp the significance of these practices. The few with the appropriate skills include notable scholars Adrienne Kaeppler and Amy Ku'uleialoha Stillman. With a dearth of scholarship on dance, however, the translation, of Pacific performative arts into a language of relevance to the studies of nation or region building, or to contemporary political and economic participation in the global marketplace, is still very slow to develop.

Despite these limits, local and regional dance festivals have become major cultural and economic opportunities for showcasing performing arts (Teaiwa, 2005). These festivals are growing fast both within the islands and the overseas diaspora (see, for example, the Culture Moves Programme, 2005). Festivals in the diaspora are often marked by the term 'Pasifika' – the Polynesian pronunciation of 'Pacific'. This was first used formally in

New Zealand to distinguish the minority Pacific Islander populations, who comprised migrants primarily from Samoa, Tonga, the Cook Islands, Tokelau, Niue, Fiji, Kiribati and Tuvalu. Today, the annual Pasifika Festival is a showcase of Pacific music, dance, food and art, and constitutes one of the biggest cultural gatherings in the region. The great economic benefits of such a gathering are not lost on the host city of Auckland.

Every four years, the nations of the Pacific gather for two weeks in a host country for the regional Festival of Pacific Arts. In addition to music and dance performance, there are displays and discussions on the visual and literary arts, navigation and canoe building, indigenous sports, museum curatorship and development, artist networks and alliance building, as well as the latest developments in fashion and textiles. Pacific countries take great pride in their participation in this forum, but its impact in the home islands in terms of government policy remains low. At the 2004 festival, the difference between New Zealand's investment in the arts – a priority under the Helen Clark government – stood in stark contrast to that of other nations: a contingent of over a hundred Maori and Pacific artists from New Zealand were flown in on a specially commissioned jet while many artists from other countries arrived by a very slow boat.

## Islands of globalization

If the Pacific is often seen by scholars as indigenous and static, the Caribbean is frequently perceived in almost the opposite terms, that is, diasporic, dynamic and profoundly shaped by a history of slavery. These opposing perceptions emphasize the differences, rather than the similarities between the island regions, and potentially exclude the indigenous element in the Caribbean and the diaspora in the Pacific.

A Caribbean scholar noted that the ways in which people move their bodies in any given time belies the diversity and layering of relationships between people, travelling ideas, various landscapes, and the sea (see Benitez-Rojo, 1996: 10). For example, if you observe closely the dance movements of a group of young men in a popular nightclub on any given Saturday in Suva, Honiara, Port Moresby, Koror or Vila, you might consider the massive impact of reggae in the Pacific.

In 2003, scholars at the University of Hawai'i at Manoa and the East-West Centre in Honolulu began a collaborative research and instructional project entitled Islands of Globalization (IOG), in an attempt to foster direct intellectual and artistic exchanges between the Caribbean and Pacific. The project, funded by the Ford Foundation, sought to understand the origins, nature and consequences of globalization from the perspective of small island societies, and in the context of changing notions of 'islandness'. IOG initiated pedagogical, policy and popular projects targeted at diverse audiences, including a postgraduate course, a public film series, a pedagogy workshop, a literary festival, several exchanges of scholars between the Caribbean and Pacific involving visits to Fiji, Hawai'i, Jamaica and

the Dominican Republic, Pacific participation in the Caribbean Studies Association Conference, and a special issue of the *Journal of Social and Economic Studies* (Lewis et al, 2007).[5]

The project exemplified the possibilities of learning between island regions. It enabled an understanding of how each space was carved out, initially by Spanish, British, French and American colonialism and imperialism, and then by globalization, through the production of material wealth and industry and the expansion of trade routes and commodities. It also contributed to an appreciation of how contemporary island societies constructed diverse and creative strategies for surviving and indeed thriving – particularly evident in the literary, visual and performance arts. Nevertheless, the stark differences in terms of the histories of slavery and creolization in the Caribbean, and the indigenous approach to Pacific identity remained a point of constant reflection and debate.

While the grouping together of island regions as Small Island Developing States (SIDS) has immense benefits, cross-regional strategies are sometimes best realized when the diversities within and between oceanic cultures are also well understood. To my understanding, the grouping of SIDS is based on geographic and economic factors. These are articulated in terms of similarities, specifically the smallness, dependency and limited nature of island economies and land bases. In short, the grouping is based on a terrestrially centred perspective, rather then an ocean-based one in which small islands are understood in terms of what they lack.

Pacific scholar Professor Epeli Hau'ofa has long-critiqued this disabling view, describing Oceania[6] as a 'sea of islands' rather then 'islands in a far sea' (1993), emphasizing a heritage that is unique and cultural, and for many, 'of' the ocean (2000).

Given UNESCO's push for the integration of cultural strengths into development policy, it is necessary to articulate specifics in terms of how island peoples and cultures are similar and different within the diverse regions, in order to produce effective policies on culture that will be useful across such varied areas. Diversity cannot merely be pronounced as valued; scholars, practitioners and policy-makers alike must have a grasp of what diversity looks like on the ground (or in the sea). Furthermore, there seems to be an urgent need to re-imagine the ways in which we just accept our economies and islands as small and dependent.

The next section focuses on the Oceania Centre for Arts and Culture in Fiji, the development of which brings together the significance of dance and performing arts in the islands with the context of constraint in which SIDS are assumed to operate.

# The Oceania Centre for Arts and Culture

*Belittlement in whatever guise, if internalised for long, and transmitted across generations, could lead to moral paralysis and hence to apathy.*

Hau'ofa, 1993: 6

The Oceania Centre for Arts and Culture was created in 1997 on a small hill near the west entrance of the University of the South Pacific's Laucala campus in Suva. Like the University of the West Indies on which it was modelled, the University of the South Pacific (USP) is a multi-national university owned by the countries of the Cook Islands, Fiji, Kiribati, the Marshall Islands, Nauru, Niue, Samoa, the Solomon Islands, Tokelau, Tonga, Tuvalu and Vanuatu. The main campus in Suva educates the largest number of Pacific Islander students in the region and satellite centres in member countries provide extension services for an even larger number of students. The university is also funded by overseas aid, primarily from Australia, New Zealand and Japan. One of its goals has always been to train students in areas important for filling the civil service ranks of its member states and it offers programmes in education, business, accounting, management, communications, the natural sciences, development, sociology, English, literature, law, history and politics. Disciplines like anthropology, cultural studies or the arts have traditionally not been considered as pragmatic or as urgent as the technical training required to run developing states. Unlike UWI, which has significant strengths in Caribbean Studies, USP's institute of Pacific Studies was not converted into a teaching programme until 2006.

The Oceania Centre's founder, Epeli Hau'ofa, was a trained anthropologist who never worked in an anthropology department. In the South Pacific, as many islander scholars joke, culture was not something one studied in a university. In the early

1980s, Hauʻofa wrote *Tales of the Tikongs* (1983), a critique of the questionable direction in which he thought independent island nations were heading. This took the form of a satire in which the institutions and forces of native government, the church, tradition, colonialism, aid and development were skilfully mocked. One of Hauʻfoa's central characters, aptly named Ole Pasifikiwei (Old Pacific Way), symbolized the vast array of creative survival strategies that islanders had developed over centuries, now hastily discarded for money and shortcuts to Western-style progress.

The University of the South Pacific had never had or desired an anthropology department, so Hauʻofa eventually found himself teaching a 'practical' social science that took for granted the smallness, isolation and dependence of Pacific islands. In *Our Sea of Islands* he wrote of his original stance on this negative characterization:

> *Initially I agreed wholeheartedly with this perspective, and I participated actively in its propagation. It seemed to be based on irrefutable evidence, on the reality of our existence [ … ]*
> *The hoped-for era of autonomy following political independence did not materialize [ … ]*

Hauʻofa, 1993: 4

Hauʻofa became Head of the School of Social and Economic Development at USP and his initial acceptance of this fatalistic approach to small island nations transformed after he began to pay attention to the reactions of his students. He wrote, 'Their faces crumbled visibly, they asked

for solutions, I could offer none' (ibid: 5). He began to ask himself,

> *What kind of teaching is it to stand in front of young people from your own region, people, you claim as you own, who have come to university with high hopes for the future, and you tell them that our countries are hopeless? Is this not what neocolonialism is about? To make people believe that they have no choice but to depend?*

ibid

Throughout his essay, Hauʻofa reimagines the Pacific not as small isolated islands, but as a sea of islands in a vast and ever-expanding Oceania. He cites indigenous cosmologies which include worlds far above, beyond and below the surface of land and sea as evidence of a vast and ever expanding indigenous worldview, boldly displayed in Pacific oral, visual and performing arts. The worldview was ever expanding, that is, until islanders arrived in universities to be told that their islands and cultures were small and dependent.

Hauʻofa declared that 'Smallness is a state of mind' (ibid: 7) and his essay moved beyond the individuality of islands to a perspective in which things were seen in terms of the totality of their relationships (ibid). He imagined Pacific cultures at their most positive and impressive, where contemporary travels and migration marked an expansion that had long been the mode of islander survival. If the world of Oceania today did not always include the heavens and the underworld, it did now include cities in Australia, New Zealand, Canada and the US, where large numbers of Polynesians, in particular, now reside. The piece became such a work of discussion that USP published a series of nineteen responses in 1993 that examined *Our Sea of Islands* from every conceivable angle. What was needed next, however, was a concrete manifestation of Hauʻofa's ideas.

As early as 1985, Epeli Hauʻofa had petitioned the Vice Chancellor of USP for a building that 'creative people could call home' (pers. comm., 2003). This was viewed as a request for some kind of 'Bohemia' and denied but Hauʻofa kept the concept in mind. When other ideas surfaced for a formal programme in Pacific Arts, Hauʻofa resisted, knowing that such a space would not be autonomous if linked to academics. While a successful writer, he felt that writing was a personal and solitary activity tied too much to the self or ego. Moreover, writing, at least on paper, was not a feature of Oceanic culture and he wanted to support forms of expression that were 'our own' (ibid). His aim was to create a space for collaboration and for the production of creative arts amongst an Oceanic community of artists.

The Oceania Centre was launched in February 1997 with just the kind of freedom Hauʻofa had envisaged. No overall plan or specific programme of action existed until 2001. He was given a small building and a modest budget for the director, an assistant and a part-time cleaner. There was no formal teaching programme and the Centre was thus autonomous but, initially, marginal to the university (Oceania Centre, 2001: 1).

What began as four small rooms and a veranda today comprises three offices, a metal workshop, an open-air painting and carving studio, a recording studio, an exhibition space, and an outdoor performance area. Permanent staff include a director, an administrative assistant, a cleaner, a sculptor, a choreographer and a composer. In addition, the community of artists now includes a large number of painters, wood carvers, musicians, sound mixers, part-time musicians, and a growing number of male and female dancers. In any given year, the Centre runs public art and dance workshops, puts on several exhibitions, dance and theatre productions in Fiji and overseas, and hosts visiting artists and choreographers from across the region.

Dancers at the Oceania Dance Theatre are exposed to choreography from a wide variety of Pacific genres which they then blend under the direction of Samoan director Allan Alo. They strive to produce something that transcends national boundaries while acknowledging specific choreographic cultures. The goals have always been to create something 'of Oceania'.

When the dance programme began in 1998 it relied on the abilities of existing performers in Suva, many of whom like myself had danced in the tourism industry and had some training in ballet and modern dance. I eventually became a founding member of the Oceania Dance Theatre collaborating with Alo on two productions: *The Boiling Ocean I* and *The Boiling Ocean II* (2000a and b). In the early 2000s, we struggled to attract versatile dancers due to a lack of formal training. Today, however, young people with dance potential are trained at the Centre and the programme has become highly disciplined. Dance productions are supported by all resident artists including visual artists and musicians, all of whom contribute to the final production.

However, certain dance movements involving the broad extension of the limbs can prove difficult for young people in the Pacific to perform. This is a result less of physical than of cultural constraints. The problem is one of progressing beyond traditional forms of choreography that in most islands prescribe restricted movement for women, and a more vigorous but still limited repertoire for men. The region below the waist is particularly taboo, and outside Trobriand, Tahitian, Hawaiian and Cook Island dance, certain pelvic movements are only employed in humour or anger. Today, the Oceania Centre has carved out a space for a growing genre of 'contemporary Pacific dance', employing in particular traditionally taboo movements for women. In the last two years in Fiji there has also been a rise in the popularity of 'krumping', an energetic dance that developed in Los Angeles, and is often likened to an ambiguous notion of 'tribal' dance. Krumping appears to map well on to the bodies of young indigenous Fijian male dancers with a convergence in the grammar of krump and traditional Fijian choreography.

Contemporary Pacific dance as practised at the Oceania Centre and increasingly across the islands and diaspora, involves an expansion of the vocabulary of the body, based on either a 'Western' choreographic or indigenous Pacific base with elements from across the region woven in. The dancers leap, roll across the floor and pirouette, yet their movements retain a Pacific flavour. Contemporary dance often attempts to transcend pan-ethnic boundaries, working across the regions of Melanesia, Micronesia and Polynesia. It is theoretically and potentially inclusive and patiently recuperative of undervalued traditions, while remaining experimental.

Several other dance companies have grown out of the Oceania Dance Theatre and are now working on their own versions of contemporary dance. Meanwhile, the Dance Theatre's productions regularly express indigenous values concerning the past, place, human relations and the environment, while commenting on rising social challenges and concerns such as domestic violence, the spread of HIV, and the growing loss of cultural identity.

The Oceania Centre's mission to practise an inclusive regionalism may still be an impossible and romantic task, but Hau'ofa has no illusions about who should participate in such a venture. He knows that such a vision does not necessarily appeal to everyone in the entire region. 'That's bloody impossible', he said to me in an interview in 2003: 'We're starting small, with a community of like-minded thinkers and artists.' Moreover, for him, art, at least today, seems to have a wider-reaching and transformative potential lacking in politics and other more direct forms of activism. There will always be a larger audience for music and dance then for reading and writing in the Pacific – a point perhaps underlined by the way in which audiovisual media (television, video, film and the internet) have been wholeheartedly embraced by our mainly oral, embodied and visual cultures. This situation, however, does not deny the critical and intellectual work of many Pacific community leaders, scholars and artists alike.

In Hauʻofa's thinking the Centre embodies a resistance to multiple pressures – ethnic, national and international – and even at the regional level, resists the term 'Pacific', which connotes passivity. 'Pacific Island states', 'South Pacific' and 'Pacific Community' are also terms Hauʻofa says are used by 'the powers that be'. He said to me:

> *The ocean is not confining though we do happen to be in the middle of it somewhere. At the moment it applies to us but it can be extended, the idea [of a sea of islands] is to include other places [ … ] but I hesitate to say too much about it as I've been accused of fantasizing. [ … ] When the 'powers that be' use the term Pacific they usually refer to the Pacific Rim and islanders are excluded. Oceania, the word itself, means the sea.*

(ibid)

Hauʻofa finds encouragement in the idea of expanding Oceania, its reach encompassing the whole world – a world 70 per cent covered by ocean, and whose leaders have hitherto focused mainly on land-based activities or simply used the ocean as resource. He says, 'The notion of Oceania cannot be contained. Metaphorically, for creative purposes, it's tremendous. For the mind it is a liberating concept, the idea of limitlessness [ … ] we can at least dream into eternity' (pers. comm.). He maintains that this in actuality is a practical exercise: creativity is what keeps us alive.

> *… You have lived long and time has passed*
> *The buzzard added*
> *Don't call the wind that will carry you away*
> *The gull counselled*
> *Don't talk to the rain that will drown you*
> *And the turtledove concluded*
> *Do not confine to the hut those who inhabit the world.*

Dewe Gorodey (1993: xvi)

## Policy recommendations

There are many more exciting programmes and activities in the performing arts occurring across the Pacific, but the infrastructure for really capitalizing and developing this potential remains loose and tenuous. The formation of the Pacific Arts Alliance based in Suva is a move by artists themselves to organize a regional network and information hub.[7] Elsewhere, I have described the potential of cultural industries in the Pacific in terms of the economic valuing of culture (Teaiwa, 2007b). Here I recommend five strategies to enable a more integrated and regional support base for performing arts development and education in Oceania.

The first is that the Pacific Arts Council under the Pacific Community be expanded into a separate regional arts foundation that would provide monetary, technical, material and human resources for the development and support of music, dance, theatre and multimedia industries. This would be added to the current line-up of organizations comprising the Council of Regional Organization in the Pacific (CROP). At present, these include the Pacific Community, the Forum Fisheries Agency (FFA), the South Pacific Regional Environment Program (SPREP), the South Pacific Applied Geoscience Commission (SOPAC), the Pacific Islands Development Program (PIDP), the South Pacific Tourism Organization (SPTO), the University of the South Pacific (USP), the Fiji School of Medicine, the South Pacific Board for Educational Assessment (SPBEA) and the Forum Secretariat.

The second is that the oral, visual and performative arts in Oceania be integrated into primary, secondary and tertiary curricula, drawing on research on the impact of the arts on educational achievement in and beyond our region. Studies supported by UNESCO have already made such recommendations but action is yet to be realized in most island countries.

Third, that anthropology, archaeology, cultural studies, dance studies, film and visual studies, theatre, music, and other oral, visual and performance-related studies also be supported as programmes of tertiary study for Pacific Islanders by the institutions, government bodies and aid agencies that currently provide scholarships in the mainly functionalist and state-building areas of economics, public policy, development studies, business management and the like. AusAID

scholarships for islanders for study in Australia, for example, can be expanded to cover these fields.

Fourth, that governments prioritize and explicitly fund the arts in their annual budgets, not just in terms of supporting troupes to participate in regional festivals, but in the building and staffing of institutions dedicated to the cultural industries. The rationale for this should be based on a sense of nation-building embedded in traditional and contemporary cultures. The Vanuatu Cultural Centre is a shining example of this.

Finally, it is imperative that SIDS devise specific strategies for exchanging knowledge between their islands, especially between the Pacific, Caribbean and Indian ocean groups. By this I mean that SIDS be approached not just as islands with similar economic and geographic limitations, but rather that SIDS learn from each other, support each other, and trade directly with each other in terms of creative strategies, materials and ideas. Within curricula this could be imagined as island children learning the histories of each others' countries rather than history primarily in terms of national or Western civilization. This approach to regional learning can take place at primary, secondary and tertiary levels. Exchanges that took place between island regions at the 2007 African, Caribbean and Pacific (ACP) festival in the Dominican Republic, and work undertaken through the Islands of Globalization Project, represent initial attempts in this field.

Implementing all of this necessitates a long-term approach, but inter-regional dialogue is a productive place to start. At the Seychelles meeting at which this chapter was first presented in 2007, I proposed a methodological question to the forum: If you were to choreograph a dance representing the Small Island Developing States, what would it look like?

# Acknowledgements

I would like to thank Tim Curtis and his staff for inviting me to participate in the UNESCO-SIDS meeting in the Seychelles in 2007. This chapter is based on my presentation at that meeting and the feedback from colleagues there was greatly appreciated. I would also like to acknowledge the members of the Islands of Globalization team at the University of Hawai'i at Manoa and East-West Centre in Honolulu, as well as Allan Alo at the Oceania Centre at the University of the South Pacific. Many more developments in dance and the culture sector have occurred since I wrote this piece and the Human Development division of the Secretariat of the Pacific Community based in Noumea, New Caledonia, is leading these initiatives with the support of the European Commission, ACP Cultures, UNESCO and the World Intellectual Property Organisation among others. Finally, I would like to acknowledge my dear friend and colleague Professor Epeli Hau'ofa who passed away in January 2009. The sections on the Oceania Centre and his ideas are based on a long interview I had with him in 2003. Epeli has inspired countless scholars, students and artists and is truly missed by much of Oceania.

# References

Alo, A. and Teaiwa, K. 2000a. Direction and performance with the Oceania Centre for Arts and Culture, Fiji, 'Boiling Ocean I' for *Bursting Boundaries*, Pacific History Association conference, Australian National University, Canberra, June.

Alo, A. and Teaiwa, K. 2000b. Direction and performance with the Oceania Centre for Arts and Culture, Fiji, 'Boiling Ocean II' for *Honouring the Past, Looking to the Future*, Pacific Studies conference, University of Hawai'i at Manoa, Honolulu, October.

Benitez-Rojo, A. 1996. *The Repeating Island: the Caribbean and the postmodern perspective*, (2nd edn). Durham: Duke University Press.

Culture Moves Programme. 2005. Culture Moves: dance in Oceania from hiva to hip hop, Wellington. Convened by Katerina Teaiwa, April Henderson and Sean Mallon. University of Hawaii at Manoa, Victoria University of Wellington, Museum of New Zealand Te Papa Tongarewa, Creative New Zealand, Pacific Cooperation Foundation, UNESCO New Zealand.

Gorodey, D. 1993. Do not confine to the hut. (Trans. E. Waddell.) E. Waddell, V. Naidu, E. Hau'ofa (eds) *A New Oceania: Rediscovering Our Sea of Islands*. Suva: School of Social and Economic Development, University of the South Pacific.

Hau'ofa, E. 1993. Our sea of islands. *The Contemporary Pacific*, Spring: 148–60.

Hau'ofa, E. 2000. The ocean in us. D. Hanlon and G.M. White (eds) *Voyaging through the Contemporary Pacific*. Oxford: Rowman and Littlefield.

Kaeppler, A.L. 1993. *Poetry in Motion: studies of Tongan dance*. Tonga: Vava'u Press.

Lewis, P., Dunn, H., Smith, M. and Prasad, B. (eds) 2007. The Caribbean and Pacific in a New World Order. *Social and Economic Studies* (special issue) 56(1/2), March/June.

Oceania Centre for Arts and Culture. 2001. *Corporate Plan*. Suva: University of the South Pacific.

Teaero, T. 2006. *Dance in Kiribati*. Guest lecture for DANCE 255 'Dance in World Cultures', Judy Van Zile, Honolulu: University of Hawai'i at Manoa, April.

Teaiwa, K. 2005. *Dance in Oceania: a historical context for 'Dances of Life'* (and six additional essays) at website 'Dances of Life', Honolulu: Pacific Islanders in Communication at http://piccom.org/home/dancesoflife/index.html

Teaiwa, K. 2007a. South Asia down under: popular kinship in Oceania. *Cultural Dynamics* 19(2): 193–232.

Teaiwa, K. 2007b. On sinking, swimming, floating, flying and dancing: the potential of cultural industries in the Pacific Islands. *Pacific Economic Bulletin* 22(2): 140–51.

Teaiwa, K. 2008. Salt water feet: the flow of dance in Oceania. A. Francis and S. Shaw (eds) *Deep Blue: reflections on nature, religion and water*. London: Equinox Publishing.

Wendt, A. 1976. The Angry Young Men of Oceania. *UNESCO Courier*, Feb: 4–12.

Whincup, T. 2002 *Akekeia! Traditional Dance in Kiribati*. Wellington: Susan Barrie.

# Endnotes

1    This chapter is a modification and expansion of a presentation given at the Seychelles meeting of a UNESCO group. The mandate was to examine the relationship between cultural diversity, cultural industries and Small Island Developing States in the Caribbean, Pacific and Indian oceans.

2    The article is based on several previously published works including Teaiwa (2005), Teaiwa (2007a and b) and Teaiwa (2008).

3    The Study Group on the Musics and Dances of Oceania recently added 'dances' to its title and is part of the International Council for Traditional Music (ICTM). Professor Philip Hayward and a cohort of Music Studies scholars have also done significant work on contemporary music in Melanesia.

4    See Matthew Spriggs' chapter for more on these histories.

5    The IOG team in Honolulu consisted of Gerry Finin, Terence Wesley-Smith, Katerina Teaiwa, Scott Kroeker, Esther Figueroa and Monique Wedderburn. Scholarly and pedagogical exchanges, including visits between the islands, were initiated with Patsy Lewis, Hopeton Dunn, Matthew Smith, Hamid Ghany, Patricia Mohammed, Jennifer Holder-Dolly, Susan Mains, Diana Thorburn and Keith Nurse of the University of the West Indies; Biman Prasad, Epeli Hau'ofa, Asenati Liki and Ropate Qalo at the University of the South Pacific; Steven Winduo of the University of Papua New Guinea; April Henderson and Alice Te Punga Somerville at Victoria University of Wellington; and Elizabeth DeLoughrey at Cornell University. Other scholars at the EWC and UHM included Tarcisius Kabutaulaka, Tim Britos, Richard Rath and Erin Weston.

6   Pacific Novelist Albert Wendt, revived the term for islanders much earlier in the 1970s when he wrote the 'Angry Young Men of Oceania' for the *UNESCO Courier.*

7   See the Pacific Arts Alliance website at: www.pacificartsalliance.com/

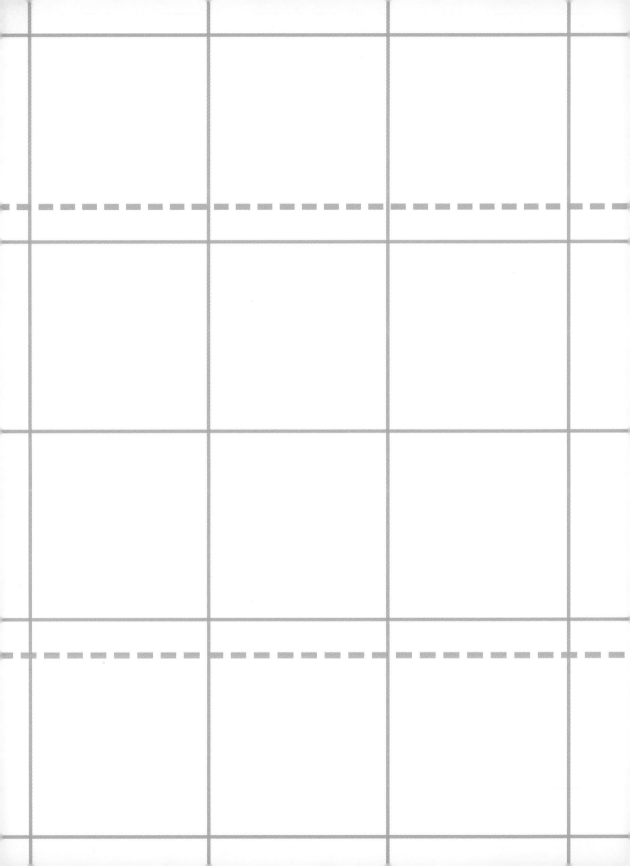

# PART 3

## ECONOMIES OF CULTURE AND CULTURES OF ECONOMY

# THE IMPACT OF THE DIASPORA ON THE SOCIETY OF THE GRAND COMORO

Aboubakari Boina, *National Centre for Documentation and Scientific Research (CNDRS) of the Comoros*

Grand Comoro or Ngazidja is one of four islands that form the Archipelago of the Comoros. When addressing the subject of the Diaspora, the island's case is of evident interest given the large number of migrants, the deep-rootedness of secular traditions linked with the *Grand Mariage* (Big Wedding) ritual, the forms of solidarity found among both families and collectives, and the dynamic forms of community development that tend to fill the gap left by the state.

The diverse origins of the Comorian population[1] give an indication of the predisposition of the island to contact with the outside world. One should add to this the strategic position of the Comoros in the Mozambique Channel, the black slave trade and French colonization. The last general census of population and housing in 2003 estimated the Comorian population[2] at 575,660 inhabitants and the Comorian Diaspora at approximately 300,000 people, of whom the overwhelming majority originate from Grand Comoro.

In order to better understand the impact of the Diaspora in Grand Comorian society, it is necessary to examine three aspects which are both distinct and complimentary: the history of migrations from the Comoros, the contributions of the Diaspora to Grand Comoro, and the lessons learned given the weak exploitation and optimization of support provided by Comorians living abroad.

## History of Comorian migrations

The particulars of the history of Comorian migrations and the exact number of Comorians abroad are not well known. However, some sources indicate that the migrations of Comorians to Madagascar and eastern Africa occurred from the fifteenth and sixteenth centuries onwards. Manicacci (1968: 33) notes a settlement of Comorians at Tamatave and its environs from the seventeenth century. But it is at the end of the nineteenth century, beginning with armed conflicts among belligerent sultans and the despoilment of lands by the French colonizers, that the Comorian migrations assume importance in Madagascar and Zanzibar.

Proximity and social, economic and political links allowed Comorians to establish themselves easily on Madagascar and Zanzibar. They were able to reconstitute the practices and tributary structures of their country while stressing the permanent concern of educating their offspring. The result seems satisfying: a large number of children born to Comorian migrants were able to attain academic and professional qualifications and have even occupied important positions of responsibility in their host countries.

Briefly, three principal periods in the history of Comorian migration can be distinguished: the pre-colonial period, the colonial period and the present period of independence.

# The pre-colonial migrations

The Comorian migrations to Madagascar and eastern Africa took place prior to French colonization of the Comoros, which began in 1841. Various factors explain these migrations; in terms of priority: geographic proximity, maritime activities, slavery in the Indian Ocean, internecine wars between belligerent sultans, matrimonial relations and connections with Islam.

The Comoros lie approximately 300 km by sea between the north end of Madagascar and eastern Africa. The islands therefore constituted a privileged port of call for commerce and slavery:

> ... *slavery was maintained by the Comorian aristocracy, the sultans and the Arab-Muslim merchants. The Arab boutres (sailing ships) from the Red Sea regularly provisioned themselves from these merchants. And in the fifteenth century, these last increased their activities thanks to the arrival of the Shirazi; the slave trade thus became an important source of wealth in the Islands.*

Translated from the French (Sidi, 2002: 89).

During this period of the city state, the Grand Comoro was 'rent' into regions by wars between belligerent sultans. Fear of these men pushed both opponents and the defeated to immigrate to eastern Africa (notably to Zanzibar and Tanganyika) and Madagascar.

Lastly, matrimonial relationships between the inhabitants of this part of the Indian Ocean and those of Eastern Africa and the strengthening and/or the spread of Islam enabled numerous Comorians to emigrate to countries in the region. Many were searching for development – material (enrichment), social and/or intellectual. Such facts concerning migrants change noticeably during the colonial period.

# Migration during the colonial period

Slavery in the Comoros continued in other guises under French colonization, in particular in the form of a labour force supplied to the colonial economies of Madagascar and Reunion. Numerous Comorians had to leave to 'work' in these French colonies. It should be noted, in passing, that Madagascar was conquered by the French in 1895 and would remain dependent until 1960.

To escape the colonial order, some Comorians chose the route of exile. In this regard, Mohamed (2007) indicates that 'the colonial administration arrived with taxes, the police, forced labour, and the draft for military service, seen as a death sentence for the most useful men in the families. It was necessary, for protection against these forces, to find a place of refuge'. (Translated from the French.)

Comorian migrations to Madagascar increased with the colonization of the Great Island by France. The Comoros were administratively attached to Madagascar from 1912 to 1946, at which time France ceded administrative and financial autonomy to the Archipelago of the Comoros. Because the two lands were integrated administratively, the period of regulated immigration was followed in the 1950s by a period of free circulation. The Comorians thus went in large numbers to Madagascar to work, learn a trade, or study given the limited possibilities of employment, training and study in the Comoros. At the beginning of the 1960s, aside from Moroni, not a single secondary school could be found in the Archipelago of the Comoros.

The trend for migration towards Reunion and France began to establish itself in the mid-1960s and early 1970s following the independence of Madagascar in 1960 and its 'socialist revolution' during the 1970s. This phenomenon accelerated with the unilateral declaration of independence by the Comoros in 1975 and has continued throughout the last thirty years. This period has been characterized by political instability, economic depression, separatism, loss of confidence in the capacity of rulers to instigate home-grown development, and weak local capacity to absorb high school graduates and diversify tertiary education.

# Migration following independence

In the wake of unilateral independence, some Comorians with French nationality preferred to migrate to Reunion or France for professional, economic and political reasons. This tendency further increased with the hardening of the new political regime of President Ali Soilihi, a self-styled 'revolutionary'. In a 1975 interview with the newspaper, *Liberation*, he affirmed:

> *We are in a country where there is a type of systematic immunity, defined by a code which is hierarchical, traditional, functioning according to age, and according to customary acquisitions and customary expenditures, which means that the whole political and social design depends on this type of hierarchy. As long as this hierarchy and this ladder of values exist in the country, we cannot speak of progress. We think that the first thing, is to continue in the coming months to always accelerate this overthrow, in the manner of placing swathes of young people in the forefront, to render the country capable of accepting and driving progress. We estimate that this work is essential; we intend to consecrate ourselves to this work almost exclusively.*

Translated from the French.

The Soilihist state had initiated reform programmes across the country. Its hope was to destroy the pillars of the previous regime and to construct a new society in a modern state. Reforms took place in many sectors – social, economic and administrative – with the country's youth considered as the spearhead of these programmes.

The reform programme was neither accepted nor understood by many among the Comorian population, and in order to escape the dictates of the new regime, entire groups of Comorian workers, managers and some students left for countries in the Indian Ocean region, eastern Africa and Arabia, as well as France.

The phenomenon of emigration was accentuated by the restoration of President Ahmed Abdallah, backed by mercenaries, from 1978 to 1989. The new regime founded 'a soft dictatorship' which did not permit democratic liberties. All opposition parties elected to relocate outside the country, notably to France.

In the final analysis, the principal reasons for Comorian emigration during this post-colonial period were 'ignorance' and flight from misery. The principal goals were to find wealth outside the country or to benefit from technical, professional or general training – the first Comorian school of higher learning only saw light in 1980 and offered a limited choice of training and studies. Moreover, young people who desired professional and technical training at the secondary level or to further their knowledge of Arabic, Islamic theology, or other disciplines related to Islam had no choice but to leave for other countries.

If the majority of immigrant workers travelled to France and Reunion, it must be emphasized that the new preferred destinations lie in the Middle East. However, students today travel to all five continents in search of college or university training.

Some choose residence in the host country, obtaining work permits after their training or through marriage. As a result, Comorian communities now exist in destinations such as South Africa or more distant countries such as the United States of America.

To summarize, Comorians continue to migrate abroad for the following reasons, in order of importance:

- to work in the host country to accumulate wealth (workers)

- to benefit from training or tertiary studies (recent graduates)

- to study professional and technical training at the secondary level or increase knowledge of Arabic, Islamic theology or other disciplines related to Islam (recent graduates), and

- to escape the established order and build political capital with migrants in order to strengthen the ability to return to power (leaders and political militants).

If a tiny minority of Comorian migrants prefer to finish their days abroad,[3] the overwhelming majority of the Comorian Diaspora are haunted by an obsession with the return home. The idea is omnipresent in the collective consciousness of Comorians living abroad and undoubtedly influences ways of life, work, consumption, saving, the maintaining of relations with the family in the home country and plans for the future.

At the individual level, items of prioritized expenditure for each migrant are generally as follows:

- financing the *Grand Mariage*

- pilgrimage to Mecca for one or more members of the family

- construction of a sturdy house, and

- multi-faceted assistance to members of the family remaining in the country to address daily needs: small expenditures, health, education, and religious and customary services.

The totality of individual ideas forms the nebula of a collective, diasporic philosophy which enables Comorians to provide an inestimable amount of assistance to compatriots that remain in the country.

# The contributions of the Diaspora in Grand Comoro

Outside their country, Comorian migrants organize themselves into many forms of association: people of the same neighbourhood, village, town, region or island come together to develop solidarity amongst themselves and with their fellows who remain on the island. Those who are most committed at the 'union' or 'political' level manage to move beyond the village environment to promote the political demands of the moment, as much within the host country as in the direction of the home country.

It must be emphasized that the Diaspora influences all sectors – social, economic and cultural. Two representative examples that illustrate our thesis are 'Twarab' and the 'Sabena'.

# Cultural influences: the examples of Twarab and the Sabena

The Comoros share Bantu culture with black Africa and Swahili civilization with eastern Africa. Twarab is the most important genre of Comorian music. The inhabitants of Zanzibar and the island of Pemba refer to it by the same name, although those who live in eastern Africa call it *musiki wa mwanbao* (music of the coast).

It was Abdallah Cheikh Mohamed who introduced Twarab to the Comoros on his return from Zanzibar, between 1912 and 1913. Played on a *fidrila* (violin), Twarab quickly established itself as the leading genre of Comorian music for extraordinary occasions: marriages and village or national celebrations. The success of Twarab can be explained by its incorporation into the *Grand Mariage*.

From ten at night until dawn, one or more orchestras play Twarab music, transporting guests with Arab melodies played on violins and lutes and black African dances, performed to drums. Twarab constitutes the pinnacle of the day's events and the audience rewards the orchestra by placing wads of bills in a small case reserved for this purpose. It should be noted that during Twarab performances, the placing of guests follows a hierarchical order. Those who merit a seat of choice always include the *bwana harusi* (the groom, his family and friends), the political authorities, and other prominent people.

In summary, Twarab music has five distinct dimensions. It acts as:

- an integral component of the *Grand Mariage*

- a community music

- a music which perpetuates songs of praise and perhaps religious songs

- a music that through its popular lyrics has become the principle vehicle for ideas, and perhaps even a site where opinions on contemporary events are forged, and

- a music which permits a simple understanding of Comorians: their aspirations, creations, capacity for openness, limits and common ideas, as well as the changes underway and those that may yet come.

Twarab endures despite the introduction of contemporary musical instruments and its detractors, who encourage people to conceive of it as a serious departure from Muslim practices and beliefs.

The Sabena are Comorians who were repatriated from the Malagasy town of Majunga by the Belgian airline, Sabena, at the beginning of 1977,

following the tragic events which occurred unexpectedly on 20 December 1976. Bourges and Vauthier, as cited by Mohamed (2007), describe the events as follows:

> *Following an insignificant event, hundreds of Comorians were pursued, killed, and mutilated at Majunga. Majunga was home to 16,000 Comorians, which was about one third of the population.*

> *The Comorians control commerce; thus they were thrown out as a result of social hatred, xenophobic nationalism, and religious fanaticism.*

> *15,000 to 20,000 Comorians were evacuated from Majunga.*

Translated from the French (2007: 67).

The white paper of the Comorian Minister of Foreign Affairs, Mouzawar Abdallah, described the massacre as follows:

> *Over there, in Majunga, our blood flowed a lot, a lot, a lot. The mosques were stained, profaned, and destroyed; the homes were sacked, looted, and set on fire. Our dead, they were piled in trucks with the destination of common graves dug for the occasion with the help of mechanical diggers. Not one of the victims benefited from the Muslim rites reserved for burials. Our wounded were scattered in various hospitals, while the survivors were crowded together in military camps and endured inclement weather.*

Translated from the French.

Since the return of those expatriates Comorian society has not ceased to change. Their contribution takes several forms, notably, the resourcefulness of the expatriates, the work undertaken by women, and the development of small trades.

The word *mkarakara* (resourcefulness) takes its importance from a Malagasy expression: *mkarakara mbo mahazu* (who searches, finds). This is the spirit which enlivens the survivors of Majunga. Indeed, the poorest of Comorian society have joined the survivors of Majunga by engaging in informal petty trade, small jobs and learning new trades to support themselves.

Before the arrival of the Sabena, Comorian women often remained cloistered in their houses or, at best, worked in agriculture. It was the women of Sabena who liberalized customs and mores by working in many small trades, notably commerce and domestic work. The Sabena also infused a new energy into crafts, mechanics, shoe-making, welding, embroidery, knitting, hairdressing and many other trades.

Despite the courage and will of the Majunga survivors, the spirit of *mkarakara* encountered major obstacles, in particular, the poor organization of administrative services and the absence of credit for financing. No state administrator took responsibility to council, organize or promote their activities.

# Political and ideological influences

The first political party to demand Comorian independence was created in 1963 in Dar es Salaam under the name, *Mouvement de Libération Nationale des Comores* (Movement for the National Liberation of the Comoros, MOLINACO). As well as campaigning for independence it also registered the problem of Comorian decolonization, before it received attention from international authorities.

Five years later, two leftist independence parties were born at the national level: the *Parti Socialiste Comorien* (Socialist Comorian Party, PASOCO) and the *Parti pour l'Evolution des Comores* (Party for the Evolution of the Comoros, PEC), both of which shared similarities with MOLINACO. The campaign for independence attracted large swathes of the population and advanced the accession of the Comoros to international sovereignty, which took place in 1975.

The 'Green' and 'White' governing parties followed suit with the incorporation of Comorian nationals from Zanzibar. On 15 June 1973, a 'common declaration on the access of the Comoros to independence' (translated from the French), better known as the Accords du 15 juin 1973, was made public in Paris. The declaration foresaw, among other things, that 'access to independence will proceed through consultation with the people of the Archipelago on a date which will be determined by common accord, in at most five years following the signing of this declaration'. (Translated from the French.)

In France, starting in 1968, the *Association des Stagiaires et Etudiants des Comores* (Association of Comorian Trainees and Students, ASEC) changed its status from that of a corporate association to a 'revolutionary union', thus providing its contribution to national mobilization. Since then, ASEC has been considered a mirror of all the contradictions within Comorian society. These Comorian students and trainees are considered 'the party of Comorian intellectuals', and the most 'aware', 'resolute' and 'loyal' to the development of proletariat interests and political groups defending workers in the Comoros.

In 1978, ASEC gave birth to the *Mouvement Communiste Marxiste Léniniste Comorien* (Comorian Marxist Leninist Communist Movement), composed of a secret inner group and a public group in France. The Communist Movement, in turn, created the *Front Démocratique* (Democratic Front) in 1982 – the principal opposition party until the end of the regime of Ahmed Abdallah Abderemane and the departure of his mercenaries in 1989. The Democratic Front adopted the following political objectives of the Communist Movement:

- to win national independence

- to restore national territorial unity

- to put an end to dictatorship by feudal lords, mercenaries and foreign meddlers

- to restore democratic liberties, and

- to lift the country out of misery and away from archaic structures.

In contrast to the case of Comorian students in France, the first wave of students to obtain scholarships to study in the Arab and Muslim countries increased in number during the mid-1970s. This group included young people who originated in the big cities and had fled the 'Marxist' regime of Ali Soilihi. These young people had parents or Koran teachers that were close to representatives of non-governmental Arab organizations, anxious to spread the Muslim faith. The majority of these students had little choice other than to follow a theological education. Saudi Arabia, the leading host country, offered a hundred scholarships, but only a few supported studies specializing in fields such as construction, electrical engineering and economics, and those were reserved for students born to aristocratic families.

Upon returning home, theology students have often found themselves limited to running small businesses or teaching classes, both unprofitable. Excluded from networks in the upper administration and state or parastatal institutions, their living conditions are frequently precarious. In many cases, young Ulemas (Muslim doctors of law) turn to promoting extreme, fundamental interpretations of Koranic verses, as representing the most 'perfect' political, economic and social 'programme'.

Such former students, educated in Arab and Muslim countries, have created two political parties which make claims on behalf of Islam: the *Front National pour la Justice* (the National Front for Justice, FNJ) and the *Parti pour le Salut National* (the Party for National Salvation, PSN).

The FNJ truly merits the adjective of a fundamentalist party. It is directed by young Ulemas educated in the great theological universities of Saudi Arabia, Egypt, Iran and Sudan. Those in charge of the party proclaim loud and strong that only the pure application of the Koran can save the Comoros from all evils. They militate for the acquisition of power without alliance and without compromise. But their 'political programme' can be summarized in five slogans: 'God is our objective', 'The prophet is our guide', 'The Koran is our law', 'Consultation is our system' and 'Justice is our slogan'.

The objectives of this party are therefore to:

- preserve and institutionalize the acquisition of Islamic morality

- develop a great Ministry of Islamic and Religious Affairs

- impose a break of twenty minutes during the hours of work at the time of the call to prayer

- impose 'Muslim clothing' on girls and women

- separate girls from boys in primary and secondary schools

- reinforce, develop and broaden religious education

- promote the teaching of Arabic in the administration and in education

- categorically prohibit the sale and consumption of alcohol

- prohibit the importation of cultural products from Europe, especially those that might 'harm the image of Islam', and

- apply the law of the Koran throughout the territory.

The fundamentalist tendency goes as far as to scorn the African cultural values of the Comoros. Everything that is linked to the African tradition is considered a persistent belief in animist or pagan faiths. In other words, it promotes a rejection of the symbiosis that has existed between tradition and religion, a rejection which promotes an Islam that is pure and hard.

# Remittances in support of families, the *Grand Mariage* and local communities

Far from politics and ideologies, the silent majority of migrants never ceases to send large sums of money to families and local communities.

An international survey of fifty-one countries places the Comoros in the top ranks with regard to the importance of cash transfers by the Diaspora, when measured in relation to the GDP (16 per cent, fourth position) or as related to exports (67 per cent, second position).

According to the 2005 Annual Report by the Central Bank of the Comoros:

> *Transfers by Comorian migrants constitute the primary source of external financing, representing approximately 15% of the GDP. These movements of funds, originating primarily from the Comorian community living in France, are estimated at about 20 billion FC in 2005. The informal circuit is the most commonly used means of transfer, with travellers coming to Comoros serving as intermediaries.*

Translated from the French.

According to the Comorian Central Bank, the preference for sending transfers through an informal route is a result of the following factors:

- the origin of the funds, linked to the traditional practice of tontines

- the relatively high cost of cash transfers through formal channels

- limited banking facilities, exacerbated by a tight banking system, and very weak geographic coverage by financial establishments

- lack of understanding of mechanisms and channels for transfers, and

- the high number of transfers of small amounts, varying from 50 to 200 euros.

In a small, poor country in which civil servants acknowledge many months of arrears in payment of salaries, these transfers represent principle sources of revenue. They serve quite often to meet the most basic needs: food, medical care, providing education for children, or paying an electricity or telephone bill.

Transfers of large amounts essentially result from contributions by people of the same village and are sent to village associations to finance social activities such as:

- the construction or renovation of community schools

- the construction or renovation of dispensaries

- the construction or renovation of mosques

- the construction of cultural centres or libraries

- the provision of equipment for these premises, and

- the furnishing of public venues or sport sites.

Sizeable transfers may also be destined for the construction of individual homes or simply for the financing of a *Grand Mariage*. Thus, these resources essentially finance household expenses and collective investments. Savings and productive investments are only concerned in small measure.

But most often, infrastructure and equipment projects are conceived without real technical expertise and with little concern for management, planning or sustainability. The absence of dialogue and planning between the state and grassroots communities is glaring. A village, for example, might decide on its own to construct a dispensary or classrooms, without the construction being foreseen in the national health plan or the national education plan.

In addition, transfers through formal channels are essentially carried out by cash transfer businesses, as banks only channel a somewhat small amount. In 2005, according to the Central Bank of the Comoros, the amount of transfers by such channels rose to 7.3 billion FC, compared with 6.4 billion FC in 2004 and 5.2 billion FC in 2003.

Discussions to support and develop a partnership between networks of micro-finance institutions and French savings and loan institutions are underway, with the goals of better organizing the circuit, reducing the costs of transfers, and familiarizing migrants with the use of more formal channels made possible through the presence of counters throughout French territory. In addition to providing advice, the Central Bank of the Comoros plans to participate equally in the circuit through the accounts of micro-finance institutions,

registered with the bank, allowing the consolidation of external deposits, and limiting the phenomena of hoarding and the circulation of euros.

It should be noted that cash transfers to the Comoros serve mainly to finance the custom of the *Grand Mariage*. The *Grand Mariage* or the *Anda Nku* is a local tradition, which shapes space (notably public places, mosques and 'customary homes'), stimulates exchanges between families, affects the behaviour of islanders, and codifies social hierarchies. The social ideal of all Grand Comorians is to succeed in attaining a *Grand Mariage*, with the objective of raising one's status to that of a member of the group of *wandru wadzima* (the accomplished people).

The *Grand Mariage* occupies a dominant position in the ways and customs of the Grand Comoro. A family anxious to maintain or conquer a privileged position in the social hierarchy follows this route with all means at its disposal. The *Grand Mariage* often requires many years of saving to gather the considerable financial resources required for the different ceremonies involved. The two families knotting the alliance sacrifice considerable sums in order to attain the top rank. Competitions often emerge between the two families with regard to expenditure, the sole concern being to outdo preceding marriages.

Society is very hierarchical in Grand Comoro. The accomplishment or not of the *Grand Mariage* allows a ranking of individuals into two large groups: the *wandru wadzima* (those who have performed the *Grand Mariage*) and the *wanamdji* (those who have not). Grand Comorians aspire to undertake the *Grand Mariage* for both psychological and economic reasons. Once having paid this customary debt, the person concerned can:

- speak at public meetings

- benefit from a choice seat in all customary festivities

- wear ostentatious clothing specially reserved for those who have achieved the *Grand Mariage*, and

- easily benefit from the respect of the *wanamdji* and from credit with businesses.

This local practice is from beginning to end clothed and enveloped by Islam. Engagements, marriages, pregnancies, births, circumcisions and deaths are all ceremonial occasions as much religious as customary.

The *Grand Mariage* therefore represents the most privileged moment of family solidarity. The pomp and outward show constitute the criteria of the *Grand Mariage,* since in order to attain the given social rank, one must furnish the proof. The *Grand Mariage* constitutes the accomplishment of a step that consecrates the family and especially the newlyweds to the highest social rank. Such a step is only possible as a result of enormous expenditure on the part of the family, which means borrowing heavily.[4]

Before the ceremony takes place, the bride's family must pay for the construction of the house and its furnishing. The uncle, father and even the youngest brothers, should all contribute. Participation is obligatory. Anyone judged able to contribute and who does not is placed in quarantine.

The construction completed, everything revolves around the wedding itself. Marriage is the fundamental aim in life for a Grand Comorian. The main fruit of a man's work is the achievement of a *Grand Mariage*. The family should work together and unite more than ever to ensure that the wedding is the most radiant, most sumptuous occasion possible, and one in which all the family's energy is best deployed to create a moment without equal in a lifetime.

It is the pomp which adorns a wedding. Such pomp reveals the easy circumstances and wealth of the two families. Thus, the most important characteristic of a successful *Grand Mariage* is investment joined to strong physical and material participation. Although physical participation is supposed to be more valued than all other types of participation, it cannot be denied that great importance is attached and great attention paid to material and financial contributions, which, finally, raise the concerned families to the highest point.

The involvement of each and everyone in the process and the ideal of attaining it within one's family, lead Grand Comorian workers who have migrated to retain as their primary objective the successful amassing of *argent de la coutume* ('bride price').

Since the 1980s, an economic and financial crisis has ravaged the population of the Comoros, rooting itself more strongly each year. The country is counted among the most indebted of the poor small island countries. As a consequence, Comorian migrants either help a member of their family to undertake the *Grand Mariage*, or attempt it for themselves. Thus, bizarrely, it is the money saved outside the country by Comorian workers that feeds, reinvigorates and perpetuates the tradition of the *Grand Mariage* within the country.

## What lessons can be learned?

For the small islands the Diaspora plays a primary role, notably at the economic level and sometimes at cultural, social and political levels, according to the characteristics of the moment or the historical stakes. If, for the most part, the migrants provide a positive plus to the small islands with regard to development, it must be emphasized that the 'imported ideologies' can sometimes undermine secular island identities, cultures and practices.

Until there is proof to the contrary, it seems that island identities (notably those of islands well anchored in customary traditions and religious practices) resist and strengthen themselves when adapting to exogenous values. For example, the Grand Comorians, having bathed for a long time in Swahili culture, now open the door little by little to new cultural elements, imported by migrants returning from France. In this way, French culture (clothing, table art, manufactured products)

becomes a part of traditional celebrations. To prove the point, it is the Grand Comorian community of France who mobilize the means necessary for the *Grand Mariage* festivities, and who generate the island's economic life from June to September, a period which corresponds to France's summer.

Moreover, the national island authorities often fail to acknowledge the importance of the Diaspora, both in terms of their cooperation with the authorities of the host country, and their manner of welcoming and rationalizing the multiple forms of contribution granted by the migrants. This raises the question of isolation, both with regard to the home country and in the host country, given the difficult living conditions and frequent marginalization. The challenge is to know how the Diaspora can figure among the important strategies of the country's development.

It would be improvident to believe that cash transfers from the Diaspora will continue indefinitely. The effects of globalization, the third generation of migrants and future generations could all constitute new factors which would change existing connections between the migrants and the home country, on the one hand, and the migrants and the host country on the other. The European Union offers an example of the transformation from national status to supra-national status. Nationals, people with double nationalities and migrants will in one manner or another no longer exist in these new spaces. This new reality once more strongly indicates the intrinsic interest of small islands in reinforcing their relations with the Diaspora, and in better preparing for current and future stakes.

It would therefore be very useful to retain some axis of ongoing intervention – from systematic studies on island diasporas and rational use of new information and communication technologies, to migrant aid, involving aid organizations in development, better cooperation between the home and host country, diversification of partnership, and participation of the Diaspora in reduction of poverty and the process of development.

It is necessary that intergovernmental organizations such as UNESCO conduct studies on island diasporas, with the objective of better understanding the phenomenon (both quantitatively and qualitatively), while at the same time, providing council to the different actors on policies in need of development. It goes without saying that such an initiative would greatly help small island nations, given the primary role played by their diasporas.

One must not forget that the primary role of national authorities is to successfully negotiate with the host country in order to assure (to the degree possible) that migrants are well integrated. The inquiry conducted in 2004 (by the ODR and the CREDOC on Reunion), 'shows that, in order to undertake this integration, the priorities are of three sorts: access to housing which assures normal living conditions, the attainment of mastery of French, and the inclusion of young people in professional courses'. (Translated from the French.)

Some development organizations (national or international) are working to link the conditions for economic growth with those for reduction of poverty, but without taking into consideration the inestimable contribution provided by migrants. It is time to rectify this way of thinking, and take better account of the interactions between the Diaspora, economic growth and the reduction of poverty. Furthermore, it is time to improve local governance, reinforce the capacities of associations, and better channel and 'direct' the cash transfers of migrants.

In addition, it is equally important that within the framework of cooperation, issues relating to the Diaspora receive equal consideration before boards whose members are drawn from the two countries concerned, or within other frameworks of negotiation. Such forums of discussion constitute the most appropriate locales for best understanding the different policies of each country and reaching compromises to benefit both sides.

Finally, the identification of digital products and the use of information highways could greatly reduce geographic isolation, help safeguard island identities, and better channel connections between migrants and the home country, to the service of all. Development of this solution will surely help protect and enliven island languages and cultures.

# References

Ali Bamba Miftahou. 1997. La communauté comorienne à Tamatave, de 1945 à 1978. Master's thesis, Faculté des Lettres et Sciences humaines, Département d'Histoire de l'Université de Tamatave.

Amartya, S. 1999 *Un nouveau modèle économique*. Paris: Edition Odile Jacob.

Boina, A. 1996. *La pensée comorienne*. Doctoral Dissertation. Paris: Université Paris X Nanterre.

Boina, A. 2001. Monographie sur la gouvernance aux Comores, working paper. UNDP, Moroni, multigr.

Central Bank of the Comoros. 2005. Annual Report. Moroni.

Centre d'Analyse Stratégique. 2006. *Mondialisation et migration internationale, les dossiers de la mondialisation*, dossier No. 5. www.rdv-mondialisation.fr.

Commissariat au Plan de l'Union des Comores. 2004. *Transfert de la diaspora comorienne*. Moroni.

DIASCOM. 2006. *Projet de Protocole d'Accord entre l'Etat comorien et la Coordination des Association de la Diaspora Comorienne*. Unpublished draft document.

Dubois, J-L. 1997. *Peut-on s'appuyer sur le capital socioculturel pour réduire la pauvreté aux Comores*, DIAL.

Haddad, Salim Djabir. 2005. *L'intégration des Comoriens à Antananarivo pendant la période coloniale*. Master's thesis in History, Faculté des Lettres et Sciences Humaines. Université d'Antananarivo.

INALCO. 2007. Les Comoriens à Majunga: histoire, migration, émeutes. *Etudes Océan Indien* 38–39.

Manicacci, A. 1968. *Les incursions malgaches aux Comores*. Tananarive: Imprimerie officielle.

Mohamed, Mzé. 2007. 'Sabena' de la Grande Comore. Cited in INALCO 'Les Comoriens à Majunga: Histoire, migration, émeutes', *Etudes Océan Indien* 38–39: 51–52.

Mouzawar Abdallah. 1976. Livre blanc [White paper]. Moroni: Ministry of Foreign Affairs of Comoros.

ODR and CREDOC (Observatoire du Développement de la Réunion et Centre de Recherche pour l'Etude et l'Observation des Conditions de Vie). 2004. *La situation des populations migrantes originaires de l'Océan Indien*, synthesis. ODR/CREDOC. Available at: www.odr.net and www.credoc.net.

Présidence de l'île de Ngazidja. 2006. Décret n° 06-07/PLAN, portant promulgation de la loi N° 05/08/05, portant composition, organisation et fonctionnement du Conseil de la Diaspora, Moroni.

Schnapper, D. 2005. De l'Etat – nation au monde transnational, *Revue Européenne des Migrations Internationales*, article published online 23 February 2005.

Sidi, A. 2002. L'esclavage aux Comores: son fonctionnement de la période arabe à 1904, E. Maestri (ed.) 2002. *Esclavage et abolitions dans l'océan Indien (1723–1860)*. Université de La Réunion: L'Harmattan.

Soilihi, President A. 1975. Interview of 08 September 1975, *Libération*. Cited in Charpentier 'Comores: la fin des sultans batailleurs – une révolution tranquille'.

Vivier, G. 1993. *Le flux migratoire Comores – France*, mémoire de DEA, Paris X – Nanterre.

# Endnotes

*1* The population of the Comoros is the result of a complex mix of people from the eastern coast of Africa, the north of Madagascar and India. Five ethnic groups are generally distinguished as today constituting a homogenous and original population: the Cafres, the Arabs, the Wamatsaha, the Makaos and the Malagasies.

*2* This figure concerns the population of the islands of Mohéli, Anjouan and Grand Comoro, since Mayotte (the fourth island of the Comoros) has been under French administration since 6 July 1975, when the Comoros gained independence.

*3* The people who prefer to stay permanently in the host countries can be categorized as follows:

- people who have acquired the nationality of the host country and are well integrated both culturally and professionally
- people who have family attachments and constitute mixed couples with mixed children, and
- people who have completely failed in fulfilling their intention to accumulate capital or to acquire knowledge, and thus for whom the return would be synonymous with 'total failure and shame' before their own people and village.

*4* At the lowest estimate for the two families, expenses are about 25,000 million Comorian Francs, or 50,000 euros. The lowest levels of expenditure are found in cities such as Moroni, due to reform of the *Grand Mariage*. The family of the bride should, at the very least, renew and furnish the nuptial home, cover the expenses linked to the customary ceremonies and invitations, not to mention the traditional ceremonial clothing, luxury toiletries and obligatory manufactured products to be sent to the groom. The groom should send to the bride collections of jewellery valued at about 22,000 euros, and provide 6,000 euros to the traditional age groups, without counting other ceremonial expenses.

# MAKING POLICY TO SUPPORT LIVING CULTURES

## A case study in 'mainstreaming culture' from Vanuatu

Ralph Regenvanu, *Vanuatu National Cultural Council and Member of Parliament*

**W**hile speaking on the panel on 'Culture' at the 2005 UN Meeting to Review the Implementation of the Programme of Action for the Sustainable Development of Small Island Developing States (SIDS) in Mauritius, Dame Pearlette Louisy, Governor General of St Lucia, remarked that,

> *A leading Caribbean academic speaks of the interlocking which exists between an understanding of one's culture and the possibilities of economic growth and the understanding of cultural heritage as the basis for economic growth and social development. There are now concerted efforts being made to 'mobilize the power of culture', as it is argued that no lasting development can be guaranteed in a society where popular cultural expressions are undervalued.*

UNESCO, 2007

This chapter describes one such 'concerted effort' – the Government of Vanuatu's declaration of 2007 as the 'Year of the Traditional Economy'. This initiative was an effort to influence macro-level development policies in the country, and transform the whole approach to national development in favour of a recognition and utilization of cultural heritage as the basis for sustainable development.

The effort described here is a bold initiative, distinctly 'home-grown', and therefore not directly transferable to many other SIDS. Nonetheless, it presents significant contributions to the current debate on culture, diversity and sustainable development. This chapter describes how this effort was initiated in Vanuatu and, in particular, the strategies used to articulate it as a priority on the political agenda. The use of the term 'culture' in this chapter refers to living culture, also understood as intangible cultural heritage (ICH). A distinction has been drawn between 'belief-based' ICH and 'economy-based' ICH, the latter referring to ICH tied to a traditional economic base and to territory and resources.

In Vanuatu, communities have expressed a desire to continue leading lifestyles based on a traditional economic base. In the context of economic globalization, however, this possibility is being ignored or denied by government policy decisions made on the basis of 'economic rationalism'. There is growing concern that these government decisions are in fact destructive of 'popular cultural expressions', and do not reflect the values of the community in relation to its development. This has raised the following questions in many people's minds: 'What is really meant by sustainable development? What if the overall approach to development is contributing to the extinction of living cultures? How do we get policies developed that support the maintenance of our culture?' In order to understand how these questions have been addressed in Vanuatu, it is necessary to step back and understand the local and national context.

## The local and national context

The Republic of Vanuatu is made up of eighty small islands in the south-western Pacific Ocean. The country has a total population of about 243,000 people, of whom over 90 per cent are indigenous. With over 100 distinct indigenous languages, Vanuatu has the highest linguistic diversity (for its population) in the world. If a language group can be considered a 'culture', then Vanuatu is the most culturally diverse nation on earth. This immense diversity characterizes the entire Melanesian region, which also comprises the Fiji Islands, New Caledonia, Papua New Guinea, the Solomon Islands and the Indonesian Province of West Papua. With a total population of less than 10 million people, this region claims about one quarter of the world's languages. The Pacific Islands region as a whole consists of over twenty states and territories in an area covering more than a quarter of the world's surface. This region is unique in having the highest rate of indigenous people within the national population of any region of the world, and also the highest

proportion of land within the state held under customary or traditional land tenure systems. Traditional land ownership is enshrined in Vanuatu's constitution, which was adopted in 1980 at the time of independence from the joint British and French colonial administration.

Key characteristics of the cultural diversity of Vanuatu are the very low level of diaspora and the very high degree of continuity with pre-colonial or 'custom' ancestral traditions ('custom' refers to cultural practices that originate prior to European intrusion and colonization). Such characteristics are in marked contrast to the situations of other SIDS featured in this publication. The great majority of the people of Vanuatu ('ni-Vanuatu') live in the rural areas of the country (about 80 per cent of the population). Almost all of this 80 per cent live in settlements (villages), with other members of their traditional extended families, on land that is theirs according to custom-based laws and the national Constitution. They satisfy most of their food and other requirements through traditional forms of land, sea and resource utilization (e.g. gardening practices) on their customary territory. They speak indigenous languages, participate in custom ceremonies which cement their place as members of their community, practise government by traditional leaders (chiefs), and resolve disputes within their communities using traditional dispute-resolution approaches. In addition, a large proportion of the other approximately 20 per cent of ni-Vanuatu living in urban areas also participate in and rely on the traditional economy to a significant degree, utilizing kinship networks to access food and other resources and dealing with disputes in the traditional way.

Today, however, even the most isolated rural dweller needs cash to pay for tea, sugar, kerosene, iron and steel implements and school fees. The fact that Vanuatu is classified as a 'Least Developed Country' by the United Nations is based on the fact that the great majority of the population use only a very small amount of cash for the necessities mentioned above. Their participation in the traditional economy is far more important and pervasive than their involvement in the cash economy. It is true to say, in fact, that the traditional economy constitutes the political, economic and social foundation of contemporary Vanuatu society.

# The benefits of the traditional economy

Vanuatu gains many important benefits from the strength of its traditional economy. One of the most significant is that everyone has access to land to cultivate, from which they can obtain food and make a living. The traditional concept of the right to use land and resources which are not your own means that individuals or families, who do not have access to their own customary land (or enough of it) to meet their needs, can be given the right to use other families' land. Another important benefit of the traditional economy is its sustainable management of the natural environment.

In 2007, a report published by the New Economics Foundation declared Vanuatu to be the 'happiest country in the world'. The main contributing factor (to quote from the report) was its 'extremely rich natural capita, with unspoilt coastlines and unique rainforests'. This rich natural capita has been achieved through thousands of years of excellent resource management embodied in ancestral traditions and practices, traditions that are still practised today. Social benefits form another important characteristic of the traditional economy. The most desired outcome of any ceremonial activity is the establishment, maintainance and mending of relationships between groups (be they families, clans or larger communities such as villages, language groups or even islands).

In short, the concrete benefits of the traditional economy are that there is more than enough food for everyone in the country, and the population enjoys a food security that only comes with growing your own food. The traditional diet uses food from the gardens and is safe, healthy and nutritious. There is no homelessness in Vanuatu, a boast that, to my knowledge, only Vanuatu, the Solomon Islands and PNG are also able to make (the three countries in which traditional economies are strongest). Vanuatu has no old peoples' homes and no mental asylums – everyone is cared for within the extended family unit. The country enjoys a general level of peace and social order that is the result of traditional values of respect, equity, the promotion of relationships and a restorative community-based system of dispute resolution.

In 2006, an 'Economic opportunities fact-finding mission' to Vanuatu was sponsored by NZAID and AusAID. Compared to earlier economic studies, it had the benefit of being undertaken *after* the concept of the traditional economy had become widely known locally. Accordingly, its report recognized that 'many of the functions of modern growth – well-being, stability, equity, social cohesion and sustainable livelihoods for an expanded population – are also well provided for through Vanuatu's strong and deeply held customary values including its custom economy', and stated that efforts to promote this economy 'should be supported'. More importantly, the report stated that

> [Vanuatu's] *most understated productive sector is the massive response within its traditional (island) economy to a rapidly growing population. [ … ] Although growth of Vanuatu's GDP has not been spectacular, it's traditional, largely non-monetarised, rural economy has successfully supported a 90% increase in the rural population in the 26 years since independence ( from about 95,000 in 1980 to an estimated 180,000 now).*

Bazeley and Mullen, 2006

# The orthodox development approach in Vanuatu

Despite the socioeconomic reality on the ground, the United Nations' designation of Vanuatu as a Least Developed Country (LDC) based on GDP per capita ranks it among the most needy countries

in the world. The benefits of the traditional economy are clearly not recognized in this assessment. The traditional economy also receives no recognition in the Government's official development agenda for Vanuatu, reflected in its two main policy documents: the Comprehensive Reform Programme (CRP) and the Priorities and Action Agenda (PAA).

The CRP was an Asian Development Bank-sponsored (soft loan) programme of reform of public services, aimed at reducing the size of the public service while strengthening state institutions of law and governance and 'private sector-led growth'. It emphasized 'opening up' the economy and integration of the country into the regional and world economy. Its targets included membership of the World Trade Organization as a 'model LDC member', and raising the standard of living through increased economic growth, defined in terms of GDP. The PAA has rather mysterious origins. It proclaims that 'the expressed wish of the people' is improved living standards through greater economic growth to be achieved through greater direct foreign investment.

Neither document recognizes other values and realities – in particular those values which underpin the reality of the lives of the great majority. Examples which illustrate this include an emphasis on 'freeing up' customary land to make it available for foreign investment, a policy which has resulted in the alienation of extensive tracts of land from customary stewardship over the past twenty years. State policy also places a high value on cash and outputs from Western economies (e.g. consumer goods), conceptualizing prosperity in terms of an urban standard of living, while either explicitly or implicitly denigrating the value of the largely rural traditional economy and its outputs. These values are also supported by the media and promoted through an education system still premised on the colonial rationale of producing administrators.

Due to the absence of abject poverty, and the objections of even state officials to describing ni-Vanuatu as living in 'poverty', new terminology now used by AusAID and the World Bank refers to 'poverty of opportunity' and 'hardship'. Such terminology serves to justify the state-adopted 'economic growth' response to globalization while obscuring the non-monetary benefits of the traditional economy. That this is possible is due in no small part to the lack of indicators to measure the contributions of the traditional economy. There are currently no measures of the non-monetary value of culture. This is despite the innovative programmes developed and implemented in the cultural heritage sector in Vanuatu, manifested in the activities of the Vanuatu Cultural Centre.

## The Vanuatu Cultural Centre and the fieldworkers programme

The Vanuatu Cultural Centre, Vanuatu's principal national heritage institution, has developed a programme for involving practitioner communities in the management of their own living intangible cultural heritage. The 'community fieldworkers

programme' is based on the rationale that the culture of the great majority of people in Vanuatu demonstrates a strong continuity with their ancestral cultures, therefore, the most effective way to safeguard and maintain this intangible cultural heritage is to encourage communities to maintain the many aspects of traditional culture in their day-to-day lives. The crucial characteristic of intangible culture is its dynamism – its continual re-creation by the people that enact it. It is essential, therefore, that practitioner communities define for themselves what they consider to be the aspects of their culture worth safeguarding, and be actively involved in deciding what safeguarding measures to take and how to implement them.

The fieldworkers programme was set up in the mid-1970s. Men and women living in the local community are selected as fieldworkers to represent different cultural groups, and receive training in using notebooks, tape recorders, and still and video cameras to record cultural information. Basic ethnographic fieldwork techniques such as dictionary-making and the recording of genealogies are also learnt, as are the more general aims and methodologies of cultural heritage preservation and development. This training takes place during annual two-week workshops held at the Cultural Centre's head office in Port Vila. At this time, fieldworkers present their individual research findings on a particular topic identified for that year's workshop, and learn of corresponding *kastom* in other areas of Vanuatu from the reports of other fieldworkers. These presentations are recorded to preserve this important information.

The workshop also includes information on programmes being developed by fieldworkers throughout the islands to encourage the maintenance and revival of cultural traditions. Most fieldworkers are involved (to varying levels) in work to transcribe oral vernacular languages into written forms, starting with the creation of word lists and dictionaries. Some of the more experienced fieldworkers have been involved in major cultural research and revival initiatives in their respective areas, often with minimal outside support. One of the most common such initiatives has been the organization and/or facilitation of performances of traditional ceremonies and rituals, and in particular, the reconstruction and revival of certain rituals from living memory as performance and part of contemporary life. Another has been the organization of community arts festivals, which provide an opportunity for the performance and learning of traditional songs, dances, practices and rituals.

Perhaps one of the more significant of such initiatives is the establishment of community 'cultural centres' (similar to Australian aboriginal 'keeping houses'). These are available for use by particular cultural communities or clans as centres for community cultural activities, and as storehouses and display areas for aspects of their cultural heritage (including old photographs and written records). To date, only two such centres have been established, however, the creation of a centre for each cultural community in the country remains a long-term priority goal for the Cultural Centre.

Fieldworkers perform an indispensable role as local community liaisons, facilitators and organizers for the programmes and work of the Cultural Centre. At the most practical level, fieldworkers organize and facilitate the recording of important rituals, practices, and cultural and historic sites by Cultural Centre staff, using written, audio, audiovisual and photographic formats. The recorded material is then archived in the main Cultural Centre building, located in the national capital, while copies of relevant material are returned to the community. All recorded material remains the property of the traditional owners.

A particularly important part of the fieldworker's liaison work is explaining the purpose of such recordings, and obtaining the approval and 'prior informed consent' of the traditional owners/custodians for such recording to take place, as well as ensuring the participation of the practitioners in the recording activities themselves. Such participation relies on a level of awareness of the Cultural Centre's cultural heritage work, which the fieldworker is responsible for imparting to the community. The fieldworker is assisted in this by the Cultural Centre's promotional programmes, including a weekly radio programme on national radio. Under the Vanuatu Cultural Research Policy, all foreign researchers and filmmakers are also required to work with fieldworkers to ensure the active participation of local communities when undertaking any work on local cultures.

All fieldworkers are volunteers – they undertake their cultural heritage work in their free time.

The principal benefit for fieldworkers is the resulting status of *filwoka*, a nationally recognized position listed in the Bislama dictionary. All fieldworkers are also members of the cultural communities they represent, speak the community language, and actually live in those communities. At present there are over 100 fieldworkers. Funding permitting, the aim is to have two fieldworkers (one man and one woman) for every cultural group in the country. This is seen as the best solution to the problems of (a) dealing with cultural diversity from within the national institution, (b) dealing with a 'living' and largely intangible culture, and (c) effecting genuine community participation in the management of their own cultural heritage.

# The 'Traditional Money Banks Project'

In June 2004, a fieldworker, James Teslo, recognized that certain traditional ceremonies in his community were not being performed due to a shortage of pigs – the most important wealth item in almost all of Vanuatu's cultures. As a result, the intangible cultural heritage that constituted these ceremonies was not being transmitted, threatening the vitality of the local culture. To remedy the situation, he suggested the establishment of a 'pig bank', which would provide the required animals. A project was initiated with the assistance of Tim Curtis, an anthropologist undertaking fieldwork in the area at the time (and later appointed to UNESCO). The 'Traditional

Money Banks Project' widened its focus to include the major traditional wealth items needed for use in ceremonies, such as dyed red pandanus mats, shell money and yams. The project partners were the Cultural Centre and the Vanuatu Credit Union League, with funding provided by the Japanese Government through the 'Japanese Funds-In-Trust for the Safeguarding of the Intangible Cultural Heritage' via UNESCO.

The stated objectives of the project were:

1. to survey and understand the production processes and investment and saving/banking mechanisms for traditional wealth items in Vanuatu

2. to raise awareness of the significance of traditional monies and the need to preserve and continue to transmit the intangible knowledge relating to skills and techniques for the production of these monies

3. to develop a strategy for promoting the use of traditional wealth items in Vanuatu

4. to develop strategies to facilitate the use of traditional wealth items to pay for services currently paid for in cash (e.g. school and medical fees), especially in rural areas

5. to establish laws and policies at provincial and national level to support the use of traditional wealth items as part of the formal economy of the country

6.  to strengthen the foundations of the tradi-tional economy within culturally appropri-ate frameworks with a view to stimulating income-generation within local populations

7.  to provide infrastructure and resources needed to establish effective and viable 'tra-ditional money banks', and

8.  to establish the viability for extending this concept to other areas of Melanesia.

At the most basic level, the principal objective of the project was to maintain and revitalize liv-ing traditional cultural practices, while stimu-lating cash income generation. This would be achieved by:

-   encouraging people involved in the produc-tion of various forms of traditional wealth (tusked pigs, mats, shell money, etc.) to con-tinue producing such wealth

-   encouraging people primarily involved in the cash economy to access traditional valuables and use them for ceremonial activities, and

-   facilitating the exchange of cash and tradi-tional wealth items between the informal and formal economic sectors, both to generate income for people involved in the traditional sphere of economic life and to encourage the revival of traditional practices amongst those primarily involved in the cash economy.

The first project activity was a survey of the situation relating to the production and use of traditional wealth items. This was completed at the end of 2004 and published in July 2005. The report found that the traditional economy was strong in some areas, while in others the know-how still existed but was no longer practised be-cause of growing monetization, specifically as a result of the need for money to pay for state health and education services. However, in spite of the greater focus on cash crops, there was still a strong and widespread interest in revitalizing traditional ceremonial exchanges and traditional cultural expressions.

By this stage, there was a growing realization that the project involved more than just cultural heri-tage issues; rather, it required a broader focus on macro-development approaches and policies. This awareness had been growing for some time within the Vanuatu Cultural Centre, as its work to assist local communities to maintain and revi-talize aspects of their cultural heritage had been consistently undermined by Government poli-cies that did not reflect these community values and concerns. The need to address the broader national development agenda led to a key deci-sion to partner with the National Council of Chiefs and cement a relationship with the Prime Minister. This partnership was to become the key strategic alliance which eventually led to the Government's declaration of 2007 as the 'Year of the Traditional Economy'.

## Strategic policy development towards 'mainstreaming' culture

The second project activity was a workshop to develop strategies to attain the project objectives at community level. It was jointly hosted by the three project partners in March 2005, and entitled the 'Workshop to recognize and promote the traditional economy as the basis for achieving national self reliance'. The title highlighted the hoped-for change in the discourse of development. In place of cultural heritage terminology the workshop used the terms 'economy' and 'traditional economy'. Most importantly, it discussed ways of recognizing and promoting existing capacities and strengths within society to achieve the set goals.

The fieldworker network was used to identify participants – key traditional experts, cultural advocates and resource people – and many fieldworkers also participated. Chiefs and community leaders from the six provinces of Vanuatu attended, as well as officers from provincial governments and different government departments (in particular, health, education, agriculture and cooperatives), officers from statutory bodies and representatives of non-governmental organizations. The President of the National Council of Chiefs officially opened the workshop and the Deputy Prime Minister (who was also Minister for Foreign Affairs) officially closed it. The Minister of Education made an address at the official closing.

The workshop produced a set of recommendations entitled 'The Action Plan to recognize and promote the traditional economy as the basis for achieving national self reliance'. These recommendations were symbolically launched in a 'canoe of self reliance' by the Deputy Prime Minister as part of the closing ceremony of the workshop. The key 'Guiding principles' of the Action Plan recognized that:

1. the production and use of traditional wealth items and customary resources always happens at the level of the household, the clan and the village

2. the production and use of these resources occurs for communal benefit and never for the benefit of individuals, and

3. a community is always understood to consist of men, women and children.

Another key guiding principle was that the production and use of traditional wealth items and customary resources must be done in the proper customary way (*stret kastom fasen*). This necessitated a respect for traditional rights and copyrights over these processes. It was further agreed that chiefs had to be represented at every level of community and state governance.

Key elements of the Action Plan included a directive not to sell or lease land, and a system for payment of government services, particularly school and medical consultation fees, using traditional wealth items. Furthermore, 2007 was declared 'the Year of Customary Wealth' (later changed to the 'Year of the Traditional Economy'). At its annual national meeting in early April 2005, the National Council of Chiefs endorsed the Action Plan in its entirety, and took a decision to change its policy regarding bride prices and the use of cash in customary ceremonies to fully implement the relevant recommendation of the workshop. This was viewed as a major policy change and was widely publicized.

The third project activity was a higher level meeting, held in July 2005, involving key policy-makers in the national capital of Port Vila. The meeting was entitled the 'National Summit for Self Reliance and Sustainability' and was hosted by the National Council of Chiefs, with invitations sent out by the Office of the Prime Minister. By this point, the language of cultural heritage was no longer apparent; instead 'sustainable development' was envisioned as the overarching objective, in addition to maintenance of culture. Primary themes included food security, social security, governance, land and land use (environmental sustainability), education, energy and health.

This Summit produced a further set of recommendations for national policy, entitled the 'Vanuatu National Self Reliance Strategy 2020'. The key recommendations were as follows:

1. The national governance system should be reformed to recognize the predominant role traditional governance plays in contemporary Vanuatu society, and to create a new system that recognizes this traditional approach and empowers it as the basis of a new structure incorporating both Western and traditional forms of governance (strengthening the National Council of Chiefs).

2. A national Land Summit should be held before July 2006 to address all issues of concern regarding land raised at the Summit.

3. Traditional resource management should become the official basis of national environmental management.

4. The national curriculum should be reformed before the end of 2006 to incorporate traditional knowledge and custom as its basis.

5. A policy facilitating the payment of school fees and health department consultation fees with traditional wealth items or produce should be finalized before the end of 2005.

6. The traditional economy should be recognized and promoted as the basis for national self-reliance and sustainability, and 2007 declared as the Year of the Traditional Economy.

7. Home-grown statistical indicators should be developed to measure and quantify economic activity (including traditional economy activities) and 'well being' or quality of life.

8. The production and consumption of traditional foods should be promoted.

9. Most imported foods and all staple foods (i.e. rice and flour) should be substituted with local foods.

10. All boarding schools and hospitals should serve local foods and set up cooperatives to accept local foods instead of cash in payment for fees.

These initiatives gave the 'National Food and Nutrition Policy' of the Ministry of Health (initially developed in 1989) and the food security focus of the Department of Agriculture a significant boost. The work of frustrated public servants in these sectors was given renewed support and they became allies in the overall initiative. As noted above, the government proceeded to declare 2007 the 'Year of the Traditional Economy'.

The Land Summit was held in September 2006. This major initiative was facilitated by the newly appointed Director General of the Ministry of Lands, who had previously worked closely with the key proponents of the Summit from within the national Environment Unit. The Steering Committee for the National Self Reliance Strategy 2020 coordinated an initiative to prepare a set of recommendations for the Land Summit, and working in collaboration with a number of key NGOs, established the 'Advocacy Coalition for Economics' (ACE) in preparation for this meeting. The two groups, working together as ACE, held a series of meetings to develop a set of recommendations for the Summit. Once these were completed, the National Council of Chiefs, the only national body with a constitutional mandate to advise the government on land matters, put its name to the recommendations on behalf of the other two groups. Of the twenty resolutions that finally emerged from the Land Summit, fourteen were taken directly from the recommendations developed through this collaboration. Following the Summit, a steering committee was appointed to oversee implementation of the resolutions. It comprised senior civil servants from key stakeholder ministries, as well a youth representative and one representative each from the National Council of Chiefs, the National Cultural Council and the National Council of Women.

By the beginning of 2007, the project was providing seed funding to support the establishment of 'pig banks' throughout the country, as well as numerous other projects to promote traditional wealth production in local communities. An awareness team comprising fieldworkers, chiefs, and national and provincial government authorities toured all areas of the islands to explain the meaning and purpose of the 'Year of the Traditional Economy', to some bemusement from local communities, who had been 'doing it all along'. Policy-makers in the national capital, ironically, were the least ready to accept what they saw as an 'about face' in national development policy, and continued to promote their more orthodox vision of development.

# Conclusion

At its most ambitious, this project aimed to establish legal, policy and infrastructural frameworks to support its objectives through the production of a new national strategy for development in Vanuatu. This strategy was one that recognized the significant economic resources and 'wealth' that already existed at the community level in the rural areas of the country, and aimed to bolster the traditional economic structures which had sustained these communities for thousands of years as the basis for future sustainable development. It encouraged the nation to look within for its development solutions, rather than accept globalized orthodoxies; the traditional adage of 'standing on the back of a turtle, looking for turtles' captures some sense of this message. In essence, the aim of the 'Year of the Traditional Economy' initiative in Vanuatu was to level the policy playing field. It addressed a concern for the need for alternative responses to economic globalization that did not follow the orthodox 'economic growth' model being taken by the government. It was an attempt to mainstream culture, seeing it as the fourth pillar of sustainable development, and build a foundation for both sustainable development and cultural development.

The initial successes of the project stemmed from the fact that it was able to articulate a populist view, particularly through the language used, which then encouraged broader political support. It also built on existing practice; for example, school fees were already being paid in certain schools with traditional wealth items. The programme capitalized on popular discontent with government development policies, especially in relation to the issue of land sales. Then, riding on the back of these concerns it built strategic alliances, in particular, with chiefs. Finally, the programme talked about preserving identity in the face of assimilationist, globalizing pressures – a discourse with recent and familiar historic precedents in the process of decolonization and independence of the country and its neighbouring states some twenty years earlier.

The challenges facing this initiative are, of course, huge. Translating these initial strategic statements and intentions into concrete political action will be very difficult. The state has always been primarily concerned with obtaining more cash in order to fulfil its mandate to provide and extend services to the population, and also (less nobly) in order to feed the excesses of its political and bureaucratic functionaries. As the traditional economy is not a source of cash, very little attention has been paid to it. This 'blind spot' on the part of the government receives support from Vanuatu's traditional bilateral partners – Australia, France, the European Union and New Zealand – as well as multilateral agencies such as the World Bank and Asian Development Bank, all of which encourage the adoption of pro-foreign investment and pro-monetization policies to increase GDP at the expense of traditional economies. Perhaps a greater challenge is the attraction of consumerism and Westernization-seen-as-betterment, an attraction which arises in no small part from a 'psychology of dependency' with deep historical roots, engrained under the colonial experience and perpetuated by the formal education system, and the 'spectre of comparisons' described by Eriksen in his contribution to this publication. While there are many fronts on which to confront these challenges, there is at the most basic level an ongoing need to reinforce our economic analysis. There is a pressing need for indicators or measures of well being that value non-monetary contributions in terms already identified, such as nutrition, food security, social security, environmental sustainability and good governance. With such indicators in place, a central role for culture in development is inevitable.

# References

Bazeley, P. and Mullen, B. 2006. *Vanuatu: Economic Opportunities Fact-finding Mission*. On Behalf of AusAID and NZAID. UK and Australia. www.ausaid.gov.au/publications/pdf/vanuatu_growth.pdf

Crowley, T. 1995. *A New Bislama Dictionary*. Port Vila. Pacific Languages Unit, University of the South Pacific.

Government of the Republic of Vanuatu, 2006. Priorities and Action Agenda 2006–2015, Ministry of Finance and Economic Management, Port Vila, Vanuatu.

Republic of Vanuatu. 27 June 1997. Comprehensive Reform Programme endorsed by the National Summit. Port Vila. Comprehensive Reform Co-Ordination Office, Office of the Prime Minister.

The Happy Planet Index, 2007 at www.neweconomics.org/gen/z_sys_Publication Detail.aspx?pid=225, New Economics Foundation, accessed 27 December, 2008.

UNESCO. 2007. *Sustainable living in Small Island Developing States*. Paris: UNESCO.

Regenvanu, R. 2007. The Year of the Traditional Economy: what is it all about? *The Vanuatu Independent* 166 (Sunday, 11–17 February).

UNESCO/Daniel Mar...

UNESCO/ Cécile Nirrengarten

UNESCO/Gary Masters

Morguefile/Xenia

UNESCO/Daniel Martin

UNESCO/Dominique Roger

# Global technologies and the business of Jamaican Culture

## Maximizing the potential of ICTs and new media

Hopeton S. Dunn, *University of the West Indies, Mona, Jamaica*

As a small developing country Jamaica has been a forerunner in the creation of cultural commodities for many decades, with music being its most significant export. In the year 2000, Jamaican music generated revenues estimated at more than US$1 billion (UNESCO, 2005: 40), however, actual or potential revenues may be much larger. Much of this income was generated by businesses and individuals operating or working outside of Jamaica – a situation that poses challenges to the harnessing of economic returns and the potential of indigenous music and other cultural products. At least part of the challenge has historically been associated with the small size of Jamaica's economy and the limited resources available for marketing, monitoring and enforcing the intellectual property, moral entitlements and other economic rights of its citizens. 'It can hardly be said that developed and developing countries are on the same footing in global capital or currency markets or in the global merchandise or service markets' (Robotham, 2005: 63).

The present information age is dominated by a double-edged form of globalization and connected by converging communication technology networks. As a result, the traditional constraints of global reach have been significantly bridged for all players. This has opened up the potential of expanded marketing in cultural artifacts from all over the world to connected consumers anywhere.

According to the United Nations' Mauritius Declaration, the key objectives for sustainable development of small developing states include recognition of the fact that 'international trade is important for building resilience [ … ] through technology transfer and development, capacity building and human resource development'. The declaration also states that attention should be focused on specific trade and development-related needs and concerns 'to enable these countries to integrate fully into the multilateral trading system in accordance with the Doha mandate on small economies' (United Nations, 2005a).

In the present global technological environment, there are lower barriers of entry for businesses and persons able to disseminate content using advanced technologies. Such entrants may also be able to benefit from plummeting costs for the enabling technologies in question. For producers, this means that there are more ways to reach consumers interested in Jamaican cultural products.

While some creative producers are taking advantage of these opportunities, the wider majority continue to encounter obstacles, including unattainable costs and limited access to capital, inadequate training in the use of these electronic networks, and the legal requirements of emerging global e-transactions regimes.

In this context, the potential exists for local production and global digital distribution of cultural products to realize real economic returns. However, this potential remains largely unfulfilled for many actors working in the creative industries in Small Island Developing States (SIDS). At the same time, both consumers and creative producers in these small yet complex societies are affected by the alternate, adverse edge of globalization and technological innovation. As I have argued elsewhere,

> the very existence of this ethnic and cultural diversity is threatened by the homogenizing, centrifugal force of the emergent global systems, which convey trans-cultural values via the new communication technologies. This approach sees the diverse lifestyles, work ethic and cultural expression of recipient societies being reached at source, within homes and communities by way of global satellite television, among other media.

Dunn, 1995: xiv

This rest of this chapter takes a conceptual and analytical look at potential ways to mitigate the challenges and maximize opportunities.

## Peoples and cultures: the essence of SIDS

In the Caribbean, as in any other region dominated by micro-states, it is the combination of diversity, cultural heritage, natural environment and the ongoing creativity of peoples that defines success, both in the present and the future. While peoples' uninhibited cultural expression is a development end in itself, the capacity to produce and market elements of this cultural expression represents an important source of value-creation and economic development. In discussing the respective roles of production and the market, Robotham makes the point that diversity and choice really begin at the point of production, not at the level of the market. 'The enormous possibility for the development of individual talent and abilities which now exist [...] only exist because of this variegated global specialization in production and global demand in consumption, including productive consumption' (Robotham, 2005: 18). The market, he argues, is the 'mechanism through which choice is exercised by those who have money to buy the goods and services available'.

In endorsing this viewpoint on the primacy of production, we must also recognize the immense power and value of effective marketing. While the developing societies of the global South are the regions most frequently associated with the contribution of new and innovative cultural practices and ideas that help to renew conventional industrial societies, they often lose out at the more lucrative end of marketing. It is true that the vast existing range of product choice is – far from being the creation of the market – the fruit of this internationally divided social labour. (Robotham, 2005: 18). However, it is vital to emphasize the importance of building capacity to manage the global marketing necessary to obtain fair financial returns on productive talent and creativity. This aspect continues to be an elusive component of the cultural development equation in SIDS.

The Barbados Programme of Action for the Sustainable Development of SIDS states that 'the survival of small island developing states is firmly rooted in their human resources and cultural heritage, which are their most significant assets; those assets are under severe stress and all efforts must be taken to ensure the central position of people in the process of sustainable development' (quoted in United Nations, 2005b: 1). The main issues facing SIDS in the area of culture relate to 'both the social and instrumental value of culture in development, and importantly, to the less emphasized economic value of cultural manifestations and expressions of SIDS' (quoted in United Nations, 2005b: 1). In short, the problem identified was the need to maximize commercial benefits while not compromising the cultural and moral fabric of these societies.

## The challenge of unequal protection

In the development of creative industries, product and process protection is always a challenge because of the conflict between WTO-driven global free trade policies on the one hand, and a country's expectations of primacy or even exclusivity in promoting and commercializing the manifestations of their cultural heritage, on the other. In attempting to globally market their unique artifacts and practices, countries often face competition from external providers with more powerful marketing capacity and global reach. The problem of cyber squatting and patenting are interesting cases in point. The pre-emption of the very names of countries and their agencies by online hacks presents a significant threat to the e-marketing and protection of goods and services that cannot be found elsewhere.

The registration in the United States of a patent on a musical instrument developed in Trinidad and Tobago – the steel pan – is another example of this challenge. The inability of affected countries, in the face of such challenges, to develop their creative sectors to their maximum potential, threatens the UN SIDS goals of wealth and job creation, reduction in poverty and crime, and reduced vulnerability to external shock impact on human capacity (United Nations, 2005b: 2–3).

Marketing and economic dissemination of some aspects of cultural production fall within the global regime of the General Agreement on Trade in Services (GATS), a treaty of the World Trade Organization (WTO). Among the sectors covered by GATS are the audio-visual category, including such cultural and creative services as film and video production, radio and television services, sound recordings, as well as educational services, recreational services and cultural and sporting services, including libraries, archives and museums.

WTO treaty commitments require signatories to liberalize their trade in services in these areas, and also require that 'most favoured nations' status or what is sometimes called 'normal trade practices', apply multilaterally to these services. The WTO justifies this open-market approach to cultural products and services on the following basis:

> *Since the services sector is the largest and fastest-growing sector of the world economy, providing more than 60% of global output and in many countries an even larger share of employment, the lack of a legal framework for the international services trade was anomalous and dangerous – anomalous because the potential benefits of services liberalization are at least as great as in the goods sector, and dangerous because there was no legal basis on which to resolve conflicting national interests.*

World Trade Organization, 2007

Translated, the industrialized countries who dominate the WTO agenda are saying that trade in these services is too lucrative to leave to the bilateral choices of the countries of origin. The change from capital-intensive to knowledge-based economies dictates greater control of indigenous cultural products and knowledge-based services by global transnational corporations and their parent governments, who are the joint net beneficiaries of these unrestricted free trade provisions.

These inequalities form the context in which Caribbean and Jamaican entrepreneurs in cultural services currently operate. Advocacy for reform mechanisms to facilitate the protection, promotion and marketing of these services by members of SIDS needs to continue, even as these countries seek to compete on unequal terms.

## Jamaica: a cultural powerhouse

Jamaica is a small developing country in global and geographical contexts. However, it has a disproportionate global influence as a result of its renowned productivity in the areas of tourism, music and sports. The country has a population of 2.6 million (PIOJ, 2006) and a total area of about 10,000 km$^2$. As is the case for many other SIDS, the local market for Jamaica's cultural goods or services is inherently small. As such, it needs to look beyond its borders to recover any significant investment in people and production tools for its cultural and other industries. This also means that local industries must identify the most cost-effective ways to market and distribute their goods and services worldwide.

Jamaica's legendary creative capacity rests upon a foundation of ethnic diversity, cultural liberty, pervasive African folk forms, minority European, Indian and Chinese traditions and an innovative, youthful population. In 2006, young Jamaicans aged 10 to 24 constituted 30 per cent of the population (PRB, 2008). In terms of ethnicity, the population is predominately African (76.3 per cent), with the remainder comprising Afro-Europeans (15.1 per cent), white (3.2 per cent), East Indian and Afro-East Indian (3 per cent), Chinese and Afro-Chinese (1.2 per cent) and other ethnic groups (1.2 per cent) (JNHT, 2008).

Daily Jamaican life is dominated by Afro-Caribbean cultural expressions in language, dance, music and cuisine. While Europe has been the dominant historical influence on education and fashion, there is a growing variation in African styles and greater educational exploration of other cultures.

Since independence from Britain in 1962, the country has cultivated an active annual Festival of Arts, which has become the cradle of new forms of cultural expression. These state-run festival seasons and the many privately sponsored stage shows, carnivals and dances represent just a part of a vibrant national cultural and entertainment calendar of activities. Such contemporary cultural forms overlay and often incorporate the established accomplishments of such cultural icons as Marcus Garvey in cultural awareness and oratory, Edna Manley in sculpture and institution building, Louise Bennett Coverley in Jamaican language, literature and comedy, Wycliffe Bennett in theatre development and visual media production, Robert Nesta Marley in songwriting and musical expression, Mortimo Planno in Rastafari and folk philosophy, Jimmy Cliff in vocal expression and acting, Charles Hyatt in theatrical performance and humour, and Rex Nettleford in dance and literary arts, among many others.

Current contributors such as Shaggy, Sean Paul, Damian Marley and Beenie Man are the leading lights in a large cast of young artists involved in the narrower genre of Jamaican popular music. They represent both an expression of widespread individual talent and an outgrowth of the legacy of their antecedents.

Political, cultural and religious freedoms have also helped to foster and maintain respect for the indigenous Jamaican language and for varied ethnic and religious practices, including the influential polito-religious tenets of Rastafarianism and such seminal folk expressions as Ska, Rock-steady, Pocomania, Gerreh, Dinki-mini and Mento.

Jamaica's also owes its increasing recognition as a cultural powerhouse to other less-developed but significant contributory factors, including the ongoing identification and celebration of political and sporting heroes, the recollection of significant historical events and ancestral sites, the development of a tradition of excellence in literary and culinary arts, and the promotion of a culture of documentation.

## Globalization and culture

According to Grant Wisdom, the global process of globalization speaks to 'the intensification of political, economic and social interconnectedness between states and peoples, thus blurring geographical boundaries' (Wisdom, cited in Dunn, 1995: 3). His definition acknowledges the preceding stages of the globalization process, in which colonial expeditionists attempted dominance of their global spheres of influence through naval, military and cultural conquests. The present phase of globalization is facilitated by new technologies in information, communication and trade, which are global in scope and potential reach.

Robotham argues that the powerful economic influence of globalization is exercised by the governments of industrialized countries in the interests of their competing transnational corporations. 'A critical part of this competition remains the battle to hold on to one's home market while seizing hold of as much of the market of other nations as possible.' (Robotham, 2005: 96) In this scramble for trade advantages both tangible and intangible assets are at stake. (Traded intangibles are becoming just as valuable as tangibles – if not more valuable). Intangible elements such as brands and copyright entitlements are increasing in value in relation to traditional products such as agricultural commodities or books. In the future, even one's wealth will be reflected in intangible resources, as wealth is increasingly being created from ideas, innovation and creativity (Hughes, 2007).

The concept of virtual wealth ties in with Nicholas Negroponte's view that

*The information super highway is about the global movement of weightless bits at the speed of light. As one industry after another looks at itself in the mirror and asks about its future in a digital world,*

*that future is driven almost 100 per cent by the ability of that company's product or services to be rendered in digital form.*

Negroponte, 1995: 12

Creative content is actually at an advantage in this context because it can usually be created in or rendered into digital formats. Once distributed digitally, the potential markets for cultural commodities are indefinite where compression capabilities and bandwidth exist. Moreover, with digital distribution, stocks are readily renewable from archived sources or ready-made digital workstations, studios or reprographic facilities operating just-in-time supply arrangements. However, in many SIDS such as Jamaica the technological tools and distribution capabilities to make this possible are as yet not widely available.

## Facilitating access, technologies and new media

The basic technologies underpinning global connectivity and the so-called information revolution have not fundamentally changed in a decade. They comprise micro-computing based on the silicon chip, satellite technology with modules operating in both low and remote orbiting slots, and digitalization – empowering more rapid and interactive transmission of higher volumes and more varied forms of information and optical and laser technologies, symbolized by the fiber optic cable often used in high-speed telecommunications (Dunn, 1995: 25).

Continuing change comes in the form of new applications of these technologies and their interactive usages in the widely acknowledged process called *Convergence*. The greatest expression of this is the internet itself and the World Wide Web, embodying the global super network, alongside capacities for data processing, storage, video streaming, sound transmission, research resources, printing, narrowcasting and electronic publication. All these capacities present valuable opportunities for news media and improved cultural production and distribution, while at the same time exposing societies to the risks of cultural imperialism and synchronization.

## The digital divide

Globally, we are observing a rapid growth in the disparity between the so-called information-rich and the information-poor. This process mirrors the economic disparities that have historically existed between the world's majority who are largely from underdeveloped regions, and many of those from the industrialized countries who form a small wealthy elite. But divergence in access to and use of information is also taking place within these countries, reflected in the rural-urban divide, race and gender disparities and social-class differentiation, in terms of availability and use of new media and information technologies (Dunn, 2006: 343).

In short, the emerging communications technologies are not global but, in reality, constitute a patchwork across the globe, with a high degree of geographic and social disparity in terms of access.

While some islands within the SIDS category have managed to become extensively connected, a majority remain on the other side of the digital divide where capitalizing on 'virtual wealth' is more difficult. Using the internet as an example, the most recent data show that just 21 per cent or about one fifth of Jamaicans, have access to the internet either at work or home (Dunn, 2007).

## Centre-periphery models

This perspective of the digital divide is consistent with the power-flows described in the centre-periphery analysis of Johan Galtung (1981), and adapted in Figure 1 below, to demonstrate the modern political economy of globalization in information services. It points to the fact that although, in many instances, communications technologies are potentially global in their availability, they are not accessible to certain social and geographical groups within the global population.

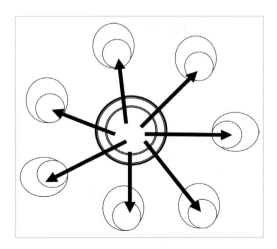

**Figure 1**: The centre-periphery model

The centre of the diagram represents the high-tech industrialized North, with the outer border of the centre representing the less well-endowed areas of the developed countries, such as rural communities, inner-city areas, and areas accommodating certain ethnic minorities. In the outer satellite circles, which represent underdeveloped economies, the urban areas with their wealthy elites are again represented by the inner circles. The outer rims reflect the majority of the poor and those without access to the technologies. The arrows radiate outwards, reflecting the dominant existing flows of media content and consumer technologies; the challenge is, therefore, to create arrows from the periphery to the centre, in significant counter-flows and a more diversified process of globalization (Dunn, 2006: 344). Such a process will challenge the one-way flows of cultural content or information – 'globalization from above' – and the global South will also be involved in disseminating their valuable cultural products, thereby creating a form of 'globalization from below'.

# Creative industries and global media

The size of the global media and entertainment industry in 2004 was estimated at US$1,350 billion, which represents 3 per cent of the global economy. Based on 1990–2004 trends, this percentage is expected to double over the next thirty-two years. The United States is the leader in the global media market with 42 per cent, followed by Europe with 26.3 per cent. This could change as developing countries such as China rapidly shift

spending to media and entertainment (Future Exploration Network, 2006: 2–3).

According to Herman and McChesney 'the media are especially important in larger and technologically advanced countries where most of the citizenry never meet 99 per cent of their fellow citizens and the media serve as a kind of proxy' (1997: 2). As such, the media form communities and linkages where normally they would not have existed. With the advent and subsequent development of the internet, anything that can be digitized can be shared across the world in real time. Global communities of persons are now being developed based on common interests. The global South needs to take advantage of this new 'networked society' where 'technological changes in the production process are presented as ushering in an entirely new historical era with a new social formation – the informational society' (Robotham, 2005: 100). This informational society is currently replacing older types of communities. Countries such as Jamaica can use the internet to focus on special targeted groups, taking advantage of global concentrations of persons and Diaspora communities interested in its cultural products.

The most recent trends in media suggest a shift in audience usage. The Future of Media Report notes that

*The history of media has been one of passive consumption. However, today one of the strongest social trends is towards participation. There are certainly many who are largely content to be 'couch potatoes', consuming the media they are given.*

*Others – particularly younger people – are keen to create, by establishing blogs or individual spaces on sites like MySpace, or sharing photos or videos online. Even clicking on a link is a creative act that can impact what other [sic] see or don't see. Yet this is not just about a social divide. Every one of us is both a consumer and a creator. Finally today we have been given the power to create for others as well as to consume what we are given.*

Future Exploration Network, 2006: 10

What the report refers to is a new phenomenon, the wiki-world, which expands audience participation by allowing people to create and disseminate their own content. Also known as Web 2.0, this new upgraded version of the World Wide Web allows for greater audience involvement. Websites such as YouTube and MySpace that allow the consumer to be the creator have grown in popularity, while sales and distribution of content have been displaced with the market no longer a predictable space. Audiences are now accessing the content they want, when they want, where they want, on whichever platform they choose (Levy and Stone, 2006: 44).

## Overview: creative industries in Jamaica

According to Jamaica Trade and Invest (JTI), formerly JAMPRO, building creative industries involves 'the range of artistic, copyright and creative goods, services and sectors, to add value and generate income by protecting and leveraging

intellectual property. The sector benefits from the conversion of ideas and skills in the arts, business and technology to create new economic value'. The span of the creative industries as purported by JTI includes music, sports, fashion, visual and performing arts, natural products and cuisine, literary arts (including publishing), heritage and cultural products, internet and computer-based technology, toys and games, events and festivals, as well as audio-visual products. In the Jamaican context, the greatest potential for earning relies again on goods and services that can be digitized, particularly music and audio-visual products.

The increased use of ICTs in the creative industries means easier access for more people to the creation and dissemination of music. It is also true that producers run the risk of greater exposure to piracy of their work, depending on the safeguards employed. There has also been argument favouring a shift in emphasis to performing services rather than record sales because of the ease with which recordings are being accessed, copied and distributed illegally (Blake Hannah, 2003: 1).

## Music in Jamaica

Reggae, Jamaica's dominant music form, grew out of a working class counter-culture that existed as far back as the 1950s, where sound systems were the main marketers, distributors and producers of authentic Jamaican music. Witter (2004: 4) describes three phases in the development of Jamaican music:

- the 1950s, prior to the recording of music, when live performances at concerts and 'stage shows' were the only means of accessing Jamaican music

- the 1950s to 1970s, when music started to be recorded and disseminated locally and sound systems were introduced, and

- the 1970s up to the present, embodied by the global distribution of Jamaican music.

While this system of classification describes different stages of development, the music scene today still reflects various characteristics of each stage. The sound system still operates in the space once called the lawn and today the Dancehall, a place more often than not a street or club venue in which reggae music dominates.

McMillan (2005: 2) considers the Jamaican music industry a 'third world business success' story. In the period between the mid-1950s and the year 2000, the island produced over 100,000 recordings. The worldwide annual sales of reggae recordings in the late 1990s stood at about US$1.2 billion, of which Jamaican musicians, producers and songwriters earned about US$300 million. Local earnings from live performances and sales of ancillary products were estimated at an additional US$50 million. This amount totalled about US$350 million and represents approximately 4 per cent of Jamaica's total GDP over the period (ibid: 2–3).

Jamaica Trade and Invest estimated the total annual revenue of the local music industry for the year 2006 as US$75 million. In excess of fifty recording studios in Jamaica are now equipped with digital audio tools and the internet is being used to deliver and promote Jamaican music. However, regular use of broadband internet in Jamaica is still too costly to allow for widespread access (WIPO-CARICOM, 2006: 7).

Jamaican artists have acquired a formidable international reputation – one that can be capitalized upon. For example, Bob Marley's posthumous album *Legend*, released in 1984, sold 12 million copies by 2003 in the US and the UK alone (McMillan, 2005: 2–3). Two decades after his death Marley was still earning about US$10 million per year, ranking fourth among *Forbes* magazine's list of top-earning dead celebrities in 2002. His earnings were surpassed only by Elvis Presley, John Lennon and George Harrison (ibid). In 1999, Marley's song 'One Love' was selected by the BBC as the song of the preceding millennium and the classic Marley album *Exodus* was named by *Time* magazine as the album of the century.

Jamaican music has achieved phenomenal success across the world with an insatiable demand in unlikely markets such as Japan and Germany. In these cases, tourism has provided both an initial conduit and a source of ongoing contact with Jamaican music and culture. Long-stay Japanese visitors to Jamaica are known to speak no standard English, but often converse fluently in the Jamaican language, learnt on the street through the recorded music and in the Dancehall itself. In 2005 alone, a local distribution company, Rockers Island, shipped more than 800,000 records to Japan (Tomlinson, 2006). Japan itself is a huge music market globally ranking as the third-largest global music market after the US and Europe in 2002 (UNESCO, 2005: 39).

Jamaican live music is another source of income in the form of 'cultural tourism'. Reggae Sumfest, for example, brought in about J$1 billion[1] of income in 2005, according to its producers (Nurse, 2006: 185). However, to update the industry to the information age, more web streaming of live performances should be done to capitalize on the potential global market for such concerts.

Witter notes that royalties constitute an important part of the total income of the music industry. The amount of royalties accruing to Jamaicans rights holders is determined by revenues from sales and the amount of airplay. Witter observes that due to the 'historically underdeveloped legal and institutional capacity in Jamaica, the percentage of royalties that is actually collected is known to be ridiculously low' (Witter, 2004: 48). Improvement in these areas for the creative industries as well as stronger awareness-building exercises among artists and entertainers should result in greater economic returns for the local music industry.

# E-commerce and mobile music

Electronic commerce in creative industries is booming worldwide with downloading, online and subscription services being propelled by demand for cultural content. In 2005, consumers bought more than 6 million portable music players, paid over US$75 billion in broadband subscriptions, and bought more than US$50 billion worth of mobile data services (Nurse, 2006: 25).

The potential of new revenue streams such as mobile music should not be underestimated, as these have taken the lead in overall mobile commerce revenue. The youth market has responded positively to the ringtone phenomenon largely because it gives the consumer the opportunity to personalize his or her mobile phone. The estimated global market in 2003 for mobile ringtones was US$700 million (Stanbury, 2004). While mobile music revenues are trending upwards, revenues from singles and albums are trending down due to the ease with which piracy can be committed. With techno-savvy youth globally constituting a large market for Jamaican culture, it suits Jamaican music producers to consider ringtones as a revenue stream and marketing tool in such environments.

# Other creative industries

The audio-visual sector is buoyant in Jamaica with total revenue from film services estimated by Jamaica Trade and Invest at J$1.37 billion, while revenue from local films was estimated to be a mere J$200 million in 2006. Production houses such as the Creative Production and Training Centre (CPTC), CTV and Mediamix have produced an impressive collection of documentary and feature programmes alongside other forms of local content such as music videos, television series and advertisements, some of which are exported to other countries.

One of the up-and-coming local cable television channels, Hype-TV, is reported to be broadcasting by satellite twenty-four hours a day, seven days a week and is available in several countries in North America, Central America, South America, the Caribbean and even some parts of Europe. Another local music channel, RETV, and its newscasting stable mate JNN were sold to the Radio Jamaica group in 2006 for US$1.75 million, reflecting the value seen to reside in local cultural enterprises. These forerunners demonstrate the demand in the global market for audio-visual products as a complement to musical products, especially with the vast spread of the Jamaican diaspora community, estimated to be close to 2.6 million Jamaicans in the US, Canada, Britain and other countries (Bennett Templar, 2008).

Book publishing is an industry that creates content which can complement other local creative industries, by providing literary and academic sources of Jamaican cultural expression. In the information age, new technologies have transformed the relationship between the writer and content. According to Nurse (2006: 99),

*the convergence of the new information driven economy has to prompt a redefinition of content providers with authors now having to shift personal paradigms from being book writers to creators of text that can assume multiple formats and generate multiple income streams as their work finds traction in specifically targeted markets.*

Authors and publishers can therefore look at their books as starting points in content creation where movies, TV shows, websites and soundtracks can add to the economic value of their text.

A leading Jamaican book publisher, Ian Randle, notes that in an industry where other types of media are drawing audiences away, local publishers need to innovate, making use of new distribution methods, such as print on demand and e-publishing, to cut out middlemen including printers and distributors. However, he argues that the financial infrastructure in the region does not adequately support e-commerce in this sector (Randle, 2004). As such, there is room for growth in the publishing industry if the right policy climate exists for use of more advanced technologies.

## Globalizing production and marketing

The foregoing data reflect the increasingly lucrative but still underperforming music and entertainment industry in one small developing country, Jamaica. This is indicative of the prospect of scientifically managed cultural industries throughout the SIDS community. Despite high individual earnings by outstanding artists, the wider industry is poorly capitalized and attracts little financial and investment resources from traditional banking and investment firms. This concern is often articulated in terms of inadequate stocks of tangible resources to serve as collateral for loans. Conventional financiers perceive the risk in terms of overly heavy exposure coupled with concerns about business documentation and the need for credible and globally understandable business processes.

While a small minority of local music entrepreneurs are making progress in spite of these constraints, the wider cultural enterprise lags behind in terms of projected national revenues, especially from the multiple global markets that have expressed an interest in the products and services generated by cultural enterprise.

Panakaj Ghemawat offers a framework for international marketing which may provide a basis for a strategy of global viability and reach for cultural industries. 'Some companies are finding large opportunities for value creation in exploiting, rather than simply adjusting to or overcoming, the differences they encounter at the borders of various markets. As a result, we increasingly see value chains spanning multiple countries' (Ghemawat, 2007: 60).

He advances three optional approaches to corporate organizational strategy for enterprises seeking to break into new global markets. The first is an *adaptation* approach, which seeks to

boost revenues and market share by maximizing a firm's local relevance. The second is a strategy of *aggregation*, involving standardizing the service or product and grouping the development and production processes together in regional or global operations in an attempt to deliver economies of scale. The third is *arbitrage*, which aims to exploit differences between national and regional markets, for example, by locating separate parts of the supply chain in different places.

Ghemawat collectively terms these approaches a 'Triple A Model'. These strategies address global integration in order to get around problems of marketing in varied cultural, economic or political environments. The arbitrage strategy, for example, would see advantages in an enterprise locating call centres in India, factories in China and retail shops in Western Europe.

> *Because most border crossing enterprises will draw from all three A's to some extent, the framework can be used to develop a summary scorecard indicating how well the company is globalizing. However, because of the significant tensions within and among the approaches, it is not enough to tick off the boxes corresponding to all three. Strategic choice requires some degree of prioritization –and the framework can help with this.*

Ghemawat 2007: 60

This strategic business-planning approach could be of relevance to existing and future efforts to produce and market cultural services and products in a wide range of emerging and established global markets. Some elements of these approaches are already implemented in certain segments of the industry. In book publishing, for example, Ian Randle Publishers employ a partial arbitrage strategy by using Jamaican literary and academic skills for the creation and editing of manuscripts; these are then printed in Asia and partially marketed online or distributed in the larger English-speaking markets of the United States and Europe through co-publishing arrangements with other publishing houses (Randle, 2004).

While the trans-regional strategy of aggregation appears to be the approach of choice for music industry entrepreneurs, an arbitrage approach in the film, video and music CD production businesses could be explored. This would imply setting up integrated Jamaican cultural outlets in various markets globally, once feasibility studies supported both their establishment and the localization marketing in each country that this approach would imply.

Defining such priority strategic approaches in corporate business plans for non-traditional music and entertainment enterprises could make investment proposals more attractive to credit managers accustomed to conventional strategic planning. While Ghemawat does not address the role of technology delivery, it is clear that choice of production and marketing delivery platforms will enhance each of the options available, depending on the nature of the enterprise. The cultural or any other type of entrepreneur is advised that 'clearer thinking about the full range of strategy

options should broaden the perceived opportunities, sharpen strategic choices and enhance global performance' (Ghemawat, 2007: 68).

## Conclusion

In an environment of pervasive creativity and cultural production, the central challenge is to harness the economic returns and potential from indigenous music and other cultural products being marketed globally. One way to begin to tackle this challenge is for cultural content producers interested in global marketing to adopt a suitable strategy consistent with the product and market being targeted.

An important part of implementing production and marketing strategies is to determine the platform and appropriate technologies to be used in production and marketing initiatives. Gaining access to regional and global markets is more complex than simply selecting the right technologies of production and distribution. Entrepreneurs will face challenging issues of intellectual property, patenting and copyright registration and enforcement decisions. In addition, managing e-transactions will require strong public policy support for electronic commerce through suitable legislation to protect the enterprises against cyber-crimes such as piracy and other electronic scams.

While use of the internet and other ICTs to market and distribute cultural products can be cost-effective, it requires initial outlays in hardware, staff support and electronic connectivity which many start-up enterprises or even established businesses in the sector do not possess. Attention, therefore, has to be placed on financing these new enterprises through government-backed loan arrangements for credible Micro, Small and Medium Enterprises (MSMEs) in the cultural industries. Special effort should be devoted to working with private banking and loan institutions to encourage these industries to invest in this non-traditional sector.

Strategic champions in the industry are a requirement. Jamaica Trade and Invest has assumed this role, adopting the task of promoting the national slogan of 'Brand Jamaica'. The agency is currently developing the Creative Industries Strategic Plan for the years 2007–2012 and is expected to involve all stakeholders in the sector. In the preparation of the plan the agency should address the concern that policy-makers and traditional managers in both government and the private sector lack the commitment or buy-in to stimulate the required investment in cultural industries. Greater commitment and support by more enlightened leaders in the private and public sectors will enable the country to use this industry to redress the slack being created by the protracted downturn in traditional agricultural sectors such as sugar and bananas.

Support for digital production, marketing and distribution through the use of ICTs is a necessity. This requires the combined efforts of the Ministry of Tourism, Entertainment and Culture and the Ministry of Industry Technology, Energy and Commerce to incorporate this emphasis in key areas of industrial policy development.

In the area of capacity-building there needs to be a stronger focus on digital rights management for IT personnel, web content developers and technicians in the sector, in order to limit the possibilities of piracy of digital content. Intellectual property and Entertainment Law are other key areas where capacity-building is required.

In the new digital era, the potential market for Jamaican cultural products is boundless and the digital world allows for unlimited distribution where infrastructure, expertise and access exist. This includes mobile technology, increasingly used as a marketing device for intangible products and services, including ringtones, SMS messaging for sports and news alerts, and international promotions. Networking must involve inter-linkage of SIDS in recognition of shared interests in indigenous content and promotional strategies. South-South cooperation among SIDS is another an important strategy that can be effected through both interpersonal and ICT inter-linkages.

While coordination of the creative industries in Jamaica is spread across some twenty-eight different departments and agencies of government, it should be accepted that such a situation is not in itself problematic. While rationalization may provide greater efficiency, the spread may indeed reflect the appropriate breadth and diversity of these innovative enterprises across a wide spectrum of government and society. What is even more important is that at least one of these agencies should rise to a clear leadership role as industry champion. The lead agency should work alongside other departments and in close association with the cultural industry leaders to further advance policies and strategies and technologies for the sustainable, long-term reach of Jamaican cultural products and services, across borders to the wider global community.

# References

Bennett Templar, S. 2008. *Engaging the Diaspora in Jamaica's development*. Retrieved on 10 July, 2008 from www.business-int.com/categories/jamaican-national-development/engaging-diaspora-jamaicas-development.asp

Blake Hannah, B. 2003. *The impact of ICTs on the Jamaican music industry*. Retrieved from www.dgroups.org/groups/isacaribbean/docs/ICT-MUSIC-JAMAICA.doc on 2 April, 2007.

Dunn, H.S. 1995. *Globalization, Communications and Caribbean Identity*. New York and Kingston: Ian Randle Publishers.

Dunn, H.S. 2006. Globalisation from below: Caribbean cultures, global technologies and the WTO. C.G.T. Ho and K. Nurse (eds) *Globalisation, Diaspora and Caribbean Popular Culture*. Kingston: Ian Randle Publishers, pp. 342–60.

Dunn, H.S. 2007. Mobile opportunities: poverty and telephony access in Latin America and the Caribbean. *Jamaica Country Report*. TPM-MSB, Jamaica: UWI Mona.

Future Exploration Network. 2006. *Future of Media Report 2006*. Sydney, Australia.

Galtung, J. 1981. A Structural Theory of Imperialism. M. Smith, R. Little, and M. Shackleton (eds) *Perspectives on World Development*. London: Routledge.

Ghemawat, P. 2007. Managing differences: the central challenge of global strategy. *Harvard Business Review*, March: 59–68.

Herman, E.S. and McChesney, R.W. 1997. *The Global Media: The New Missionaries of Corporate Capitalism*. London and New York: Continuum.

Hughes, W. 2007. *Globalisation and Culture*. UWI Public Lecture, Mona Jamaica. 22 February, 2007.

JNHT. 2008. *Jamaica – People*. Retrieved on 10 July, 2008 from www.jnht.com/jamaica/people.php

Levy, S. and Stone, B. 2006. The Web's New Wisdom. *Newsweek*, 3 April, pp. 44–47.

McMillan, J. 2005. *Trench town rock: the creation of Jamaica's music industry*. Graduate School of Business, Stanford University, Stanford, CA.

Negroponte, N. 1995. *Being Digital*. London: Coronet Books.

Nurse, K. 2006. The cultural industries in CARICOM: trade and development challenges. Draft prepared for the Caribbean Regional Negotiating Machinery.

PIOJ. 2006. *Economic and Social Survey Jamaica 2005*. Kingston: PIOJ.

PRB. 2008. Population Reference Bureau. Jamaica – Statistics. Retrieved 10 July, 2008, from www.prb.org/Countries/Jamaica.aspx.

Randle, I. 2004. *The impact of trade and technology on the Caribbean publishing industry*. Retrieved on 5 April, 2007 from www.crnm.org/documents/private_sector/creative_industries/Publishing%20Paper%20-%20Randle.pdf

Robotham, D. 2005. *Culture, Society and Economy: Bringing Production Back In*. London and New Delhi: Sage Publications.

Stanbury, L. 2004. *Mobile entertainment and the*

*Jamaican music industry*. Retrieved on 2 April, 2007 from www.ict4djamaica.org/content/home/detail.asp?iData=32&iCat=291&iChannel=Articles

Tomlinson, R. 2006. *Jamaica and Japan see reggae ties*. BBC News. Retrieved on 4 April, 2007 from http://news.bbc.co.uk/2/hi/americas/5199504.stm

UNESCO Institute for Statistics. 2005. *International Flows of Selected Cultural Good and Services, 1994–2003*. Montreal: UNESCO.

United Nations 2005a. *Mauritius Declaration*. International Meeting to review the Implementation of the Programme of Action for the Sustainable Development of SIDS. Port Louis, Mauritius.

United Nations. 2005b. *Background Paper: Role of Culture in the Sustainable Development of SIDS*. International Meeting to review the Implementation of the Programme of Action for the Sustainable Development of SIDS. A/CONF.207/1.

WIPO-CARICOM. 2006. *Mapping the Creative Industries – The Experience of Jamaica. Georgetown Guyana*. WIPO-CARICOM/IP/GET/05/INF.10.

Witter, M. 2004. *Music and the Jamaican Economy*. Prepared for UNCTAD/WIPO.

World Trade Organization (WTO). 2007. *GATS – Fact and Fiction*. Retrieved on 4 April, 2007 from www.wto.org/english/tratop_e/serv_e/gats_factfiction2_e.htm

# Endnote

1    Exchange rate in 2005: US$1.00: J$64.00.

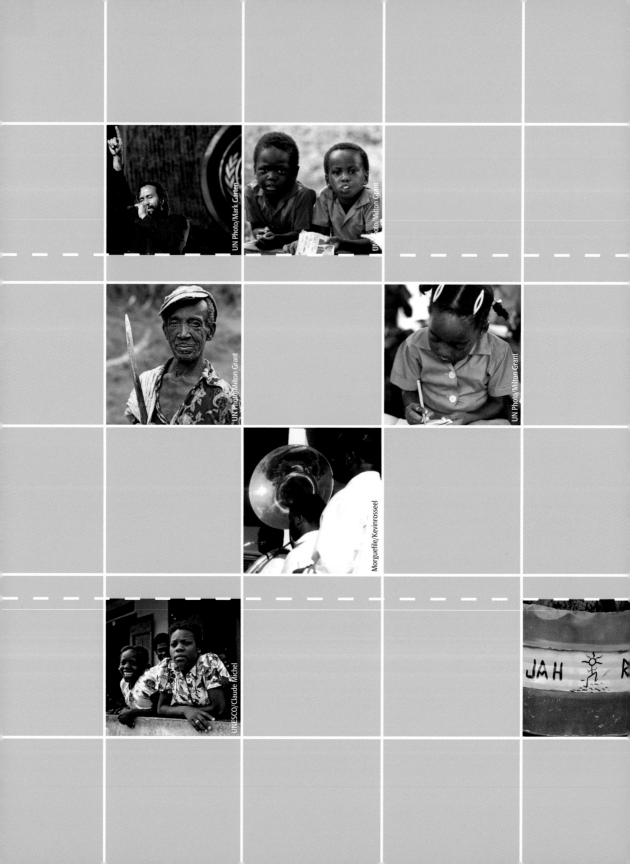

UN Photo/Mark Garten

UN Photo/Milton Grant

UN Photo/Milton Grant

UN Photo/Milton Grant

Morguefile/Kevinrosseel

UNESCO/Claude Michel

JAH R

# THE GLOBAL CREATIVE ECONOMY AND SMALL ISLAND DEVELOPING STATES

Keith Nurse, *University of the West Indies, Barbados*

Creative and cultural industries are a growth area in the global economy. For Small Island Developing States (SIDS) this sector has the potential to help diversify their economies, especially given the rise of the digital economy and increasing commercialization of the arts. It is thought that cultural industries may offer more sustainable development options since they draw on the creativity and enterprise of local artists and communities. It is also argued that cultural industries play a dual role, constituting both an economic sector with growth potential and an arena for identity formation.

This chapter provides an analysis of the cultural and creative sector by first elaborating upon the key characteristics of the creative economy. Thereafter, it outlines the structure of world trade as it relates to technological change, and examines the rise of new business models, transformations in corporate structure, and the consequent implications for the trade policy context. It then identifies the main challenges and opportunities for SIDS within the framework of the global cultural economy in terms of trade in goods, services, intellectual property and cultural tourism flows. The chapter concludes with broad recommendations on how SIDS can enhance their contribution to the creative sector.

## The creative economy

The creative and cultural sector embodies artistic, creative and copyrightable works that function as identifiable products (i.e. goods, services and intellectual property) for sale or display in marketplaces or public arenas. In short, the term 'cultural or creative industries' describes the economic activities of artists, arts enterprises and cultural entrepreneurs, for-profit as well as not-for-profit, in the production, distribution and consumption of film, television, literature, music, theatre, dance, visual arts, broadcasting, multimedia, animation, fashion and so on.

The sector is not just a commercial arena, it is a symbolic and social space where spiritual values, psychic meaning and bodily pleasures are displayed, enacted and represented. From this perspective, the cultural/creative industries play a dual role: they constitute an important area for investment in the new knowledge economy, and a means of bolstering spiritual values and cultural identity. For these reasons, UNESCO recommends that countries 'maximize potential economic contribution' as well as 'facilitate national, regional and world dissemination of endogenous cultural creativity' (UNESCO, 1999).

Certain key features distinguish cultural/creative industries from other economic sectors, thereby shaping their policy context and operations. In broad terms, the main contextual features of cultural/creative industries can be summarized as follows:[1]

- Intellectual or artistic production lies at the heart of the process, while reproduction is a manufacturing operation responding to the logic of industrial production.

- Intellectual and artistic production largely concerns betting on talent and investing in novelty. Market risk is high because consumer taste is volatile and difficult to anticipate.

- The life cycles of products and services are very short with a need for constant innovation. Each entertainment product is typically a 'one-off'.

- Producers and media firms tend to economize on marketing costs and consumers tend to economize on search and information costs, resulting in the replication of hits and high investment in 'superstars'.

- It is difficult to build consumer loyalty. For each product run, consumer taste must be nurtured and channelled.

- The costs of reproduction are low in relation to initial production costs, which grant high returns to economies of scale in distribution, or audience maximization.

- Products can be easily reproduced and companies can be considerably hurt by copyright infringement.

- Cultural goods are rarely destroyed in use. They resemble semi-public goods in that the act of consumption by one individual does not reduce the possibility of consumption by others.

- Public investment and corporate sponsorship in cultural industries are often blocked for socio-political reasons, because popular culture genres often embody anti-establishment themes.

It is the resistance component in popular culture that explains its popularity, and hence its commercial potential; this is what accounts for its contradictory social and business context. Cultural industries are not just informed by societal mores and habits, they also shape society through the ways in which they represent these mores and habits in text, sound and images.

In economic terms, the cultural/creative industry sector can be categorized depending on the extent of copyright embodied in the product or service.[2] The *creative core* refers to industries for which copyright is the central feature of manufacture, performance, broadcasting, distribution, retail and so on. The second category, *interdependent copyright industries*, encompasses those that generate equipment that service the creative core (e.g. musical instruments). The last category consists of *partial copyright industries*: those activities in which only a portion of their production is attributable to copyright, including industry sectors such as fashion and costuming.

The creative and cultural industries sector is also distinctive in that it is characterized by several different transaction networks and income streams. The sector generates income from the sale of goods (e.g. merchandise sales), the provision of services (e.g. professional fees), and the licensing of intellectual property (e.g. royalties). Cultural/creative industries also create circular goods, services and intellectual property. For example, a book can be adapted into a screenplay for a movie, which would then generate a soundtrack (e.g. CD recording) and possibly even specialty merchandise. In this sense, the creative economy allows for greater synergies as it does not produce final goods. Consequently, measuring the economic impact and performance of the sector calls for a sophisticated range of measurement tools and analyses. In most developing countries this challenge is exacerbated by the lack of an institutional framework for the collection and publication of relevant data on the sector.

# The creative economy and world trade

The creative economy has experienced a process of expansive growth and transformation on account of the digitalization of content (e.g. e-commerce, e-books, iTunes, YouTube) that allows for easier production, distribution and consumption as well

as infringement (e.g. piracy, file swapping) of cultural products, services and intellectual property (Nurse, 2000: 53–81). Further impacts include the increasing commercialization of intellectual property, particularly copyright; the shift towards a post-industrial economy where personal, recreational and audio-visual services have expanded as a share of the economy; strong cross-promotional linkages with sectors like tourism (e.g. heritage and festival tourism); and the convergence of media and the increasing concentration of large firms. All of these changes relate to a shift in the techno-economic paradigm and the rise of new business models (e.g. clicks, not bricks) which affect production, distribution and marketing in the creative economy. These transformations are complimented by the emergence of an inter-governmental trade policy framework and regime in the following areas:

- WTO GATS – covers a range of services that relate to the cultural sector: news agency services, the motion picture industry, theatrical services, libraries, archives, museums, etc.[3]

- WTO GATT – covers market access in relation to goods.

- WTO TRIPs – covers copyright, geographical indications, trademarks, traditional knowledge, etc.

- E-commerce – an increasing share of international trade takes place through online transactions linked to the digital arena.

- WIPO – deals with the harmonization and internationalization of copyright regulations through the copyright and digital treaties.

- The 2005 UNESCO Convention on the Protection and Promotion of the Diversity of Cultural Expressions.

- The Economic Partnership Agreements between the EU and the ACP (e.g. CARI-FORUM-EU EPA).

Cultural and entertainment goods, services and intellectual property are captured in a range of international regimes and instruments in the multilateral and regional trading system.[4] For small island developing states the introduction of culture into global trade rules and governance is an issue of immense concern. In many respects it is a contest between the liberalization of trade in cultural goods and services under the WTO, as well as through regional trade agreements and the promotion of cultural diversity through the UNESCO Convention.[5] The Convention calls for the parties to incorporate culture into sustainable development and for international cooperation to support the development of the cultural industries and policies in developing countries through technology transfer, financial support and preferential treatment.

The creative and cultural industries sector is one of the fastest growing sectors of the world economy. Best estimates value the sector at 7 per cent of the world's gross domestic product (UNCTAD, 2004). In most developed market economies, the cultural industries account for 2 to 5 per cent of GDP and have generated consistent and stable growth over the last decade, as exemplified in a rising share of employment and exports. Similar trends are observed in some large developing countries, such as India, Mexico and Brazil, which have strong capabilities in the audio-visual sector and large home and diasporic markets. Table 1 provides data on GDP and employment impact of cultural industries in Latin America and shows that the sector is making a sizeable contribution to these economies. As to be expected, Brazil ranks the highest with a GDP contribution of 6.7 per cent and an employment share of 5.0 per cent. However, even a smaller economy like Uruguay has impressive figures to report with 6.0 per cent and 4.9 per cent shares in GDP and employment, respectively.

**Table 1:** Cultural industries' contribution to select Latin America economies

| Country | Base year | Cultural industries' impact | |
| | | GDP | Employment |
| --- | --- | --- | --- |
| Argentina | 1993 | 4.1% | – |
| | 1994 | – | 3.5% |
| Brazil | 1998 | 6.7% | 5.0% |
| Columbia | 2001 | 2.01% | – |
| | 1999–2002 | – | 27,724* |
| Chile | 1990–1998 | 2.0% | 2.7% |
| Uruguay | 1997 | 6.0% | 4.9% |
| Venezuela | 1997–2000 | 3.0% | 35,329** |
| | 2001 | 2.3% | – |

*Source*: OAS (2004)

\* Jobs in three sectors: publishing, phonography and filmmaking.

\*\* Jobs in four sectors: graphic arts, radio, advertising and filmmaking.

# Creative goods

Recent estimates show that trade in the cultural economy over the last decade has increased at an unprecedented average annual rate of 8.7 per cent. Exports of creative products were valued at US$424.4 billion in 2005 up from US$227.5 billion in 1996 (UNCTAD/UNDP, 2008). Using customs-based and balance-of-payments data, UNESCO (UIS, 2005) estimated that world trade in cultural goods grew rapidly between 1994 and 2002 from US$38 billion to approximately US$60 billion. UNESCO uses a different methodology and definition of the sector to PricewaterhouseCoopers (PWC) by excluding activities like sport, advertising, video games and broadcast sectors. In contrast, it includes activities such as production of heritage goods. Based upon this methodology, the United Kingdom was the biggest producer of cultural goods with US$8.5 billion, followed by the United States with US$7.6 billion and China with US$5.2 billion. The United States was the biggest consumer of cultural goods in 2002 with US$15.3 billion, twice more than United Kingdom imports, which was the second largest consumer with US$7.8 billion. Germany was the third-largest importer of cultural goods with US$4.1 billion.

What is evident from the UNESCO data (1994–2002) (UIS, 2005) is that the world trade in cultural goods is highly concentrated in a few developed and emerging market economies. The structure of world trade in the cultural/creative industries in 2002 was such that Europe (EU 15) was the major exporter, accounting for approximately 52 per cent of the market. Asia is the next biggest exporter and fastest rising region (largely because of rapid expansion in East Asia and China in particular) with 20.8 per cent of the world market. North America's relative share declined from 25 per cent in 1994 to 17 per cent in 2002, which makes it the third-largest export region. The 'Other Europe' region is next with 6 per cent. Latin America and the Caribbean have expanded their share from 1.9 per cent to 3.0 per cent over the same period. Oceania and Africa together share 1 per cent of the market.

Europe is the main importer, accounting for 40 per cent of world demand, compared to the North American share of approximately 30 per cent. Both regions had 4 per cent changes in share with the United States rising and the EU dropping. Asia is third with approximately 15 per cent of global imports – a slight improvement over 1994. The LAC and Oceania regions' share has declined marginally from 4.4 per cent to 3.6 per cent and from 3.9 per cent to 2.5 per cent, respectively. Africa has stayed steady at about 1 per cent. The United States has an impressive trade balance with the rest of the world (UIS, 2005). The top ten sales territories, primarily North America, Europe and Japan, account for 80.7 per cent of the world market.

In the realm of creative goods most developing countries are net importers except for China, Hong Kong and India. Singapore and the Republic of Korea are the next best performers but have

**Figure 1:** Top developing countries – balance of trade in creative goods, 2005 (US$mn)

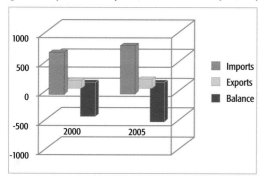

*Source:* UNCTAD/UNDP (2008)

minor deficits (see Figure 1). What this illustrates is that while the creative industries sector is making an increased contribution to GDP, exports and employment in developing countries, most operate with large trade imbalances in cultural goods.

For Small Island Developing States the picture is very much in keeping with the developing country scenario. Figure 2 provides export and

import data on cultural merchandise trade for SIDS and a comparison between 2000 and 2005 shows a significant and rising deficit in the trade of cultural goods.

The case of Caribbean-SIDS is instructive. Figure 3 demonstrates that although several Caribbean countries (e.g. Cuba, Dominican Republic, Haiti, Jamaica, and Trinidad and Tobago) are known for

**Figure 2:** Small Island Developing States – creative goods, imports and exports, 2000 and 2005 (US$mn).

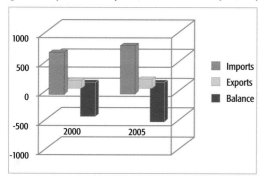

*Source:* UNCTAD/UNDP (2008)

**Figure 3:** Caribbean trade in creative goods, 2004

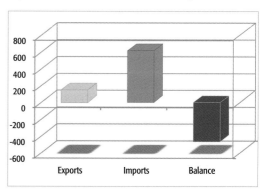

*Source:* UNCTAD (2008)

**Table 2:** Reported exports of creative services, 1996, 2000 and 2005 (US$ billions)

|      | All creative services | Architectural | Advertising | Audiovisual | R&D | Cultural & recreational | Other cultural |
|------|-----------------------|---------------|-------------|-------------|------|-------------------------|----------------|
| 1996 | 38.2                  | 9.8           | 5.0         | 6.3         | 13.3 | 10.5                    | 1.0            |
| 2000 | 55.2                  | 17.3          | 5.1         | 13.3        | 9.6  | 20.7                    | 2.8            |
| 2005 | 88.9                  | 27.7          | 15.7        | 17.5        | 18.0 | 27.5                    | 3.5            |

*Source:* UNCTAD/UNDP (2008)

their arts and cultural exports, they still have a significant deficit in the trade of cultural goods. Part of the explanation is that the table reflects data only for merchandise trade and does not include trade in services, royalties earnings and earnings from cultural, heritage and festival tourism, where these economies are able to generate some earnings.

# Creative services

The analysis of trade in the creative sector needs to move beyond the goods sector to incorporate trade in the services sectors, as well as trade in copyright and royalties. Data on trade in creative services are largely undeveloped on account of the weak informational infrastructure, particularly in developing country regions. The services sector has enjoyed a growth rate of 8.8 per cent in recent years. Best estimates put the size of the creative services sector at US$89 billion in 2005 up from US$52.2 billion in 2000, an 11.2 per cent annual growth rate. In terms of regional shares, the developed economies accounted for 82 per cent of total exports while developing countries' share was 11 per cent and that of transition economies was 7 per cent (UNCTAD/UNDP, 2008: 134). In 2005, the top exporting services were architectural services (US$27.7 billion) followed by cultural and recreational services (US$27.5 billion) (see Table 2).

Services trade is manifested in different modes. Table 3 outlines the various modes of services supply as these would apply to the creative sector. Mode I

**Table 3:** Modes of supply in trade in creative services

| Mode I: Cross-border supply | Supply of services from one country to another, for example, sound engineering services or architectural services transmitted via telecommunications. |
|------------------------------|------------------------------------------------------------------------------------------------------------------------------------------------------|
| Mode II: Consumption abroad | Consumers from one country using services in another country, for example, cultural, festival and heritage tourism. |
| Mode III: Commercial presence | A company from one country establishes a subsidiary or branch to provide services in another country, for example, setting up a booking agency. |
| Mode IV: Movement of natural persons | Individuals travelling from their own country to offer services in another, for example, an artist or band on tour. |

is cross-border supply, which refers to services transmitted via some form of telecommunications, for example, sound engineering (a soundtrack) or architectural services (e.g. blueprints) sent to a client via email. This is an area where developing countries do not have capacity and are likely to be net importers or downloaders. Consumption abroad (Mode II) refers to consumers from one country travelling to use services in another country. This involves tourism-related activities such as cultural, heritage and festival tourism, where developing countries and particularly SIDS have export capabilities given the importance of the tourism sector to their economies. Mode III refers to a firm establishing a commercial presence in another country to provide a service, for example, setting up a radio station or a booking agency. This is another area where developing countries are weak in terms of trade and exports. The last Mode (IV) speaks to the movement of natural persons, for example, a visual artist or a music band on tour. This is the area where a large share of services exports for developing countries come from. As this activity often involves independent professionals it is very difficult to collect data.

## Intellectual property

Intellectual property is a key growth area in the global economy and one of the core features of the creative sector. Copyright and related rights are the main forms of intellectual property through which creative goods and services are protected and commercialized. Royalties earnings and licensing fees are a key source of income for rights-owners such as authors, composers and producers.

In terms of global trade in intellectual property in the creative sector, the most recent data for global authors' rights and royalty collections worldwide gives a figure of 7,155,532,807 euros for 2006, which represents a 6 per cent increase over 2005.[6] Of this amount, Europe accounts for approximately 63 per cent or 4.48 billion euros. North America is the next-largest region in terms of collections with 1.55 billion euros. Developing country regions such as Asia-Pacific collected 878 million euros, Latin America and the Caribbean, 211 million euros, and Africa, 34 million euros (see Figure 4). These data only cover royalty collections from national societies and not royalty payments between collection management organizations, for example, inflows and outflows to foreign collections societies.

Prospects for royalty-based creative trade (i.e. digital content like internet TV and mobile music) appear to be very strong, based on recent data from a

**Figure 4:** Global royalty collections, by region, 2006

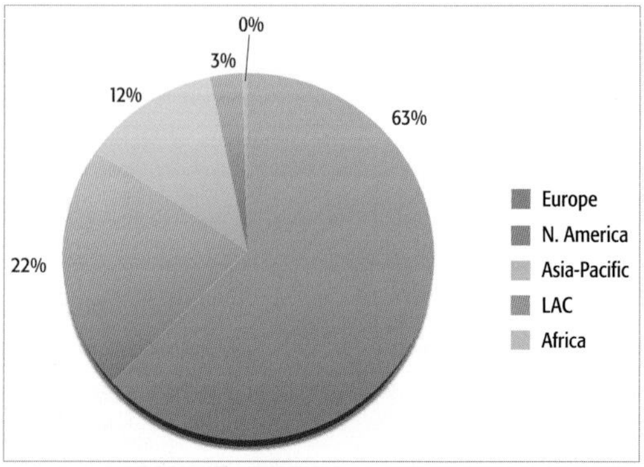

*Source:* CISAC (2008)

CISAC study (CISAC, 2008). This is a burgeoning element of the creative economy from which only a few developing countries are benefiting. For example, estimates from UNCTAD show that the top exporters of new media from the developing world are key industrial economies in Asia (China, Singapore, Korea, Taiwan, India and Malaysia), while other developing country regions such as Latin America and Africa are not active participants. The scenario for Least Developed Countries and SIDS is even more marginal with regard to these growth trends (UNCTAD/UNDP, 2008: 134).

## Cultural tourism

The tourism sector, which is the mainstay of most SIDS, is faced with increased competition and new demand conditions. One of the key growth trends in the global tourism industry is the diversification of the tourism product away from high-impact mass tourism toward specialty or niche markets like cultural tourism. Cultural tourism includes a broad range of activities such as tours of historical, heritage and archaeological sites; visits to art galleries, museums and craft exhibitions; and attendance at arts performances, live entertainment and festivals. Cultural tourism has emerged as an important innovation and a new source of competitive advantage in the global tourism industry. The World Tourism Organization estimated that 37 per cent of all trips have a cultural element (EIU, 1993). The relationship between the tourism industry and cultural industries is increasingly appreciated as one in which cultural

industries generate demand for tourism, while tourism generates additional markets and income for the cultural sector.

Appreciation of this relationship has grown with increased attention to the economic importance of the arts. For SIDS, cultural tourism is an effective means by which to generate national, regional and international appreciation of indigenous arts and popular culture, and so build cultural industries and local cultural confidence. It is also effective in diversifying the tourism product as well as generating destination and intellectual property branding. The latter largely emerges from the media impact gained from successful festivals and heritage sites, attractions and experiences. From this standpoint broadcasting has emerged as a critical asset for cultural tourism marketing and promotion. Media is essential to delight and build audience support, win corporate sponsorship and expand artists' careers. The growth of the internet presents new options for production, marketing and broadcasting, for example, through webcasting and podcasting of festivals and other arts events.

In the Caribbean, festivals have been pivotal, especially carnivals and indigenous music festivals, to the development of the cultural industries and arts sector. Festivals give a fillip to the entertainment sector by creating new clients, markets and media exposure, thereby facilitating export expansion. They also stimulate infrastructure development, heritage conservation and investment in the arts (Nurse, 2003). Many festivals are observed to have a significant impact on visitor arrivals, airlifts and hotel occupancy rates with spillover effects on media industries, local transport (e.g. car rentals) and the food, beverage and restaurant sectors.

Caribbean festivals have a significant impact on the regional tourism sector in terms of creating a new tourism season and/or filling the void in the tourism calendar. These Caribbean festivals have done much to generate new tourism demand from the short-break travel market, as well as from diasporic and intra-regional tourists – groupings that are largely omitted in the tourist marketing plans of most Caribbean tourism organizations. The spending of festival tourists, which is considered 'new' or incremental and counts as an export industry, has been very significant as a share of total visitor expenditure, where data on visitor arrivals have been documented by exit surveys.

Caribbean festivals create a strong demand-pull for visitors (see Table 4). The best case is that of Trinidad Carnival. The carnival is the largest festival in the region in terms of visitor arrivals and expenditure. Arrivals have grown by 60 per cent

since the late 1990s, such that by 2004 there were over 40,000 visitors, who spent approximately US$27.5 million – over 10 per cent of annual visitor expenditure. The growth in total expenditure has come largely from the increased average length of stay for carnival visitors: from nine days in 2000 to fourteen days in 2004. Average daily expenditure per carnival tourist has remained in the US$50.00 range for several years, although this is considered to be a very conservative estimate (Nurse, 2003).

The festival with the next best performance in the region is that of St. Lucia Jazz, which has grown from averaging 9,000 visitors in the late 1990s to averaging 12,000 in recent years. Visitor expenditure has grown steadily throughout the period from US$14.1 million in 1998 to US$17.3 million in 2003 (Nurse, 2003).

An economic impact assessment of the St. Kitts Music Festival was undertaken in 2002 and 2003. In 2002 there were 1,164 visitors and in 2003 there was a significant increase to 2,562 visitors.

**Table 4:** Festival tourism economic impact

| | 1997 | 1998 | 1999 | 2000 | 2001 | 2002 | 2003 | 2004 | 2005 |
|---|---|---|---|---|---|---|---|---|---|
| Trinidad Carnival | | | | | | | | | |
| Festival arrivals | 27,414 | 35,665 | 34,907 | 42,646 | 35,221 | 33,487 | 38,537 | 40,455 | 40,555 |
| Visitor exp. US$mn | 10.2 | 14.0 | 18.1 | 17.7 | 21.4 | 22.7 | 26.2 | 27.5 | |
| St. Lucia Jazz | | | | | | | | | |
| Festival arrivals | n.a. | 9,929 | 9,909 | 11,041 | 8,421 | 11,203 | 12,164 | 12,553 | |
| Visitor exp. US$mn | n.a. | 14.1 | 13.9 | 14.8 | 12.0 | 12.5 | 17.3 | | |

*Source:* Data taken from K. Nurse (2003) and recent surveys

The findings from the 2003 festival put visitor expenditure at EC\$3.1 million. Of this, 26 per cent (US\$0.81 million) was spent in the hotel and accommodation sector and a further 20 per cent (US\$0.61 million) was spent on festival-related activities and merchandise. The remainder of US\$1.7 million (55 per cent) was spent on the wider economy, including meals, transportation and shopping (Sahely and Skeritt, 2003).

## Analysis and policy

The creative sector is a major growth pole in the knowledge economy. For developing countries, the above analysis indicates their status, in relative terms, as small traders in the global creative economy, even when the weak informational infrastructure is taken into account. Another key finding is that the developing world should not be viewed as a monolithic group. Instead, an understanding of differentiation among developing countries and regions is needed. Asian economies are fast-rising players in the creative economy as represented by the growth of China in goods exports. The Asia region is also expanding global market share in services exports, royalty income, digital trade and new media. Other regions like Latin America and the Caribbean and Africa generate significant cultural art forms, but this is not reflected in trade expansion and global competitiveness.

In many respects the problem in these countries is that there is no adequate support from a trade, industrial and innovation standpoint for local or regional cultural enterprises and industries. Moreover, in the realm of copyright and royalty collections many developing countries are faced with the problem of under-reporting in relation to public performance of copyright works by the collective management organizations in OECD countries, particularly the US (Nurse, 2000). Furthermore, given the nature of cultural industries, the challenge is essentially one of creating demand for alternative genres and creating new tastes.

Governments and corporations in most SIDS have not fully appreciated the new directions of the global economy and the ways in which their economies can diversify to meet new challenges and take advantage of emerging opportunities. Often, the cultural industries are not seriously regarded as an economic sector, the key stakeholders are poorly organized, and overall economic value remains largely undocumented. In this context policy measures have typically been absent. Changing this mindset is the first key recommendation.

In broad outline, the key policy interventions would entail a number of initiatives from a wide array of stakeholders: the state, including various ministries and agencies along with industry associations; non-governmental development organizations; and international development agencies. A short list of the main recommendations for fostering a local environment conducive to the development of the cultural industries includes the following:

- Improve government-industry relations through the harmonization of government policy on trade and industrial and intellectual property policies. Proactive policies aimed at promoting cultural diversity and investment in the cultural sector should be preserved in bilateral and multilateral negotiations (e.g. WTO) and in inter-regional arrangements (e.g. Economic Partnership Agreements).

- Document the economic impact of cultural industries and establish benchmarks, targets and policy measures to promote employment generation, enterprise development, industrial upgrading and export expansion.

- Increase local and regional content on the airwaves (radio and TV) through local content legislation/regulation, where needed. Encourage and facilitate the 'uploading' of local and regional content onto the World Wide Web, for example, through the webcasting of festival and events.

- Develop cultural industry associations to represent the interest of the sector and also to develop a code of ethics and standards for remuneration rates and work practice (e.g. in the hotel, hospitality and advertising sectors).

- Improve access to finance, credit and business support services for emerging and export-ready firms and artists. Establish booking agencies and trade/export facilitation centres. These measures should be matched by market-development grants and financing for participation in trade fairs.

- Copyright protection and collective administration must form a vital component of the policy agenda, including an anti-piracy enforcement and a public awareness campaign. National and regional rights management centres should be established for multiple areas of the creative industries (e.g. music and book publishing).

- Expand the linkages between the creative industries, the tourism sector and the wider economy, for example, through festivals such as the Caribbean Festival of Arts and the Pacific Festival of Arts. Facilitate and encourage new marketing strategies targeted at the diasporic and intra-regional markets, as well as cultural tourists.

- Develop internet-readiness for alternative broadcasting, marketing and distribution of cultural goods, services and events. Establish an e-commerce platform and a regional warehousing system for sales and distribution.

- Upgrade the human resource capabilities of the cultural sector through training in the arts, as well as training in arts administration, management and cultural entrepreneurship.

# Conclusion

Achieving the above policy goals does require some resource mobilization, which can only be determined on a case-by-case basis. Some SIDS have more commercialized arts and cultural industries, and some have stronger export capabilities and the required institutional and organizational resources. SIDS have small markets, which can be a disincentive to investment. Exports to regional and extra-regional markets are critical to overcoming dis-economies of scale. Cultural industries are also often viewed as risky investments due to the volatility of consumer tastes and difficulties in predicting market demands. Consequently, the main source of capital has tended to come from private individual and family savings rather than banks and credit facilities. Development grants and small-business financing are appropriate for emerging sectors of this sort.

Historically, the cultural arena has not been seen as a priority area in national budgets or international development assistance when compared to the problems of poverty and hunger, or the resource demands of traditional economic activities. Furthermore, when resources are available for the cultural sector, they tend to be allocated to tangible and built heritage. Intangible heritage has traditionally attracted fewer resources – an issue which UNESCO has begun to address with the Intangible Heritage Award scheme.

This chapter argues that the creative sector is a critical catalyst for identity formation, nation-building, and reinforces and expands the cultural confidence of former colonial societies and their diasporic communities. It also argues that investing in the creative industries provides worthwhile returns because the sector generates new and indigenous forms of employment, production and exports; aids in the diversification of the tourism product; and facilitates a more competitive development platform. The conclusion is that the creative industries should be viewed as a critical strategic resource in the move towards creating sustainable development options in SIDS.

# References

CISAC. 2008. *CISAC Annual Report 2007.* International Confederation of Societies of Authors and Composers (CISAC). www.cisac. org . Last accessed June 2008.

EIU. 1993. *The Market for Cultural Tourism in Europe.* London: EIU Travel and Tourism Analyst No. 6.

Gans, H.J. 1999. *Popular Culture and High Culture,* New York: Basic Books.

Graber, C.B. 2004. Audiovisual Media and the Law of the WTO. C.B. Graber, M. Girsberger and M. Nenova (eds) *Free Trade versus Cultural Diversity.* Schulthess: Zürich, 15–65.

Hesmondhalgh, D. 2002. *The Cultural Industries.* London: Sage Publications.

Nurse, K. 2000. Copyright and music in the digital age: prospects and implications for the Caribbean. *Social and Economic Studies* 49(1).

Nurse, K. 2003. *Festival Tourism in the Caribbean.* Washington DC: Inter-American Development Bank.

OAS. 2004. *Culture as an engine for economic growth, employment and development.* Second Inter-American Meeting of Ministers of Culture and Highest Appropriate Authorities. 7 June, Washington DC.

Sahely, L. and Skeritt, S. 2003. St. Kitts Music Festival 2003: economic impact assessment and visitor profile. July.

UNCTAD. 2004. *Creative industries and development.* Paper presented at UNCTAD Eleventh Session, Sao Paulo, June (TD(XI)BP/13).

UNCTAD/ILO. 1995. *Media Services: a survey of the industry and its largest firms,* Geneva: UN.

UNCTAD/UNDP. 2008. *The Creative Economy Report 2008. The Challenge of Assessing the Creative Economy: towards informed policy-making.* UNCTAD/UNDP, Geneva. www.unctad.org/creative-economy. Last accessed May 2008.

UNESCO. 1999. *The value of culture.* Position paper for the forum 'Development and Culture', Inter-American Development Bank/UNESCO, Paris, 11–12 March.

UNESCO Institute for Statistics (UIS). 2005. *International Flow of Selected Cultural Goods and Services, 1994–2003.* UNESCO Institute for Statistics. www.uis.unesco.org accessed 02/03/2006.

Van den Bossche, P. 2007. *Free Trade and Culture: A Study of Relevant WTO Rules and Constraints on National Cultural Policy Measures.* Amsterdam: Boekmanstudies.

Voon, T. 2007. *Cultural Products and the World Trade Organization.* Cambridge: Cambridge University Press.

WIPO. 2003. *Guide on Surveying the Economic Contribution of the Copyright-Based Industries.* Geneva, Switzerland.

WTO. Council for Trade in Services. 1998. 'Audiovisual Services: Background Note by the Secretariat', S/C/W/40, 15 June.

# Endnotes

1 This list is drawn from Hesmondhalgh (2002), Gans (1999), UNCTAD/ILO (1995) and WIPO (2003).

2 For further details, see WIPO (2003).

3 For further discussion see Graber (2004: 15–65); see also WTO, 1998.

4 See Van den Bossche (2007).

5 Voon (2007).

6 This data is based on the earnings of CISAC members.

# AFTERWORD

Katerina Stenou, *UNESCO Paris, France*

## Director of the Division of Cultural Policies and Intercultural Dialogue, Culture Sector

BY bringing together multi-disciplinary expertise from the main Small Island Developing States (SIDS) regions of the world (Caribbean, Indian and Pacific Oceans), UNESCO wished to develop greater reflection on the issue of cultural diversity as a guarantee for sustainable development. Substantial discussions addressed the main current challenges, such as the need to:

- emphasize the nature of SIDS as sanctuaries of cultural diversity and laboratories of genuine dialogue. This means transcending the view of island populations as isolated, and stressing instead the continued interactions resulting from cultural encounters throughout history;

- stress the links between 'culture, diversity and development'; development being understood as both economic growth and the flourishing of human beings benefiting from their cultural resources, whilst maintaining openness to choices provided by modern communication technologies;

- defend the creative capacity of people through their many different tangible and intangible forms of culture, whilst ensuring the harmonious coexistence of individuals and groups from diverse cultural backgrounds living in the same space. The protection and promotion of SIDS' rich diversity is doubly challenging, since culture refers not only to the arts and literature but also lifestyles, value systems, traditions and beliefs;

- compound 'culture, international solidarity and mutual understanding' by encouraging exchanges and partnership. This is particularly important for populations whose cultural expressions face difficulties related to the contemporary challenges of creation, production, distribution, access and enjoyment.

This very reflection on cultural diversity is intended to make a considerable contribution to the United Nations (UN) Mauritius International Meeting to Review the Programme of Action for Sustainable Development of the 54 SIDS (2005), which identified culture as a priority. Concrete commitments were made to develop national cultural policies and legislative frameworks; measures to protect the natural, tangible and intangible cultural heritage; and increase resources for the development and strengthening of national and regional cultural capacities.

In light of this achievement it is surprising that five years later, the recent High-level Review Meeting on the implementation of the Mauritius Strategy for the Further Implementation of the Programme of Action for the Sustainable Development of SIDS held in New York (24–25 September 2010) was silent on the issue of culture. The outcome document of the SIDS Review Meeting records that States demonstrated their commitment to promoting sustainable development in fields such as protected areas, protecting biodiversity and adopting strategies for promoting renewable energy, and to mitigating the negative impact of the global financial and economic crises on their economies. However, there is no equivalent demonstration of their commitment to protect and promote cultural diversity through policy and programmes, as foreseen in the comprehensive and multidisciplinary SIDS Mauritius Strategy.

Nevertheless, despite this silence, there is a strong commitment to culture in future strategies and action for sustainable development. Prior to the SIDS Review Meeting the UN High-level Plenary Meeting on the Millennium Development Goals (MDG Summit, 20–22 September 2010) stressed the importance of culture for development and its contribution to the achievement of MDGs, recognizing that all cultures and civilizations contribute to the enrichment of humankind. The same outcome document also renews Member States' commitment to the full and effective implementation of the Mauritius Strategy.

Furthermore, the recent UNESCO Executive Board meeting (October 2010) adopted a resolution on UNESCO's contribution to the Mauritius Strategy for the Further Implementation of the Programme of Action for the Sustainable Development of SIDS. It is explicit about the need to strengthen capacity and expertise in safeguarding tangible and intangible heritage, and in promoting creativity, cultural

industries and tourism as part of sustainable development efforts. By doing so, the importance of culture in SIDS sustainable development strategies is recognized, as it represents peoples' expression and identity, and the foundation of the richness of their cultural diversity, traditions and customs.

These new commitments invite UN agencies, Member States and civil society to join hands, create synergies between different disciplines, knowledge systems and approaches to ensure that culture, in its rich diversity, finds its ample place in concrete actions for the sustainable development of SIDS. Cultural diversity itself carries the answers to these challenges. By encompassing plural, dynamic and diverse identities, it allows creativity to blossom with infinite variety. Each form of creativity is a meeting-place, providing new horizons and perspectives, increasing our capacity to exchange, and forging solid links between and among regions, groups and individuals. As an open-ended process, culture constantly remodels the legacy of skills, knowledge and wisdom – a process which is handed down and reinvents new forms of expression across time and space, thus demonstrating its endless diversity.

The present publication wishes to restore the missing link between the interrelated issues of culture and development, that is, cultural diversity recognized by the Earth Summit (2002) as a collective force for development. This is the way to strengthen SIDS' resilience to overcome their unique and specific vulnerabilities, accentuated by the negative impact of the economic and environmental crises that threaten their very survival.